Leading Works in Law and Religion

Leading Works in Law and Religion brings together leading and emerging scholars in the field from the United Kingdom and Ireland. Each contributor has been invited to select and analyse a 'leading work', which has for them shed light on the way that Law and Religion are intertwined. The chapters are autobiographical, reflecting upon the works that have proved significant to contributors, and also offer critical analyses of the current state of the field, exploring in particular the interdisciplinary potential of the study of Law and Religion. The book also includes a specially written introduction and conclusion, which critically comment upon the development of Law and Religion over the last 25 years and likely future developments in light of the reflections by contributors on their chosen leading works.

Russell Sandberg is Professor in Law at the School of Law and Politics at Cardiff University, UK, where he specialises in Law and Religion, Legal History, Family Law and interdisciplinary approaches to Law. He is editor of Routledge's *Leading Works in Law* series.

Leading Works in Law

Series Editor:

Russell Sandberg, Cardiff University, UK

In an age where legal education is undergoing considerable change and facing a number of challenges, the *Leading Works in Law* series is designed to explore how the study of Law and legal sub-disciplines have developed so far and their likely future. The purpose of the series is to fire critical light at the way in which sub-disciplines within Law understand themselves and perpetuate their identity.

Each book focuses upon a different legal sub-discipline. It asks leading and emerging scholars in the field to select and analyse a 'leading work'; one which has contributed internationally to the development of the sub-discipline as a whole. The chapters explore the likely implications and applications of the leading work upon the sub-discipline in question. The discussion may be in part autobiographical, exploring how the work in question has impacted upon the contributor's own scholarship and understanding of the sub-discipline in question.

The books in this series are intended to assess the development of the sub-discipline in question and examine its potential future development. The leading works chosen are not meant to be exhaustive; they are simply illustrative and a means by which the contributors reflect upon the often unspoken question about how and why a sub-discipline has developed in the way that it has and the way in which it could develop in the future.

Titles in this series:

Leading Works in Law and Religion
Edited by Russell Sandberg

For more information about this series, please visit: www.routledge.com/Leading-Works-in-Law/book-series/LEADINGWORKS

Leading Works in Law and Religion

Edited by
Russell Sandberg

Routledge
Taylor & Francis Group
LONDON AND NEW YORK

First published 2019
by Routledge
2 Park Square, Milton Park, Abingdon, Oxon OX14 4RN

and by Routledge
52 Vanderbilt Avenue, New York, NY 10017

First issued in paperback 2020

Routledge is an imprint of the Taylor & Francis Group, an informa business

British Library Cataloguing-in-Publication Data
A catalogue record for this book is available from the British Library

Library of Congress Cataloging-in-Publication Data
Names: Sandberg, Russell, compiler.
Title: Leading works in law and religion/[compiled by] Russell Sandberg.
Description: Abingdon, Oxon [UK] ; New York, NY : Routledge, 2019. | Series: Leading works in law | Includes bibliographical references and index.
Identifiers: LCCN 2018036226 | ISBN 9781138244467 (hardback)
Subjects: LCSH: Religion and law. | Religious law and legislation. | Freedom of religion. | Laicism. | Religion and state. | Convention for the Protection of Human Rights and Fundamental Freedoms (1950 November 5)
Classification: LCC K3280 .S26 2019 | DDC 344/.096—dc23
LC record available at https://lccn.loc.gov/2018036226

ISBN 13: 978-0-367-66425-1 (pbk)
ISBN 13: 978-1-138-24446-7 (hbk)

Typeset in Galliard
by Apex CoVantage, LLC

Contents

Notes on contributors

Sylvie Bacquet is a Senior Lecturer in Law at the University of Westminster in London. Sylvie's recent publications in the area of Law and Religion include: 'Religious Freedom in a Secular Society: An Analysis of the French Approach to Manifestation of Beliefs in the Public Sphere' in P Cumper and T Lewis (eds), *Religion, Human Rights and Secular Society in Europe* (Edward Elgar Publishing, 2012); 'Religious Symbols and the Making of Contemporary Religious Identities' in R Sandberg (ed), *Religion and Legal Pluralism* (Ashgate, 2015); and 'Non-Religious Views in the RE School Curriculum: What Can We Learn from *R (Fox and Others) v Secretary of State for Education*?' [2016] *Education Law Review*.

Anthony Bradney is Professor in Law at Keele University. He is author of *Law and Faith in a Sceptical Age* (Routledge/Glass House Press, 2009); *Conversations, Chances and Choices: The Liberal Law School in the Twenty-First Century* (Hart Publishing, 2003); (with Fiona Cownie), *Living Without Law: An Ethnography of Dispute Avoidance and Resolution in the Religious Society of Friends* (Ashgate, 2000); and *Religions, Rights and Laws* (Leicester University Press, 1993). He is a Fellow of the Academy of Social Sciences and a Fellow of the Royal Society of Arts.

Frank Cranmer is an honorary Research Fellow at the Centre for Law and Religion at Cardiff University, a Fellow of St Chad's College, Durham, and Secretary of the Churches' Legislation Advisory Service. His recent publications include 'Religion and Belief in United Kingdom Employment Law: An Introduction to the Case-Law' (2017) 1:3 *Brill Law and Religion*; 'Reasonable Accommodation for Religion in Employment and Provision of Services' (2017) 179 *Law & Justice*; and (with David Pocklington), 'Banns of Marriage: Their Development and (Possible) Future' (2017) 19:3 *Ecclesiastical Law Journal*.

Eoin Daly is a Lecturer above the Bar at the School of Law, NUI Galway. He is author of *Rousseau's Constitutionalism: Austerity and Republican Freedom* (Hart, 2017); (with Tom Hickey), *A Political Theory of the Irish Constitution* (Manchester University Press, 2015); and *Religion, Law and the Irish State* (Clarus, 2012).

Peter W. Edge is Professor of Law at Oxford Brookes University. His publications in the area of Law and Religion include *Legal Responses to Religious Difference* (Kluwer, 2001); *Religion and Law: An Introduction* (Ashgate, 2006); and (with Lucy Vickers), *EHRC Report 97: Review of Equality and Human Rights Law relating to Religion or Belief* (2015).

Méadhbh McIvor is Assistant Professor of Religion, Law and Human Rights at the University of Groningen, the Netherlands. She received her PhD in Anthropology from the London School of Economics in 2016, where her research focused on the politics of religious freedom in the contemporary United Kingdom.

Ed Morgan is a Barrister, canonical advocate and ecclesiastical judge. He is a Visiting Professor at the Faculty of Canon Law, Katholieke Universiteit, Leuven and a Fellow at the Centre for Law and Religion at Cardiff University. He has contributed to *Sweet & Maxwell's Encyclopaedia of Employment Law* and is principal author of the *Directory on the Canonical Status of Clergy – Rights, Obligations and Procedures* (Catholic Bishops' Conference of England and Wales, 2009).

Megan Pearson is a Teaching Fellow in the School of Law, University of Southampton. She is the author of *Proportionality, Equality Laws and Religion* (Routledge, 2017) and several articles on Law and Religion. Her research interests are primarily in Discrimination Law, Law and Religion, Human Rights and Comparative Law.

David Pocklington is an independent researcher whose primary interests lie in the fields of Ecclesiastical Law and Environmental Law. In addition to his books and publications, he has a long-established column in *Environmental Law and Management* and co-edits the Law and Religion UK blog with Frank Cranmer.

Russell Sandberg is Professor in Law at Cardiff University. He is the author of *Law and Religion* (Cambridge University Press, 2011); *Religion, Law and Society* (Cambridge University Press, 2014); and (with Mark Hill QC and Norman Doe), *Religion and Law in the United Kingdom* (2nd edn, Kluwer Law International, 2014). He is Series Editor for Leading Works in Law, a series editor for Transforming Legal Histories and the Managing Editor of the ICLARS Series on Law and Religion, published by Routledge.

Sharon Thompson is a Senior Lecturer in Law at Cardiff University. She is the author of *Prenuptial Agreements and the Presumption of Free Choice: Issues of Power in Theory and Practice* (Hart, 2015), which was cited and applied by the High Court of Australia in *Thorne v Kennedy* [2017] HCA 49. She researches the areas of divorce, family property, prenuptial agreements and mid-twentieth-century legal history, with a particular focus on feminist perspectives.

Lucy Vickers is Professor of Law at Oxford Brookes University. She is the author of *Religious Freedom, Religious Discrimination and the Workplace* (2nd edn,

Hart Publishing, 2016), and (with Peter Edge), *EHRC Report 97: Review of Equality and Human Rights Law relating to Religion or Belief* (2015).

John Witte, Jr is Robert W Woodruff Professor of Law, McDonald Distinguished Professor, and director of the Center for the Study of Law and Religion at Emory University. A leading specialist in legal history, family law, religious liberty, human rights, and law and Christianity, he has published over 250 articles, sixteen journal symposia, and thirty books. Recent book titles include *The Western Case for Monogamy over Polygamy* (Cambridge University Press, 2015); *Religion and the American Constitutional Experiment* (4th edn, Oxford University Press, 2016); *Christianity and Family Law: An Introduction* (Cambridge University Press, 2017); and *Church, State, and Family: Reconciling Traditional Teachings and Modern Liberties* (Cambridge University Press, 2018).

Acknowledgments

As with any edited collection, I am beholden first and foremost to the contributors to *Leading Works in Law and Religion*. Many of the contributors presented early drafts at the Law and Religion Scholars Network Conference at Cardiff University in May 2016 and presented later drafts at a specially convened workshop in Cardiff in December 2016 attended by Professor John Witte Jr prior to a lecture he gave to launch Cardiff's new Law and History research group. I am obliged to the research group and the Centre for Law and Religion at Cardiff University for hosting and providing funding for these events and to the Events team at the School of Law and Politics at Cardiff University, Sarah Kennedy and Antoinette Samuel, for their outstanding support.

I am also indebted to Dani O'Connor for her work in helping to edit the volume. I am also extremely grateful to Dr Celia Kenny with whom I first developed the Leading Works format and to Dr Sharon Thompson with whom I have refined it. I am also in the debt of Alison Kirk and her team at Routledge for their sterling support and professional dedication to the text and to developing Leading Works into a book series.

The development of this book coincided with my term of office as Head of the Law Department at Cardiff University and that experience has taught me a considerable amount about the quality, value, distinctiveness and vividness of legal education. I am extremely grateful to a number of colleagues in the Law Department not only for conversations that have helped shaped the contents of this book but also for their personal support which has allowed me some time to complete this volume. I am especially grateful to Dr Sharon Thompson, Dr Katie Richards, Dr Lydia Hayes, Professor Elen Stokes and Dr Leanne Smith as well as my colleagues at the Centre for Law and Religion, most notably Professor Norman Doe, Mark Hill QC and Frank Cranmer.

I would like to dedicate *Leading Works in Law and Religion* to all the legal educators that I have had the good fortune to work with.

Russell Sandberg, July 2018

Series introduction

Russell Sandberg

As Anthony Giddens has noted:

> 'Every recognized intellectual discipline has gone through a process of self-legitimization not unlike that involved in the founding of nations. All disciplines have their fictive histories; all are imagined communities which invoke myths of the past as a means of both charting their own internal development and unity, and also drawing boundaries between themselves and other neighbouring disciplines'.[1]

The world of higher education is changing. Old stereotypes of lone scholars residing in timeless ivory towers, if ever true, no longer resonate in an age of mass university attendance where students are regarded as consumers and where great (perhaps overriding) emphasis is placed upon the impact of research as the manifestation of its worth. In our 'on demand' era an excess of content is always available, waiting to be binged at a time and place that suits the consumer. An individualised consumption culture exists that is intuitively at odds with the collective learning activity that a university has traditionally encapsulated. Researchers are cast adrift in a sea of scholarly outputs. Buckled shelves in libraries have been superseded by an online world where a plethora of books, articles and blog-posts are consulted (and perhaps read) only after they have been found by search engines. This culture of excess arguably makes universities even more important. In the lightning-paced, ultra-superficial world where information (but not knowledge) is at our finger-tips, where social media algorithms reinforce our own biases and where everyone is a journalist liking, tweeting and blogging content with little attention paid to sources or the correctness of the information, it is arguably even more important to have spaces to think, to pause and to critique; places where questions are even more important than answers and where not only all options are on the table but it is even questioned whether or not there is a need for that table.

1 A Giddens, *Politics, Sociology and Social Theory* (Polity Press, 1995) 5.

These changes have impacted upon legal education. The place of the law school within the academy remains characterised by some ill-ease. Law schools' links with the legal profession but location within universities means that law schools are often torn between being academic and vocational.[2] Their increased emphasis upon research in recent years, shaped by the Research Excellence Framework and its predecessors, has been manifest in the way that law lecturers are now more likely to possess a PhD than have experience in legal practice. This now sits uncomfortably with their need to teach a body of knowledge and a skill-set prescribed by regulatory bodies of professions that many law students will follow their tutors in not entering. Though the closing years of the twentieth century and opening years of the twenty-first century has seen an explosion of interest in interdisciplinary research (reflected most clearly perhaps in doctoral research), the law school and the law library are often regarded as being isolated from other parts of the university. There remains a suspicion that their activities are distinct. Erroneously, legal reasoning and analytical skills are still not commonly regarded as being research methods. And tensions remain within law schools surrounding divisions between (and the perceived relative value of) doctrinal work that situates legal academia within the world of legal practice and the socio-legal work that situates legal scholars within the wider context of the academy. Even where academic isolationism has been overcome, the plurality of disciplinary perspectives that can be applied to law has often been overwhelming. The work of Mathias Siems and Daithi Mac Sithigh seeking to 'map legal research' in the United Kingdom found that legal scholarship was faced by a choice as to 'whether to "go American" in moving closer to social sciences, or "go German" in remaining closer to the humanities'.[3] This dilemma is reflected in the way in which funding for legal research projects is available from both the Arts and Humanities Research Council (AHRC) and the Economic and Social Research Council (ESRC). Law schools are increasingly characterised by a plurality of approaches, presumptions and values which at first glimpse often appear to be contradictory.

The pace of change within higher education as a whole and within legal education in particular has meant that there has been little chance to take a step back to explore, analyse and question the overall trajectory, to look at how legal education has changed and how it is likely to develop in the future. However, the pace of change also makes such an analysis timely and important. This is particularly true at the level of legal sub-disciplines.[4] Both academics and practitioners recognise and perpetuate (albeit slightly different) sub-disciplines within law, including the distinction between private and public law, the identification of bodies of law relating to distinct legal actions (such as the law of Tort, Contract and Trusts) as well

2 See further F Cownie (ed) *Stakeholders in the Law School* (Hart, 2010).

3 MM Siems and D Mac Sithigh, 'Mapping Legal Research' [2012] *Cambridge Law Journal* 651, 673.

4 A term used by, for example, A Bradney, 'The Rise and Rise of Legal Education' (1997) 4 *Web Journal of Current Legal Issues*. Available at http://webjcli.ncl.ac.uk/, accessed 3 September 2018.

as sub-disciplines that focus on certain legal relationships (such as Employment Law, Sports Law or Family Law). Such labels – like all labels – are, of course, rough and ready classifications of convenience that are the product of history, culture and politics with the distinctions made never being absolute. However, although overlap and movement between sub-disciplines is commonplace, legal sub-disciplines are entrenched. Like any typology or classification, the use of legal sub-disciplines is a helpful means of identifying and sorting primary and secondary sources. However, it is vital that the artificial and constructed nature of the categorisation is not forgotten. The labels we give legal sub-discipline invariably identify not only a bespoke body of law and practice but also an identifiable scholarly community. Academic lawyers tend to self-identify by reference to one or more legal sub-disciplines ('I am an expert in Tort Law', 'I teach Employment Law' and so on) and much activity occurs at a sub-discipline level both in terms of teaching (note the overabundance of textbooks) and research (with academic books and legal conferences being divided more often than not upon sub-disciplinary lines).

As Roger Cotterrell has pointed out, academic disciplines need to be understood 'primarily as social phenomena'.[5] This is equally true of sub-disciplines; they need to be understood as the social creation of those who work in each knowledge field. In the words of Anthony Giddens, disciplines (and by implication sub-disciplines) develop their own 'fictive histories'.[6] They form their own identities, deciding what is included and what is excluded, what is valued and devalued and what methodological and theoretical approaches are to be embraced and which are to be shunned. Sub-disciplines define themselves in both positive and negative terms and by distinguishing themselves from others. Most of this is achieved implicitly, the unspoken decisions that inform the content of syllabuses, textbooks, journals and book series. Yet, this can be hugely influential, perpetuating a particular way of studying the sub-discipline. And it can also be constraining, excluding work and approaches.

The Leading Works book series is designed to fire a critical light at the way in which sub-disciplines regard themselves and perpetuate their identity. It asks leading and emerging scholars in the field to select and analyse a 'leading work'. The intention is to use these leading works as a means to explore, analyse and critique the development of the sub-discipline. The objectives of the Leading Works series are:

(i) to map current understandings of legal sub-disciplines by identifying leading works in them;
(ii) to show how these works give identity to the legal sub-disciplines, shaping them and plotting their development; and
(iii) to provide a vehicle for critique of the way the works constitute the legal sub-disciplines.

5 Cotterrell cites the work of Michel Foucault, particularly M Foucault, *The Archaeology of Knowledge* (Routledge, 2002 [originally published in 1969]), as a highly influential way of thinking of academic disciplines as social constructs: R Cotterrell, *Law's Community* (Clarendon Press, 1995) 42.

6 A Giddens, *Politics, Sociology and Social Theory* (Polity Press, 1995) 5.

The chapters explore the likely implications and applications of the leading work upon the sub-discipline in question. Most leading works will have been chosen because they have contributed internationally to the development of their sub-discipline as a whole. Following the insights of Cotterrell and Giddens, discussion of those works is likely to be in part autobiographical, exploring how the work in question has impacted upon the contributor's own scholarship and understanding of the sub-discipline in question. However, leading works will also include works that have had little influence on the field but should have done. In these chapters, contributors will explain why the work has been important for them, the consequences that ignoring the work has had upon the sub-discipline and how the work could transform the field. The Leading Works series will also include chapters by contributors who are critical of works that have limited the sub-discipline. Contributors will discuss how such works have reduced the sub-discipline by what they exclude either implicitly or explicitly.

The Leading Works series is designed to unpack and critique the architecture of law school understandings of law and of particular legal sub-disciplines. The questions of what constitutes a discipline and sub-discipline and how these fields of knowledge develop in rapidly changing times will be central. The format provides a critique of the conventional canons within legal sub-disciplines and some chapters will explicitly focus on gender, race, class, disabilities or age inequalities to critique the way in which the sub-discipline has developed. Each book, as a whole, is intended to assess the development of the sub-discipline to date and comment on its potential future development. This will come to the fore in the introductory and concluding chapters: the introductory chapter provides an account of the development of the sub-discipline, highlighting the main tensions, while the concluding chapter reflects upon what the nominated leading works suggests in terms of the future development of the sub-discipline.

It should be noted that the leading works chosen are not meant to be exhaustive; they are simply illustrative and a means by which the contributors reflect upon the often unspoken question about how and why a sub-discipline has developed in the way that it has and its likely and desired future development. The approach rather is akin to Radio Four's *Desert Island Discs* or BBC One's *Room 101*. Each contributor has been given a free choice in his/her selection of leading works. The definition of the term 'leading work' is determined by each contributor. It includes books, book chapters, articles and any other medium that has been or should have been influential in the sub-discipline. There is no restriction on the choice of leading works in terms of geography or discipline. However, since the way in which sub-disciplines develop varies geographically, in most books the contributors themselves will be sought only from the UK and Ireland so that the book as a whole can reflect upon the development of the sub-discipline there.

Contributors have also been asked to follow a prescribed format so that comparisons can be drawn. The 'leading works' essays are presented according to the names of the contributors in alphabetical order. The title of each chapter includes the name of the leading work in italics. Each chapter follows a set grid and will consist of four sections. The first, 'The Work', introduces both the author and the leading work. The second, 'The Context', situates the chosen work within the literature and within the sub-discipline as a whole. The third, 'The Significance', is the main part of each chapter: the analysis and discussion of the reason that the chosen work *leads* scholars in new directions. The fourth and final part, 'The Legacy', provides the conclusion, summarising the arguments of the chapter as to whether, and if so why, it is a leading work and also reflecting on the likely effect the leading work will have in the future.

***

This first book in the Series seeks to explore and critique the development of Law and Religion as a legal sub-discipline. As the next chapter will explain, Law and Religion is a relatively recent addition to the law school curriculum. It may be questioned whether it should be regarded as a sub-discipline or rather regarded as an interdisciplinary interaction such as Law and Literature. The trend so far has been largely to regard it as a sub-discipline, taught and researched mainly in law schools. One of the key questions that this book will address in looking at the development of Law and Religion in this jurisdiction will be to explore the extent to which Law and Religion has become a sub-discipline, the effect of this and what the future may hold for the study of Law and Religion.

1 Prologue

Russell Sandberg

The interdisciplinary ideal of Law and Religion

Writing in 2012, the esteemed American scholar of Law and Religion John Witte Jr described how 'a new interdisciplinary movement has emerged in the United States dedicated to the study of the religious dimensions of law, the legal dimensions of religion and the interaction of legal and religious ideas and institutions, norms and practices'.[1] This increase in interest in the interaction between Law and Religion has been felt not only in the United States. Continental Europe, where aspects of Law and Religion have long been studied and taught recent years, has seen the topic become increasingly controversial and the focus evolve beyond the study of Church and State. In other jurisdictions, such as the United Kingdom, Australia and South Africa, Law and Religion has become established as an area of study for the first time, with research clusters and courses being set up and academics defining themselves as Law and Religion scholars.

However, it can be questioned whether the US experience described by Witte has yet come to exist on this side of the Atlantic. Witte's interdisciplinary conceptualisation of Law and Religion studies has much in common with work on Law and Literature where a familiar distinction has been drawn between 'law in literature' (the examination of 'the possible relevance of literary texts . . . as texts appropriate for legal scholars') and 'law as literature' (which 'seeks to apply the techniques of literary criticism to legal texts').[2] This entails reading law as literature and literature as law. Witte's schema suggests that similarly the interdisciplinary study of Law and Religion can be understood as involving the study of law as religion (the study of how laws and legal mechanisms can be understood religiously) and the study of religion as law (the study of how religious texts and practices can be understood legally). Understood as an interdisciplinary endeavour, Law and Religion involves both reading law religiously and understanding

1 J Witte, Jr., 'The Study of Law and Religion in the United States: An Interim Report' 14 (2012) *Ecclesiastical Law Journal* 327.

2 I Ward, *Law and Literature: Possibilities and Perspectives* (Cambridge University Press, 1995) 3.

religion legally. In the words of Witte, a 'dialectical interaction' between Law and Religion is required:

> This study is predicated on the assumptions that religion gives law its spirit and inspires its adherence to ritual and justice. Law gives religion its structure and encourages its devotion to order and organisation. Law and religion share such ideas as fault, obligation and covenant and such methods as ethics, rhetoric and textual interpretation. Law and religion also balance each other by counterpoising justice and mercy, rule and equity, discipline and love. This dialectical interaction gives these two disciplines and dimensions of life their vitality and their strength.[3]

For Witte, 'law and religion are distinct spheres and sciences of human life, but they exist in dialectical interaction, constantly crossing over and cross-fertilising each other'.[4] There is a need to study Law and Religion as two distinct spheres, not only in how they interact with one another but also how they see and reconstruct one another on their own terms. To date, however, the field of Law and Religion in the United Kingdom has rarely achieved this ambition. Though there are notable exceptions, the study of Law and Religion on this side of the pond has not yet developed into an interdisciplinary endeavour.[5] Law and Religion has mostly developed as an area of study within law schools. It has developed as a legal sub-discipline focusing very much on understanding religion legally rather than understanding law religiously. The focus has tended to be on understanding how national and international laws regulate religion (which I have labelled as 'Religion Law')[6] and the challenges that religious conviction (both individually and collectively held) pose for the State. There has been some growing focus upon how religious groups use law to regulate their own internal affairs (which I have referred to as 'Religious Law') but even there the focus has been very much upon debating the proper role of the State.

A reason for this is that political and social changes have shaped the agenda of Law and Religion studies. The rise in scholarly writing and teaching on religion in law schools has coincided with significant changes which have challenged conventional assumptions that predicted the social decline of religion, especially post-September 11th. As Julian Rivers has noted, there has been 'a new loss of consensus about the role and significance of religion'.[7] There are numerous causes of this.[8] The notion of religion as a benign force has been challenged in

3 J Witte, Jr., 'The Study of Law and Religion in the United States: An Interim Report' 14 (2012) *Ecclesiastical Law Journal* 327, 327–328.

4 Ibid 328.

5 See further, R Sandberg, *Religion, Law and Society* (Cambridge University Press, 2014) ch. 1.

6 R Sandberg, *Law and Religion* (Cambridge University Press, 2011) ch.1.

7 J Rivers, 'The Secularisation of the British Constitution' (2012) 14 *Ecclesiastical Law Journal* 371, 385.

8 See further Sandberg, *Religion, Law and Society*, ch. 5.

an age when all authority is questioned, where populations are more diverse than ever before, where individual's identities are more multifaceted and where acts of terror in the name of religion dominate the news headlines. Neither talk of secularisation nor of religious revival come close to adequately describing the situation in which we find ourselves. A complex cocktail of constantly changing causes has created an age of uncertainty, which has meant, amongst other things, that the place of religion in the public sphere has become ever-controversial, divisive and disputed.

The conventional account has drawn a line of causation between these political and social developments and the rise of Law and Religion studies. It has been commonly assumed that Law and Religion blossomed as an area of study as its subject-matter has become more controversial. This account sees the development of Law and Religion as a pragmatic development. The early years of the twenty-first century saw a number of moral panics about the place of religion in the public sphere: media and political heat roasted such topics as religious dress and symbols, the operation of religious tribunals and the clash of rights between religious freedom on the one hand and freedom of expression or homosexual rights on the other. Given this backdrop, the growth in scholarly literature on issues concerning religion and the law was unsurprising. This was particularly predictable given that many of the social and political changes of the late twentieth and early twenty-first century concerning religion had a legal dimension. An abundance of new laws were passed regulating religion, followed by a multitude of cases seeking to define the contours of the new religious rights and how the new laws interact (or not) with earlier provisions and older understandings. These changes, both novel and newsworthy, meant that legal scholars began to pay attention to religion. Elsewhere I have referred to these developments and the general acceptance that religion was a problem that could be understood and solved by legal means as constituting the juridification of religion.[9]

The growth of Law and Religion

There is ample evidence to support this conventional account of the recent rise of Law and Religion. The English Reformation of the 1530s resulted in the side-lining of religious law. The termination of Papal jurisdiction was accompanied by a prohibition on the teaching of Canon Law at the Universities of Oxford and Cambridge.[10] The ban on the study of Catholic canon law did not result in the infant ecclesiastical law of the Church of England becoming a subject of study. Although lawyers in the Church courts continued to appeal to

9 Sandberg, *Law and Religion*, 193–195 and Sandberg, *Religion, Law and Society*, ch. 1.

10 Injunctions were issued in 1535 which substituted lectures in Civil Law for lectures in Canon Law and in 1545 an Act (37 Henry VIII c. 17) allowed judgeships in the ecclesiastical courts to be held by laymen who were doctors only of Civil Law.

Roman Canon Law,[11] the developing ecclesiastical law of the Church became solely the subject of professional training at a learned society which came to be known as Doctors' Commons.[12] As the centuries wore on, the law of the Church was occasionally the subject of professional texts but almost no attention was given to the general interaction between Law and Religion. Even when alternative forms of religiosity became lawful following the slow and piecemeal march of toleration, there was no discrete law on religious freedom to comment upon and no identifiable social problem. As Maitland expressed it in his lectures subsequently published as *The Constitutional History of England*, 'religious liberty and religious equality [was] complete'.[13] The powers of the ecclesiastical courts of the Church of England had 'very much declined'.[14] And the feeling was that there was very little to say about the interaction between Law and Religion, at least in England.

This was still true by the mid- to late twentieth century. Legal textbooks seldom mentioned religion;[15] and while works on the law of the Church of England were occasionally published these were mostly practical guides rather than academic treatises.[16] Moreover, the literature rarely extended beyond the study of the law of the established Church.[17] Questions concerning how English law facilitated the exercise of religious freedom by groups other than the Church of England or by individuals went largely unasked. However, by 2000, this had significantly changed. An academic industry devoted to Law and Religion had come into

11 R Helmholz, *Roman Catholic Law in Reformation England* (Cambridge University Press, 1991). The Submission of the Clergy Act 1533 provided that the Roman canon law was to continue to apply unless it was 'contrariant or repugnant to the law, statutes or custom' of the realm or to the King's prerogative.

12 See GD Squibb, *Doctors' Commons: A History of the College of Advocates and Doctors of Law*, (Clarendon Press, 1977); P Barber, 'The Fall and Rise of Doctors' Commons' (1996) 4 (18) *Ecclesiastical Law Journal* 462; D Polkington, 'The Continued Relevance of Doctors' Commons' (2011) 166 *Law and Justice* 52. For a discussion of the term 'Ecclesiastical Law' see R Sandberg, *Law and Religion* (Cambridge University Press, 2011) 7–9.

13 FW *Maitland, Constitutional History of England* (Cambridge University Press, 1908) 520. It is worth noting that Maitland did dedicate a twenty-page section to 'The Church' which examined the legal historical development of the Church of England, the history of toleration, the present condition and powers of the ecclesiastical courts and the status of the established church: ibid 506–526.

14 Ibid, 523. On which see RB Outhwaite, *The Rise and Fall of the Ecclesiastical Courts, 1500–1860* (Cambridge University Press, 2006).

15 J Rivers, 'The Secularisation of the British Constitution' (2012) 14 *Ecclesiastical Law Journal* 371, 372.

16 See, e.g, W Dale, *The Law of the Parish Church* (Butterworths, 1932); G Moore, *Introduction to English Canon Law* (Clarendon, 1967); G Moore, T Briden and K MacMorran, *Handbook for Churchwardens and Parochial Church Councillors* (Mowbray, 1989); J Pitchford, *An ABC for the PCC* (Wyche 1980).

17 The 1975 edition of the Ecclesiastical Law volume of *Halsbury's Laws of England* (4th edn, vol. 14, London, 1975), for instance, dealt with 'other religious denominations' as an afterthought.

existence.[18] There were now specialist journals, book series, research clusters and conferences as well as academics that identified their research interest as being Law and Religion. To a lesser extent, there were now courses and textbooks dedicated to the subject, though it remained largely true that legal textbooks on areas such as Public Law, Family Law and Employment Law seldom mentioned religion. It is tempting to see the post-9/11 tide of legislation and litigation as the main cause of this; to say that the sub-discipline of Law and Religion was created by new laws formally regarding religion as a human right actionable in domestic courts and laws expressly and specifically prohibiting discrimination on grounds of religion or belief.[19] However, this would be a simplification. The early twenty-first century clearly saw a significant increase in Law and Religion activity.[20] But the birth of the sub-discipline came much earlier.

Developments in the 1980s and 1990s awakened interest in the law of the Church of England and treated it as the subject of academic analysis for the first time.[21] Moral panic concerning the publication of *The Satanic Verses* lit a fuse which continues to burn today. And even earlier, the impact of what Charles Taylor has referred to as the 'individuating revolution' of the 1960s was to have significant long-term ramifications.[22] Maitland's assumption that religious freedom was 'complete' was questioned way before 9/11. The rise of Law and Religion studies was not the overnight sensation it is often assumed to have been. Tensions between secular authorities and religious convictions are a constant throughout history. It is correct that the early twenty-first century saw a renewed focus upon the place of religion, and Islam in particular, in the public sphere. However, laws

18 The language of 'industry' is derived from R Grillo, *Muslim Families, Politics and the Law* (Ashgate, 2015).

19 By virtue of the Human Rights Act 1998, the Employment Equality (Religion or Belief) Regulations 2003 and the Equality Act 2006 (now see the Equality Act 2010).

20 A bibliography compiled for the Ecclesiastical Law Society's silver jubilee indicated that whilst between 1987 and 1997 there were on average two to three books published per year, this figure grew to an average of six books between 1997 and 2000 and to ten books after 2007. This rise was even more accelerated in the case of edited books. See R Sandberg, 'Silver Jubilee Bibliography: Ecclesiastical Law Publications 1987–2011' (2012) 14 *Ecclesiastical Law Journal* 149.

21 In 1987, the Ecclesiastical Law Society was formed 'to promote the study of ecclesiastical and canon law particularly in the Church of England and those churches in communion with it'; while in 1991, the LLM in Canon Law degree was launched at Cardiff University, the first degree to study the laws of the Church of England and Catholic Canon Law since the Reformation. Throughout the 1990s the focus of both institutions broadened. The Ecclesiastical Law Society's journal, the *Ecclesiastical Law Journal*, published articles on the laws of other religions and faith communities and on national and international laws affecting religion while the success of the LLM programme led Cardiff University to establish its Centre for Law and Religion in 1998. See N Doe, 'The First Ten Years of the Centre for Law and Religion, Cardiff University' (2008) 10 (2) *Ecclesiastical Law Journal* 222.

22 C Taylor, *Varieties of Religion Today* (Harvard University Press, 2002) 80. See further Sandberg, *Religion, Law and Society*, ch. 5.

have long prohibited, constrained, tolerated, enabled, privileged and burdened both religious groups and the religious beliefs and actions of individuals. Moral panics that once concerned Catholicism have been superseded by moral panics about Islam. The growth of the Law and Religion industry is not purely attributable to the wider political and social change. The increase in academic attention is also in part attributable to cultural change within the academic world whereby research has become more central to the mission of Law Schools and a growing move towards interdisciplinary and innovative work. The conventional account of the twenty-first century juridification of religion is therefore something of a simplification.

The limits of Law and Religion

The commonly assumed context of the juridification of religion which is seen as providing the catalyst for the expansion and development of Law and Religion scholarship has also constrained it. As Anthony Bradney has observed, Law and Religion scholarship has tended to assume and characterise the relationship between Law and Religion 'as a problem that is capable of solution'.[23] The moral panics of the early twenty-first century have meant that attention has often been narrow with much attention being afforded to particular spots of conflict. Law and Religion scholarship has tended to be narrow and rather parochial.

The study of Law and Religion has developed as a legal endeavour, what Witte calls 'the legal dimensions of religion';[24] the study of religion performed legally almost mainly within law schools.[25] The development of Law and Religion as a *legal* sub-discipline has itself gone largely unquestioned. While literature in other 'Law and' areas have developed with close interaction with people, literatures and methods from other disciplines, academic lawyers have dominated the study of Law and Religion and the work in the field remains characterised by academic isolationism; throw-away references to work completed outside the law school is commonplace but the synthesis of work and approaches from other parts of the academy within works of Law and Religion scholarship remains exceptional.[26] In short, the 'and' in the term 'Law and Religion' has too often been overlooked.

The legal nature of Law and Religion scholarship has narrowly construed and interpreted religion. Writing over twenty years ago, Michael King accurately predicted that law would reconstruct religion 'essentially as those customs, rites and rituals which in the public domain come to symbolize statements of faith and

23 A Bradney, 'Politics and Sociology: New Research Agenda for the Study of Law and Religion' in R O'Dair and A Lewis (eds), *Law and Religion* (Oxford University Press, 2001) 65, 68.

24 J Witte, Jr., 'The Study of Law and Religion in the United States: An Interim Report' 14 (2012) *Ecclesiastical Law Journal* 327.

25 And there are important questions about the identity of the scholars who have done much of this work in terms of their religion, race, gender, sexuality and geography.

26 See Sandberg, *Religion, Law and Society*, ch. 1.

holiness . . . as rights of worship and performance of ritual' and that law would likely see religion 'as constituting for law a set of rights' which would often result in judges 'seeing it in terms of some external authority' such as 'a law, God's law, Islamic law'.[27] This prediction has come true. This is underlined by the work of Suhraiya Jivraj which has criticised what she refers to as 'socio-legal law-and-religion scholarship' for 'conceptualizing religion in predominately theological terms such as belief/faith and practice' which 'tends to marginalize [the] racialization of non-Christianness' and understands religion 'as a contingent concept that can come to be produced within law'.[28] Jivraj argues that this is equally true of Law and Religion scholarship that accepts 'more complex notions of religious identity' in that these works perpetuate 'an onto-theological model of belief and ritual practice' that is 'so often left un-interrogated'.[29] She argues that a critical approach deriving from Anthropology, Religious Studies and Critical Race Studies is required that understands religion contextually and historically 'as contingent upon and as part of particular political, economic, and other circumstances' to 'challenge not only the onto-theological notion of religion through various methodological routes, but also the idea that there can be any fixed concept of religion at all'.[30] Her work therefore underlines the cosy consensus of taken-for-granted assumptions about the nature of religion and religious behaviour that is commonly found within the Law and Religion literature and for Jivraj can 'often be influential on legal developments'.[31] Jivraj's critique underscores the problematic consequences of the isolated way in which Law and Religion scholarship has developed. The moral panics that provided its context have narrowed its focus and its ambition.

These concerns are rarely discussed in the Law and Religion literature. There has been a huge growth in both the amount of literature and the institutional framework surrounding it (consisting of journals, book series, societies and so on). However, little attention has been paid to questioning how the field has developed and how it may develop in the future.[32] The near absence of textbook or student-friendly texts has meant that, unlike other legal sub-disciplines, there have been only a few attempts to map the field as a whole or even to formulate a conception (either explicitly or implicitly) of what is taught and researched under

27 M King, The Muslim Identity in a Secular World' in M King (ed) *God's Law Versus State Law* (Great Seal, 1995) 91, 108, 110.

28 S Jivraj, *The Religion of Law: Race, Citizenship and Children's Belonging* (Palgrave, 2013) 82.

29 Ibid, 28.

30 Ibid, 6–7.

31 Ibid, 3.

32 For notable exceptions see A Bradney, 'Politics and Sociology: New Research Agenda for the Study of Law and Religion' in R O'Dair and A Lewis (eds), *Law and Religion* (Oxford University Press, 2001) 65; the essays in N Doe and R Sandberg (ed) *Law and Religion: New Horizons* (Peeters, 2010); Sandberg, *Law and Religion*; Sandberg, *Religion, Law and Society* (Cambridge University Press, 2014) and the essays published as part of the 25th anniversary of the Ecclesiastical Law Society in (2012) 14 *Ecclesiastical Law Journal.*

the banner of Law and Religion in law schools. There remains a lack of identity and a suspicion that it may not be more than the sum of its parts – an undeveloped Frankenstein's monster of other 'proper' legal areas.[33] A suspicion remains that what we are dealing with is not the development of a new area of study but rather a number of separate areas of interaction between religion and discrete and well-established areas of law. Although some works have sought to identify an overarching legal framework concerning religion,[34] most of the time the only connection that unites Law and Religion work is its focus on religion. Developments concerning religion in Criminal Law, Discrimination Law, Human Rights Law, Family Law and so on can be understood solely in those terms. They are not interrelated to the degree that they ought to be understood as part of an overall body of law concerning religion.

The question remains of whether the study of Law and Religion amounts to more than the sum of its parts. The juridification of religion – the rise of positive religious rights articulated in human rights and discrimination provisions – has undoubtedly stimulated the growth of Law and Religion as an area of research and teaching within law schools. It has also helped to create a body of law which is often but not always referred to in other developments concerning religion.[35] Yet, the way in which Law and Religion has developed as a sub-discipline remains uneven. There are some signs that Law and Religion is as well established (if not more established) than some other newly formed legal sub-disciplines such as Sports Law or Education Law. This is evident in terms of the number of specialist journals, the sheer number of academic publications and the thriving societies formed at both national and international level. However, there are other signs that Law and Religion is less well established than other sub-disciplines. Law and Religion lags behind other sub-disciplines in terms of the number of courses taught and the quantity of works aimed at a student readership, for instance. Taken as a whole, Law and Religion is currently in a state of flux; it shows some signs of developing into a sub-discipline but is not there yet.

The ghettoisation of Law and Religion

This state of flux is very damaging for Law and Religion scholarship. Although Law and Religion has not to date become a fully-formed legal sub-discipline,

33 Similar concerns have been raised in relation to Family Law as discussed by G Douglas, *An Introduction to Family Law* 2nd edn (Clarendon Press, 2004) 3–4 and in relation to Sports Law, see, e.g., M James, *Sports Law* (Palgrave Macmillan, 2010) 19; and S Gardiner *et al*, *Sports Law* 3rd edn (Cavendish, 2006) 88–91.

34 Most notably J Rivers, *The Law of Organized Religions* (Oxford University Press, 2010) and Sandberg, *Law and Religion*.

35 For analysis of this in relation to the definition of religion where there has been some movement towards a common definition which recent cases have departed from see R Sandberg, 'Clarifying the Definition of Religion Under English Law: The Need for a Universal Definition' (2018) 20 *Ecclesiastical Law Journal* 132.

ironically the structures set up in order to help grow the sub-discipline, such as specialist journals and associations, have ended up constraining it. Much Law and Religion work is being disseminated in ways and in places that limit its appeal to those already within the clique. There is a real risk of ghettoisation: there is a danger that Law and Religion scholars will speak only to one another and will be immune from and unable to shape wider debates within the discipline of Law (not to mention the wider risks caused by the academic isolationism of Law and Religion scholarship that comes from such work being mainly situated in law schools).This means that Law and Religion scholarship has not benefited as much as it could have done from wider expertise and insights (both in and outside of law schools). There are, of course, exceptions, especially where the Law and Religion scholar is also an expert in the wider area of law, such as Lucy Vickers' work on religious discrimination and Malcolm Evans' work on Religion and International Human Rights Law.[36] However, overall, Law and Religion writers on religion and Criminal Law, Discrimination Law, Human Rights Law, Family Law and so on do not engage with or place their work within the wider context of those legal sub-disciplines.

This can be illustrated by my work co-authored with Sharon Thompson (an expert in Family Law). Our collaborative research argued the need to place the concerns about the operation of religious tribunals (a significant focus of Law and Religion scholarship following Rowan Williams' speech on religious and civil law)[37] within the context of wider developments within Family Law. It argued that the concerns raised by Sharia debate can be addressed by three general reforms to the law on adult relationships which are also merited in Family Law generally.[38] First, numerous studies of Islamic tribunals have highlighted concerns about marriages that are not registered under State law meaning that where that relationship breaks down the couple have no remedy under State law and have to rely upon Islamic tribunals and other forms of dispute resolution.[39] There is no clear answer as to why such marriages are not legally registered but this could be due in part to current laws concerning where and how people can get married.

36 Most notably MD Evans *Religious Liberty and International Law in Europe* (Cambridge University Press, 1997) and L Vickers, *Religious Freedom, Religious Discrimination and the Workplace* (2nd edn, Hart, 2017).

37 R Williams, 'Civil and Religious Law in England – A Religious Perspective' (2008) 10 *Ecclesiastical Law Journal* 262. See R Grillo, *Muslim Families, Politics and the Law* (Ashgate, 2015).

38 R Sandberg and S Thompson, 'The Sharia Debate: The Missing Family Law Context' (2016) 177 *Law & Justice* 188; R Sandberg and S Thompson, 'Relational Autonomy and Religious Tribunals' (2017) *Oxford Journal of Law and Religion* 237; and S Thompson and R Sandberg, 'Common Defects of the Divorce Bill and Arbitration and Mediation Services (Equality) Bill 2016–17' (2017) *Family Law* 447.

39 S Shah-Kazemi, *Untying the Knot: Muslim Women, Divorce and the Shariah*(Nuffield Foundation, 2001) S Bano *Muslim Women and Shari'ah Councils* (Palgrave, 2012) and G Douglas et al, 'Social Cohesion and Civil Law: Marriage, Divorce and Religious Courts', http://www.law.cf.ac.uk/clr/research/cohesion.html, accessed 17 August 2018.

Placing this within the Family Law context points to a need to revisit the current law on the formalities required for marriage. Recent work by the Law Commission suggested that the current law was complex, out of date and uncertain.[40] The Law Commission's Scoping Paper noted that the number of unregistered Islamic marriages was a reason for reform, but it was by no means the only one.

Second, and related to this, the Sharia debate points to a need to look again at the rights and protection given to cohabiting couples. Those who have a religious marriage but are not married under State law have the same legal status as cohabiting couples. Users of Sharia councils, such as unmarried cohabitants, also often assume that they have more legal rights than they do. The problem of the non-registration of Islamic marriages is, therefore, related to the problem of the prevalence of the myth of 'common law marriage'. Although reform of has long been mooted,[41] England and Wales currently has no legislative provision that specifically provides unmarried cohabitants with financial relief in the event of the ending of a relationship that has generated economic disadvantage. Couples dividing assets in this situation must instead navigate complex trust law principles that depend on direct financial contribution. Again, awareness of the wider Family Law context shows that concerns about religious tribunals would be best dealt with by general reform of the legal protection of unmarried cohabitants.

Third, the use of religious tribunals needs to be placed as part of a wider trend of what Gillian Douglas has referred to as 'the general de-juridification of family matters and the drive to encourage alternative dispute resolution'.[42] The severe cuts to legal aid for Family Law disputes as a result of the Legal Aid, Sentencing and Punishment of Offenders Act 2012 have reduced the legal assistance available in Family Law disputes, with the effect that people increasingly represent themselves or seek solutions out of court.[43] This means again there is a need to broaden the focus from just religious tribunals to explore the growing number of legal, quasi-legal and non-legal means of solving family disputes. The concerns about gender equality expressed in much of the work on religious tribunals are also likely to apply to non-religious forms of alternative dispute resolution. The gender biases across different legal and quasi-legal systems need

40 Law Commission, *Getting Married: A Scoping Paper* (Law Com, 17 December 2015). On which see C Barton, 'Weddings: The Law Commission's "Scoping" Paper' [2016] *Family Law* 719.

41 The Law Commission advocated reform similar to the legislation introduced in Scotland in its report to Government in 2007 (*Cohabitation: The Financial Consequences of Relationship Breakdown* (Law Com No 307) and these proposals have received public support from Lady Hale in *Gow v Grant* [2012] UKSC 29 and Resolution (an organisation of family lawyers in England and Wales).

42 G Douglas, 'Who Regulates Marriage? The Case of Religious Marriage and Divorce' in R Sandberg (ed) *Religion and Legal Pluralism* (Ashgate, 2015) 53, 61.

43 See further, e.g., L Trinder and R Hunter, 'Access to Justice? Litigants in Person before and after LASPO' [2015] *Family Law* 535; E Hitchings and J Miles, 'Mediation, Financial Remedies, Information Provision and Legal Advice: The Post-LASPO Conundrum' (2016) 38(2) *Journal of Social Welfare and Family Law* 175.

attention. Assumptions that individuals are equally free to reach mutually beneficial agreements can be especially harmful to women because research shows that economic dependencies created by unpaid work in the home (which is still disproportionately undertaken by women) is not appropriately addressed in private agreements.[44] The Family Law context shows that there is a need to revisit the regulation of mediation and alternative dispute resolution; the need for such reform is not constrained only to Sharia tribunals.[45]

Integrating and contextualising the Law and Religion debate about religious tribunals into wider debates and concerns within Family Law scholarship clearly shows that concerns about the operation of Sharia tribunals can be understood as part of a number of general trends in Family Law where reform is desperately needed and where that general reform would help to remedy, if not fully remedy, the concerns expressed in the Law and Religion literature.[46] This provides a case study which warns against the ghettoisation of Law and Religion. There is clearly a need for experts in Religion Law and Family Law to collaborate.[47] And there is a similar need for Law and Religion scholars to collaborate (or otherwise glean insights from) experts in Human Rights, Discrimination, Education Law and so on.

The partial development of Law and Religion as a legal sub-discipline has, therefore, created the worst of both worlds. On the one hand, the fact that Law and Religion is not sufficiently advanced as a legal sub-discipline means that there is still a lingering perception that it is not stronger than the sum of its parts; that it is a Frankenstein's monster of discrete areas of law that happen to interact with religion but which ultimately have little in common with each other and do not collectively constitute a legal framework. On the other hand, the attempt to formulate Law and Religion as a legal sub-discipline has meant that the field has become ghettoised with Law and Religion scholars increasingly just talking to one another and with their work becoming isolated from developments and trends within the wider areas of law that they are writing about. Moreover, this has meant that Law and Religion has developed as an activity largely situated within law schools. Rather than developing as the interdisciplinary study

44 See S Thompson, *Prenuptial Agreements and the Presumption of Free Choice: Issues of Power in Theory and Practice* (Hart/Bloomsbury 2015) and S Thompson, 'In Defence of the "gold digger"' (2016) 6(6) *Oñati Socio-Legal Series* 1225. For a move towards an alternative approach see the Australian decision in *Thorne v Kennedy* [2017] HCA 49, as discussed by S Thompson, '*Thorne v Kennedy*: Why Australia's Decision on Prenups is Important for English Law' (2018) 48 *Family Law* 415. See also S Thompson, 'Feminist Relational Contract Theory: A New Model for Family Property Agreements' (2018) 45(4) *Journal of Law and Society* (forthcoming).

45 See also K O'Sullivan and L Jackson, 'Muslim Marriage (Non) Recognition: Implication sand Possible Solutions' (2017) 39(1) *Journal of Social Welfare and Family Law* 22.

46 Sandberg and Thompson, 'The Sharia Debate: The Missing Family Law Context' (2016) 177 *Law & Justice* 188.

47 There are other areas outside the religious tribunal context where such collaboration is needed, for example, in relation to marriage and divorce generally as well as legal disputes concerning the religious upbringing of children.

envisaged by Witte,[48] on this side of the pond the study of Law and Religion has largely been constrained to the study of the legal dimensions of religion, the extent to which the State can and should accommodate religious difference.

The adolescence of Law and Religion

The study of Law and Religion on this side of the Atlantic is therefore at a transitional stage. Law and Religion is no longer in its infancy; it is now in its adolescence. Now is the time when Law and Religion will decide how it wants to develop; what it wants to grow into. As the study of Law and Religion advances from its current state of adolescence, there are a number of challenges and uncertainties but there is also the potential to build upon the successes of the sub-discipline. To achieve this, there is a need to take a step back. There is a need to make explicit the distinctions, choices and assumptions that are usually implicit. There is a need to articulate how the sub-discipline has developed, its identity, its values and its potential. It is necessary to ask questions about what the study of Law and Religion includes and excludes in terms of content, methodology and ambition. This debate will occur (and is already occurring) subconsciously anyway. Editors of Law and Religion journals, edited volumes and book series as well as individual authors, researchers and teachers are all reflecting upon these growing pains and shaping the way in which the endeavour develops. However, these issues can be properly scrutinised and debated if what is already happening implicitly is made explicit; if the past, present and future of the study of Law and Religion is critiqued, discussed and reformulated. Now is precisely the time to discuss whether, and if so how, the interdisciplinary vision of Law and Religion can be realised here as part of the continuing development of Law and Religion studies.

The book that you have in your hands is part of an attempt to begin to do precisely that. The Leading Works format brings together leading and emerging voices within Law and Religion to identify what they consider to be the formative works of the field, and in so doing to reveal their thoughts about the nature and development of Law and Religion studies. The selection is not intended to be comprehensive. The purpose is not to describe a canon of definitive works on Law and Religion. Rather, it is to use works that the contributors deem to be leading in order to map and ask questions about the development of this field of study and research. The chapters are arranged alphabetically by the surnames of the authors and so can be read in any order. Yet, taken as a whole, they develop a range of ideas and themes about how Law and Religion scholarship has developed, both positively and negatively.

The next chapter by Sylvie Bacquet provides an example of the Leading Works format being used to critique the field, examining a work that has been neglected

48 J Witte, Jr., 'The Study of Law and Religion in the United States: An Interim Report' 14 (2012) *Ecclesiastical Law Journal* 327.

by Law and Religion scholars and exploring the ramifications of this. Bacquet highlights the work of Kevin Boyle, most notably the chapters he contributed to *Striking a Balance*, a collection which explored the interaction between hate speech, freedom of expression and non-discrimination.[49] She argues that this should have been regarded as a leading work because not only was it a forerunner for the debates about the clash of rights which have come to the fore in recent years but it also highlights perspectives that have been missing in debates on Law and Religion. In pointing out this gap in Law and Religion scholarship, Bacquet argues for greater dialogue with experts in international human rights and calls for an 'International Law and Religion'.

On the surface, Anthony Bradney's chapter is on a more conventional leading work focusing on a book that has been foundational to the development of Law and Religion as an academic field. It focuses upon St John Robilliard's *Religion and the Law*,[50] an early and influential work on Law and Religion in England. Bradney's account, however, casts this familiar book in a new light, which is likely to encourage us to take it off the bookshelf more frequently. In dealing with the law's interaction with religion as a topic worthy of its own monograph, *Religion and the Law* could be seen as sowing the seeds for the ghettoisation that was to come. Yet, as Bradney shows, Robilliard's work focused on the ways in which laws interacted with religion rather than identifying a body of law. Perhaps, had this trend continued, the risk of ghettoisation would have been reduced. Moreover, Bradney discusses the extent to which Robilliard used sources and ideas from other areas of law, most notably Trusts and Family Law. This may suggest that one reason why Law and Religion developed as a separate sub-discipline was that experts in other areas of law which interacted with religion paid little interest to such interactions. Moreover, Bradney also places *Religion and the Law* within the intellectual development of law schools and this again provides an explanation for the way in which Law and Religion has developed. The increased emphasis upon research (or to be more accurate, research outputs) has led to a situation where areas of law which are not commonly taught can now be the subject of research agendas. This disconnect has meant that the questions about the identity of such sub-disciplines are not addressed and little attention is given to the shape of the field as a whole and questions of inclusion and exclusion.

Bradney's chapter is followed by two chapters by Frank Cranmer. The first provides a Scottish perspective arguing the importance of Francis Lyall's *Of Presbyters and Kings*.[51] This is perhaps the Scottish equivalent of Robilliard's *Religion and*

49 S Coliver, K Boyle and F D'Souza, *Striking a Balance: Hate Speech, Freedom of Expression and Non-Discrimination* (Article 19, Intl' Centre against Censorship, 1992).

50 St John Robilliard, *Religion and the Law: Religious Liberty in Modern English Law* (Manchester University Press, 1984).

51 F Lyall, *Of Presbyters and Kings: Church and State in the Law of Scotland* (Aberdeen University Press, 1980).

the Law in that it is a much cited foundational work which is often seen to be the first modern academic work on the topic and a precursor to the twenty-first century literature. As Cranmer's chapter shows, in addition to providing a groundbreaking account of the interaction between religion and the State in Scotland, the emphasis upon history in *Of Presbyters and Kings* is also noteworthy. History is not entirely absent from Robilliard but that book, like some of its twenty-first century successors, uses history to set the scene.[52] By contrast, in Lyall's book the rich historical account is central to his analysis. Perhaps this reflects the greater emphasis upon Legal History within Scottish law schools but the need for and importance of historial analysis of law is a theme that is developed further in later chapters of this book. Cranmer's second chapter appears to stretch the Leading Works format to its breaking point. He suggests that the obvious leading work on Law and Religion is the European Convention on Human Rights itself. What begins as a humorous subversion (starting with a touch of Rumpole), however, soon gives way to a convincing argument of the importance of the Convention and the fact that its importance extends far beyond Article 9 on freedom of thought, conscience and religion.

Cranmer's second chapter reminds us of the international context in which Law and Religion occurs and echoes Bacquet's call for more attention to be given to this. This is underscored further by the next chapter, written by Eion Daly, which highlights the importance of comparative law and interdisciplinary work. There is a rich tradition in Law and Religion studies of comparative work which classifies and distinguishes different models and approaches of religion–State relations especially in different European States. The European Consortium for Church and State Research holds annual meetings exploring the interaction in a particular context and these papers have been published.[53] And Norman Doe has written the first synthesis of this material, exploring the contours of and major principles concerning law on religion in Europe.[54] The proposition that there are distinct models of church–State relations proves to be unsustainable the minute the focus moves from the letter of the constitutional text to either its implementation in practice or to sub-constitutional Religion Law rules.[55] Yet, common misconceptions still exist about the differences in Religion Law in different European countries with the postures of countries being caricatured. This is perhaps particularly true in relation to France, where the doctrine of *Laïcité* is commonly cited for the proposition that French Religion Law is distinct and distinguishable. Daly's chapter focusing on Jean Baubérot's 2006 book translatable

52 See also J Rivers, *The Law of Organised Religion* (Oxford University Press, 2010); Sandberg, *Law and Religion*.

53 Note, in particular, G Robbers (ed), *State and Church in the European Union* (2nd edn, Nomos, 2005).

54 N Doe, *Law and Religion in Europe* (Oxford University Press, 2011).

55 See ibid, R Sandberg and N Doe, 'Church-State Relations in Europe' (2007) 1(5) *Religion Compass* 561, and R Sandberg, 'Church-State Relations in Europe: From Legal Models to an Interdisciplinary Approach' (2008) 1(3) *Journal of Religion in Europe* 329.

as *Republican Fundamentalism Against Laïcité*[56] is important in its own right in introducing the English-speaking readership to Baubérot's nuanced and revisionist understanding of *Laïcité*. It also highlights the importance not only of comparative works but also of interdisciplinary study, a theme that is developed further in later chapters of this book.

The international dimension and the importance of international human rights guarantees is underlined further in the chapter by Peter Edge and Lucy Vickers which focuses on Carolyn Evans' *Freedom of Religion under the European Convention on Human Rights*.[57] Edge and Vickers focus on the ways in which Evans' then academic concerns about the way in which the jurisprudence of the European Court of Human Rights, at a time when it was very early days in relation to the Article 9 jurisprudence, have been borne out in subsequent case law. The chapter highlights fundamental and often unresolved tensions that go to the very heart of questioning why and how religion should be protected by law. This theme is central to the next chapter, authored by Méadhbh McIvor. She examines Winnifred Fallers Sullivan's *The Impossibility of Religious Freedom*,[58] which, as the title suggests, argues that religion cannot be distinguished and so should not be separately protected. Although debates about definition and whether protection should be afforded to religion *qua* religion is present in almost every situation where religion and the law coincide, it has rarely been brought to the fore in the way that Sullivan does so. It would also be fair to say that the work, though moderately well known, has not been as influential on Law and Religion scholarship on this side of the Pond as it could be. Recent work by Silvio Ferrari dialoguing with and questioning Sullivan's thesis underlines the need to engage with *The Impossibility of Religious Freedom*.[59] This is underlined by McIvor's chapter which also provides a further example of the value of and need for interdisciplinary approaches, since Sullivan presents an ethnographic account of the application of laws guaranteeing religious liberty in the contemporary United States. Although there has been a general dearth of empirical work in legal studies in the United Kingdom, it remains a matter of regret that work that has taken place has not been as central to the development of Law and Religion as it has with other fields.[60]

56 J Baubérot, *L'intégrisme républicain contre la Laïcité (Editions de l'Aube, 2006)*.

57 C Evans, *Freedom of Religion under the European Convention on Human Rights* (Oxford University Press, 2011).

58 WF Sullivan, *The Impossibility of Religious Freedom* (Princeton University Press, 2005).

59 S Ferrari, 'Who Needs Freedom of Religion?' in Frank Cranmer et al (eds), *The Confluence of Law and Religion: Interdisciplinary Reflections on the Work of Norman Doe* (Cambridge University Press, 2016) 185.

60 Note the reduction in the number of empirical legal studies identified by the Nuffield Inquiry on Empirical Legal Research: http://ucl.ac.uk/laws/socio-legal-empirical, accessed 17 August 2018.. Family Law may be considered exceptional in this regard. It is noticeable that a significant proportion of empirical work in Law and Religion concerns matters that overlap with Family Law, most notably the role of religious tribunals in determining marital status.

Different but equally large and often neglected 'big' questions come to the fore in Ed Morgan's chapter. This looks at Harold J Berman's *Law and Revolution – The Formation of the Western Legal Tradition*,[61] a work of undeniable importance and influence. Berman's book is a renowned classic. So, given that Morgan's case for labelling his chosen text a leading work is relatively straightforward, he chooses instead to focus on Berman's argument taking a trip through both time and space to highlight the thesis. *Law and Revolution – The Formation of the Western Legal Tradition* is obviously not only of relevance to Law and Religion scholars and so Morgan's chapter also develops the argument that the concerns relating to the interaction between Law and Religion are of much broader concern and should not be relegated to a specialist sub-discipline. The chapter again underlines the need to place current controversies and current laws on religion into their context. A historical approach is crucial in this regard showing that the law is contingent.

On the surface, the next chapter by Megan Pearson provides a contrast to McIvor and to Morgan in particular by focusing in on the details of a particular interaction between Law and Religion rather than upon general and underlying principles. Pearson examines Lucy Vickers' *Religious Freedom, Religious Discrimination and the Workplace*,[62] regarding it as a ground-breaking work focusing on the protection of religion and belief within the specific context of the workplace. Vickers' work may be seen as a successor to Robilliard's *Religion and the Law*, suggesting that the existence a body of international legal norms and domestic statute and case law on this topic has not meant that one particular area of study now merits a monograph-length discussion in its own right. This underlines how much has changed in the interim period. This again raises the issue of ghettoisation: is Vickers' book best read alongside works on Religion Law or Discrimination Law or both? Moreover, despite first impressions, it would be wrong to distinguish Pearson's chapter from Morgan's. Pearson's focus on the issue of proportionality, its nature and its application, provides another example of the 'big' questions that Law and Religion scholars are looking at and that academics from other legal sub-disciplines are also engaging with.[63] This again underscores how many of the concerns of Law and Religion are not specific to Law and Religion and this increases the fear of the risk of ghettoisation.

All of the Leading Works discussed so far fall comfortably under the Religion Law umbrella. They are all largely concerned with laws and norms created by national and international bodies that apply to religion as opposed to the Religious Law created by religious groups themselves. This distinction, however, cannot and is not intended to be watertight: the Religion Law/Religious Law

61 HJ Berman, *Law and Revolution – The Formation of the Western Legal Tradition* (Harvard University Press, 1983).

62 L Vickers, *Religious Freedom, Religious Discrimination and the Workplace* (2nd edn, Hart Publishing, 2016).

63 This has been further developed in Pearson's seminal monograph: M Pearson, *Proportionality, Equality Laws and Religion* (Routledge, 2017).

labels are applied to show that both are needed rather than to create a binary distinction.[64] This is especially true in the English context where the fact that the Church of England is established by law means that its regulation is a complex fusion of both Religion Law and Religious Law.[65] The next two chapters look at leading works that focus on Religion Law and Religious Law and the interaction between the two. David Pocklington's chapter focuses on an aspect of the regulation of the Church of England. Pocklington discusses *A Note on the Theology of Burial in relation to Some Contemporary Questions*, which was written by Christopher Hill following a request by the Dean of Arches in the case of *Re Blagdon Cemetery*.[66] Like Cranmer's chapter on the European Convention on Human Rights, Pocklington's chapter raises questions about the definition of the term 'work' and also highlights the sometimes complex relationship between primary and secondary sources given that a 'slightly expanded' version of the note was published in the *Ecclesiastical Law Journal* in 2004.[67] The chapter shows how legal texts are relied upon and interpreted by courts, adding another dimension to the understanding of a leading work. Citation, either in academic outputs or in legal sources, does not alone give any indication of the quality of the piece and its importance over time. Determining the issue of legacy is difficult and something which the contributors have all dealt with in different ways. However, the practical and grounded nature of Pocklington's chapter provides a reminder that, more so than other disciplines, writings about law can have significance outside the university since non-academic actors play a considerable role in shaping the legal discourse.

The legacy of the subject of my chapter is probably beyond dispute. It looks at Frederic Maitland, who is regarded as one of the greatest writers on the common law and as the founder of Legal History as we know it today. My chapter, however, examines his relatively little-known collection of essays, published as *Roman Canon Law in the Church of England*,[68] and argues that these should be reclaimed as a seminal work in Law and Religion. Not only do these essays show the importance of historical analysis (something that, as we have seen, is a theme in several of the chapters in this book), it also shows the value of and need for analysing the law of the Church of England (and by implication religious law generally) with the same rigour as is applied to national and international law. The chapter concludes by unpacking this further, exploring the dual nature of Religious Law as being both religious and legal before exploring what Maitland's approach tells us about the nature and importance of Legal History. The concluding pages of this chapter draw together a major theme that is found not only in the discussion of Maitland but in this book as a whole: whether the way in which Law and

64 Sandberg, *Law and Religion*, ch. 1.
65 For further discussion see ibid, ch. 3.
66 *Re Blagdon Cemetery* [2002] Fam 299, [2002] 4 All ER 482.
67 C Hill, 'A Note on the Theology of Burial in relation to Some Contemporary Questions' (2004) 7 *Ecclesiastical Law Journal* 447.
68 FW Maitland, *Roman Canon Law in the Church of England* (Methuen & Co, 1898).

Religion has developed as a sub-discipline has adversely affected its potential. The chapter returns to the issue of the ghettoisation of the sub-discipline, linking this to prevalent narratives of secularisation. It concludes by suggesting that the development of Law and Religion as a specialism has led to a closed approach. The chapter argues for the need for Law and Religion scholars to interact with other legal sub-disciplines and other disciplines within the university and calls in particular for bringing in methods, insights and approaches from elsewhere.[69]

The final substantive chapter provides an indication of one way that this could work. Sharon Thompson and I explore the need for a feminist approach to Law and Religion through considering Ayelet Shachar's *Multicultural Jurisdictions: Cultural Differences and Women's Rights*[70] as a leading work. On account of its being discussed during Rowan Williams' infamous lecture on 'Civil and Religious Law in England',[71] Shachar's book is widely cited. Our chapter illustrates, however, that Shachar's diagnosis of the situation shows what a feminist approach to Law and Religion could achieve; but ironically, Shachar's proposed solution of transformative accommodation suffers from many of the defects of which she is rightly critical. We suggest instead that a feminist approach, derived from Thompson's previous work on prenuptial agreements,[72] can provide a way forward. More generally, the chapter suggests that a feminist approach provides one way in which the Law and Religion field could be developed and rejuvenated.

This is developed in the concluding afterword which returns to the question of the future development and ambition of Law and Religion. This is appropriately authored by John Witte Jr, who places the development of Law and Religion in the UK and Ireland in an international context. Witte shifts focus to explore matters of content, sketching out areas that are ripe for study. Some of these are familiar to the Law and Religion community on this side of the Pond but many are not. Again, this suggests that there is a need for the legal study of religion to develop further here beyond its current adolescent state. The development of Law and Religion on this side of the Atlantic has already produced works of great scholarship, reaching new insights and questioning the direction and effectiveness of the law. However, the message of this book is that a wider, deeper and more audacious interdisciplinary study of the 'dialectical interaction' between Law and Religion awaits.[73] The chapters in this book show the clear potential for

69 For further discussion of this see R Sandberg, *Religion, Law and Society* (Cambridge University Press, 2014).

70 A Shachar, *Multicultural Jurisdictions: Cultural Differences and Women's Rights* (Cambridge University Press, 2001).

71 R Williams, 'Civil and Religious Law in England – A Religious Perspective' (2008) 10 *Ecclesiastical Law Journal* 262.

72 Thompson, *Prenuptial Agreements and the Presumption of Free Choice: Issues of Power in Theory and Practice*. See also S Thompson, 'Feminist Relational Contract Theory: A New Model for Family Property Agreements' (2018) 45(4) *Journal of Law and Society* (forthcoming).

73 Cf. J Witte, Jr., 'The Study of Law and Religion in the United States: An Interim Report' 14 (2012) *Ecclesiastical Law Journal* 327, 328.

Law and Religion scholarship to develop. This is true not only of the chapters by established scholars in the field whose work is pushing the subject into new areas, but also the chapters by ground-breaking up-and-coming academics who constitute the new generation of Law and Religion scholars. This means that, despite the significant challenges and criticisms of how the field has developed, there is much cause for optimism. What has happened so far may be just the prologue.

2 *Striking a Balance*

Restoring a neglected leading work

Sylvie Bacquet

The work

The chosen work was edited by Sandra Coliver, Frances D'Souza and Kevin Boyle, who were all associated with Article 19, the international London-based human rights NGO with particular focus on fighting censorship and defending freedom of expression.[1] Coliver was then a Legal Officer at Article 19 while D'Souza had succeeded Kevin Boyle as Executive Director in 1989. This chapter will mainly focus on Boyle's contribution to the book in chapters 1 and 8 and more generally on his legacy, not because the remaining chapters of the book are irrelevant to the field of Law and Religion, quite the contrary, but as a way of honouring the memory of a great man who passed away too soon. This chapter is an opportunity to highlight Kevin's contribution to the field of Law and Religion even though he is traditionally seen as pertaining to the field of International Human Rights Law.

The late Professor Kevin Boyle (1943–2010) was an internationally respected human rights lawyer, activist and academic. He left a long list of publications and case law in the field of International Human Rights. Kevin Boyle was born in a Catholic Northern Irish family. He began his academic career in Northern Ireland during the early years of the conflict and played an important role in the Civil Rights Association. Fighting religious discrimination was already his priority and continued to be at the heart of his work throughout his life. In 1986 he was appointed Founding Director of Article 19 and initiated a high-profile campaign on behalf of Salman Rushdie, denouncing censorship and blasphemy laws. In 1989, he developed a 'World Statement' in support of Rushdie, denouncing the fatwa as 'armed censorship'. As a Barrister, Kevin Boyle brought many human rights cases before the Human Rights Commission and European Court of Human Rights (ECtHR) including many successful prosecutions against Turkey which formed the basis for scholars' work in the field of international human rights. In particular, Boyle defended Kurdish villagers against Turkey and

1 S Coliver, K Boyle and F D'Souza, *Striking a Balance: Hate Speech, Freedom of Expression and Non-Discrimination* (Article 19, Intl' Centre against Censorship, 1992).

acted in numerous cases before the ECtHR.[2] In 2001 he was Senior Advisor to Mary Robinson when she was UN High Commissioner for Human Rights in the direct aftermath of September 11 and he denounced the events as a crime against humanity rather than solely a breach of human rights. When he returned to the UK he became Chair of Minority Rights Group International, the international NGO working to secure the rights of ethnic, religious and linguistic minorities. Better known for his fight for freedom of expression, Boyle also leaves an important but often neglected academic contribution in the field of Law and Religion with his work on non-discrimination and minority rights. In 1997, he co-edited with Juliet Sheen a ground-breaking study on Freedom of Religion and Belief. The work exposes denials of freedom of religion throughout the world and constituted the ground work for further research and campaigning in the field. It was amongst the first publications on how freedom of religion was understood, protected or denied around the world. The book covers Africa, the Americas, Asia-Pacific, Europe and the Middle East and for each country studied provides an account of the state of religious freedom. It looks at themes such as church and state, women and religion, education and religion and religion and the law. The book played an important role in exhibiting violations of religious freedom in many parts of the world and gave an impetus for religious freedom to be taken more seriously by scholars.

Striking a Balance, the chosen work, is an earlier piece and is at the intersection of expression and religion. In that sense, it is illustrative of Boyle's combat throughout his life both as a defender of free speech and actively engaged in the combat against racism and religious discrimination. The book was the first of its kind on hate speech. Boyle's input to *Striking a Balance* in Chapter 1 'Overview of a Dilemma: Censorship v Racism', and Chapter 8 'Religious Intolerance and the Incitement of Hatred' provide a good account of his contribution to the field of Law and Religion. Chapter 1 sets out the nature of a debate which was at the heart of Boyle's preoccupation throughout his career. It looks at the dilemma between two seemingly conflicting rights: freedom of expression and freedom from religious and racial discrimination. While Boyle was a defender of freedom of expression he was equally preoccupied with combatting racial and religious discrimination while at the same time a strong opponent of censorship. Chapter 8 is also at the intersection of religion and expression and provides an overview of the international legal framework on anti-discrimination including a critical appraisal of the approach of the Human Rights Committee and international human rights standards in the field of religious discrimination. It sets the tone for calls for the abolition of blasphemy laws both nationally and internationally. The work also makes a case for the separation of church and state. Boyle advances the proposition that separation is essential for freedom of religion to flourish. Despite being part of Boyle's earlier work, the ideas developed in those chapters paved the way for further research on religious freedom around the world and in that

2 *Akdivar and Others v Turkey* (application No 21893/93).

sense Boyle's work is a leading timeless work with a strong influence on Law and Religion. This chapter will develop some of Boyle's arguments in light of current developments in order to demonstrate the timeless nature of the work.

The context

The chosen leading work is a relatively early piece on the issue of Law and Religion. It predates the bulk of the Law and Religion literature in the UK which emerged only at the beginning of the twenty-first century.[3] As such, Boyle's large body of work on racism, religious intolerance and anti-discrimination, including his legal work in the field of religious freedom, provided the framework for future work in the field despite being overlooked by more contemporary UK Law and Religion scholars such as Edge, Doe or Sandberg.[4] This is deeply to be regretted as Boyle was a leading figure on the international human rights scene and inspired many lawyers, academics and campaigners[5] in the field of religious discrimination.[6]

The chosen piece is of particular significance to the field of Law and Religion; it identifies the struggle for religious liberty as being at the core of the international human rights machinery, thus demonstrating that religious freedom and non-discrimination more generally are the tenets of human rights. Boyle at the outset highlights that religion has been at the centre of conflicts and sufferings throughout history and that the struggle for religious liberty has been the driving force behind the human rights' machinery. International Human Rights treaties indeed emerged in the aftermath of World War Two and the horrors of the holocaust. Freedom of religion therefore and freedom from discrimination on the grounds of religion are key aspects of International Human Rights Law and as such, International Human Rights Law cannot be separated from Law and Religion. Yet, as discussed further below, the two disciplines have emerged and developed in parallel.

Boyle also highlights the intimate connection between freedom of expression and freedom of religion and advocates church and state separation as a pre-condition for religious freedom. He denounces the denial of freedom of conscience, which is still an occurrence in Islamic countries where the law of the land is the religious Sharia law. In 2015, the young Saudi blogger, Raif Badawi, was condemned to a prison sentence and a thousant lashes for promoting secularism on his blog;[7] this is far from an isolated case. Countries which deny religious freedom also deny

3 See Chapter 1 of this volume and R Sandberg, *Law and Religion* (Cambridge University Press 2011).

4 P Edge, *Religion and Law: An Introduction* (Ashgate, 2006), N Doe, *Law and Religion in Europe, A Comparative Introduction* (Oxford University Press, 2011) and Sandberg, *Law and Religion*.

5 Minority Rights Group, 'Article 19' (2016) Amnesty International.

6 G Gilbert, F Hampson and C Sandova, *Strategic Vision for Human Rights: Essays in Honour of Kevin Boyle* (Routledge, 2011).

7 A Brown, 'Ten years in jail and 1,000 lashes: why we must defend Saudi blogger Raif Badawi' (18 June 2017) *The Guardian*, available at https://www.theguardian.com/commentisfree/2017/jun/18/raif-badawi-saudi-arabia-blogger, accessed 17 August 2018.

free speech since religion and the state are fused and only the religion of the state is the accepted religion. All others are not tolerated and any attempt to speak against the state and against religion leads to persecutions.

In short, the piece evokes many of the themes which are later developed separately in further literature either by Boyle himself or by others. These include the definition of religion in international law, the struggle for religious liberty as the driving force behind human rights law, the intimate connection between freedom of religion and freedom of expression, the need to abolish blasphemy laws and the challenge posed by hate speech as well as the separation of church and state as a pre-requisite for religious freedom. These themes are disturbingly current and it is particularly timely to revisit Boyle's legacy in light of more recent developments.

The significance

It is Boyle's work and Kevin himself who inspired me and many others of his students at the University of Essex to begin research in the field of racism and religious discrimination. It led me to reflect on the French model of church–state relations as well as doing research in the area of anti-Semitism, hate speech[8] and religious freedom.[9] Yet, the work of Kevin Boyle has mainly been seen as pertaining to International Human Rights Law rather than Law and Religion itself and in that sense it is oblique to the field. This is mainly an issue of timing, with the bulk of Kevin's work predating 9/11. Yet Boyle's work brings a significant contribution to the field by focusing on religious discrimination, defending religious minorities and providing a thorough interpretation of international human rights standards.

Many leading Law and Religion scholars (less so in the UK) have seen, and continue to see, Boyle's scholarship on international religious anti-discrimination standards as the leading work in the field.[10] The findings of his *World Report* provided the basis for further studies in individual countries.[11]

8 S Bacquet, 'An Analysis of the Resurgence of Anti-Semitism in France' (2004) *Journal of Diplomatic Language* 4, available at: https://papers.ssrn.com/sol3/papers.cfm?abstract_id=1337662, accessed 17 August 2018, and S Bacquet, *Freedom of Expression v. Hate Speech* (VDM, 2011).

9 S Bacquet, 'School Uniforms, Religious, Symbols and the Human Rights Act 1998: The "Purity Ring" Case' (2008) 9 (1) *Education Law Journal* 11.

10 See for instance the work of Ferrari, Aldridge, Taylor, Shah and Evans: S Ferrari, *Routledge Handbook of Law and Religion* (Routledge, 2015); A Aldridge, *Religion in the Contemporary World* (Polity, 2007); PM Taylor, *Freedom of Religion: UN and European Human Rights Law and Practice* (Cambridge University Press, 2005); Niaz A Shah, *Women, the Koran and International Human Rights Law: The Experience of Pakistan* (Martinus Nijhoff Publishers, 2006); Carolyn Evans, *Freedom of Religion under the European Convention on Human Rights* (Oxford University Press, 2001).

11 J Rehman and SC Breau, *Religion, Human Rights and International Law: A Critical Examination of Islamic State Practices* (Martinus Nijhoff Publishers.2007) 23, and N Lerner, *Religion, Secular Beliefs and Human Rights* (2nd edn Martinus Nijhoff Publishers, 2012).

The significance of the work and of Boyle's legacy for the field of Law and Religion lies in his fight for freedom of expression which is an essential feature of religious freedom, as Boyle himself advanced: 'freedom of expression is the child of freedom of religion and the two remain intimately connected'.[12] It is the struggle against religious absolutism in Europe that paved the way for freedom of speech.[13] As well as being an advocate for freedom of expression, Boyle was a defender of religious intolerance and racism. In Chapter 1 of *Striking a Balance* Boyle highlights the seeming conflicts between those two human rights, freedom of expression and freedom from discrimination on the basis of race and religion, hence the necessity to strike a balance, which is the title of the book. Boyle sets out the challenge of racism and the timeless aspect of those chapters is striking. While the work dates back to 1992, it evokes many themes which are still very current. Boyle, highlights the articulation of prejudice, the fomenting of hatred, the urge in Europe to limit immigrants and asylum seekers, the espousal of racism by mainstream democratic political parties which are all themes that resonate within liberal democracies.[14]

At the outset, Boyle is a defender of freedom of expression but not at the expense of compromising the fight against racism. In Chapter 1 he highlights some of the challenges faced by the defenders of freedom of expression, in particular the challenge of racist speech which is still a challenge today. Throughout his work Boyle questioned how to reconcile free speech with racist speech without resorting to censorship, which he strongly opposed. Boyle argued that censorship was dangerous mainly due to the impossibility of controlling who oversees the censor.[15] Boyle developed the idea that dialogue, democracy and education may be the answer to hate speech rather than laws seeking to limit hate speech such as censorship; this is discussed further below. In the wake of recent events such as the attack on the French satirical newspaper *Charlie Hebdo* in January 2015, the debate as to whether there should be a right not to be offended in one's religious conviction has been reignited with some arguing that it may be time to reintroduce some form of blasphemy laws that would apply equally to all. Such comments were immediately condemned by defenders of the freedom of expression, such as the National Secular Society, who advance that in a pluralist society religion should be open to criticism and debate. This is in keeping with Boyle's combat against blasphemy laws.

The abolition of blasphemy law in the UK is one of Boyle's important legacies. He played a crucial role in exposing the discriminatory aspect of English blasphemy laws which protected only Christians and as such the law made a claim that it was possible to defame other religions but not Christianity, thereby placing

12 K Boyle and F D'Souza, 'Striking a Balance: Hate Speech, Freedom of Expression and Non-discrimination' (Article 19, International Centre Against Censorship, Human Rights Centre, University of Essex, 1992) 61.

13 K Boyle, 'The Danish Cartoons' (2006) 24/2 *Netherlands Quarterly of Human Rights* 185.

14 Boyle and D'Souza, 'Striking a Balance: Hate Speech, Freedom of Expression and Non-discrimination', 2.

15 Ibid 4.

Christianity on a superior level. Boyle highly criticised the courts' approach in the *Lemon* case,[16] as well as the unsuccessful outcome of its challenge before the ECtHR in *Gay News v UK*[17] which he argued amounted to people having a right not to be offended in their religious feelings. *Lemon* concerned the successful challenge of a poem published in *Gay News* which depicted the Christ as a homosexual. Boyle's campaign for the abolition of the blasphemy laws continued after the Rushdie affair. With Article 19, Boyle and D'Souza led the International Campaign for the defence of Salman Rushdie, following the publication of his book *The Satanic Verses* in 1988 which created outrage within the Muslim community and accusations of blasphemy as well as death threats from the Ayatollah Khomeini, who published a fatwa against the author. The book, despite being a work of fiction, is critical of Islam and was received by Muslims around the world as blasphemous. Boyle argued that Iran's fatwa against Salman Rushdie was the revival of the same principle in Islam as the blasphemy laws which had been defended in the *Gay News* case.[18] He accused the West of applying double-standards and of hypocrisy for denouncing laws in the Muslim world which protect Islam against other faiths yet defending an offence protecting only the majority religion. The campaign for the defence of Salman Rushdie was an opportunity to continue the campaign for the abolition of blasphemy laws in England and Wales. As Chair of the International Committee for the Defence of Salman Rushdie, Boyle initiated a pamphlet to advocate the abolition of blasphemy. In the pamphlet the Committee denounced blasphemy laws as impeding tolerance, understanding and respect for minority faiths.[19] Blasphemy laws were eventually abolished in England and Wales in 2008. While Boyle welcomed this move as a step in the right direction he nonetheless continued his fight against the archaic offence in other countries. In February 2016, Iran renewed its fatwa against Rushdie, showing that Kevin's battle is not yet over.[20]

Boyle also spoke out against some UN members' attempts to create an offence of defamation of religion. Between 1999 and 2010, the Organisation of Islamic States sponsored a number of UN Resolutions protecting religion itself from defamation.[21] In 2009 Boyle equated those resolutions to an attempt to create an international blasphemy law:

> Twenty years on from the fatwa, the threat to freedom of expression and artistic freedom remains. The abolition of the crime of blasphemy last year in

16 *Whitehouse v Lemon* [1979] AC 617.

17 *Gay News v UK* 5 (1983) EHRR 123.

18 Boyle and D'Souza, 'Striking a Balance: Hate Speech, Freedom of Expression and Non-discrimination', 67–68.

19 K Boyle, 'Article 19' (1989) International Centre Against Censorship.

20 S Osborne, 'Salman Rushdie: Iranian state media renew fatwa on Satanic Verses author with $600,000 bounty' *The Independent* (21 February 2016).

21 See for instance Resolution 4/9 of 2007 combating defamation of religion, or Resolution 7/19 of 2008.

> the UK was one positive development. But the current campaign at the UN over defamation of religion is in essence an effort to legislate an international blasphemy law. It must be resisted.[22]

Boyle's fight for freedom of expression continued, following another international crisis in February 2006 over what became known as the 'Danish cartoons' affair. The Danish newspaper *Jyllands-Posten* in September 2005 published twelve cartoons depicting the prophet Mohammed – the purpose of this was to challenge self-censorship, which had been occurring in Denmark especially from illustrators asked to depict the Prophet Mohammed which is strictly forbidden in Islam. Flemming Rose, the editor of the newspaper's cultural magazine where the cartoons were published, wrote in an article accompanying the cartoon:

> Some Muslims reject modern secular society. They demand a special position, insisting on special consideration of their own religious feelings. It is incompatible with secular democracy and freedom of expression, where one has to be ready to put up with scorn, mockery and ridicule.

The cartoons were perceived as blasphemous and insulting by Danish Muslims and by Muslims around the world, and there were public protests worldwide which resulted in hundreds of deaths and numerous wounded. However, the Danish Public Prosecutor decided that the cartoons did not warrant prosecution as the intention of the publication was to provoke public debate rather than to insult or degrade the Muslim faith.[23] The offence of blasphemy in Denmark which has since been abolished[24] was contained in Article 140 of the Danish Penal Code and punished anyone who publicly 'ridicule[d] or insult[ed] the dogmas or worship of any lawfully existing religious community'. As Boyle pointed out, it should not be for a legal officer to have to determine the extent to which the cartoons had ridiculed or insulted a particular religion and, as such, the case was another opportunity to call for the serious scrutiny of any surviving blasphemy laws in Europe and elsewhere.[25] Boyle advocated a more productive approach which would involve building a deeper understanding of human rights principles between Muslims and other citizens in Europe and promoting mutual and equal respect for different values and beliefs. He notably criticised the Danish authorities for failing to explain the situation to the Muslim minority, who did not fully grasp the rationale for the decision of the Danish Public Prosecutor.[26]

While the offence of blasphemy no longer exists in England and Wales, blasphemy laws remain popular in many parts of the world and therefore Boyle's fight

22 Boyle 'Article 19' (2009) International Centre Against Censorship.

23 Boyle, 'The Danish Cartoons' (2006) 24/2 *Netherlands Quarterly of Human Rights.*

24 See further 'End Blasphemy Laws', 2, June 2017 at https://end-blasphemy-laws.org/2017/06/blasphemy-law-abolished-denmark/, accessed 17 August 2018.

25 Boyle, 'The Danish Cartoons' (2006) 24/2 *Netherlands Quarterly of Human Rights* 189.

26 Ibid, 190.

is not over. In 2017 Stephen Fry, the English comedian, writer and activist, was investigated by the police in Ireland for negative comments he made about God on an Irish TV show in 2015, which a viewer reported as breaching section 36 of the Irish Defamation Act 2009 which makes it an offence to 'publish or utter blasphemous matters'.[27] The case was eventually dropped but it reignited the debate about blasphemy laws and calls for their abolition. The problem is that those laws lead to many persecutions on the ground of religious and political dissent. This is particularly common in the Middle East, notably in Afghanistan, Egypt, Pakistan and Iran.[28] In Islamic countries with autocratic governments, blasphemy laws are a tool to suppress dissidents of the regime. Blasphemy laws, however, are not confined to Islamic countries and even in Europe some countries retain laws criminalising criticism of religion despite their rarely being used. These include Ireland, Italy, Greece and Poland, where the Christian church has traditionally had a strong political influence.

Blasphemy laws deny people's freedom of expression and the freedom to criticise religion which in a modern pluralist society is necessary. They represent a step backwards, reminiscent of a time when religious freedom was accorded only to the majority religion and dissidents were strongly persecuted as there was a failure to recognise that different religious groups could co-exist in the same geographical area. Boyle denounced blasphemy laws as an offence to both freedom of expression and freedom of religion.[29] In addition, blasphemy laws deny the right to be free from religion by imposing religious ideologies over non-religious ones, thereby breaching the freedom of conscience.

Boyle's combat is continued by human rights organisation, lawyers and academics. In *Otto-Preminger-Institut v Austria*[30] the Strasbourg Court upheld the decision of the Austrian Court to ban a film in which the majority religion was satirised on the ground that there had been a violation of Article 9 of the ECHR. The Court considered that 'respect for religious feelings of believers'[31] had been affected even though, as rightly reminded by Boyle himself and other advocates of Freedom of Expression, there is no right to have one's religious feelings respected within Article 9. Article 9 does not give protection against mockery, satire and criticism of religion itself. Instead, it protects individuals against discrimination based on their religion and belief.

This does not mean however, that freedom of expression can never be restricted. The balance metaphor Boyle used in *Striking a Balance* illustrates that it is acceptable in certain instances for the right to be free from discrimination to take precedence over freedom of expression. The aim of the book, in particular, was to

27 Irish Defamation Act 2009 s.36.

28 AE Theodorou, 'Which countries still outlaw apostasy and blasphemy?' (2016) Pew Research Centre. Available at http://www.pewresearch.org/fact-tank/2016/07/29/which-countries-still-outlaw-apostasy-and-blasphemy/, accessed 17 August 2018.

29 Boyle, 'The Danish Cartoons' (2006) 24/2 *Netherlands Quarterly of Human Right* 189.

30 *Institut v Austria* Application No. 13470/87.

31 Ibid, para 47.

identify those circumstances which should warrant limiting freedom of expression. Religious discrimination and hate speech are examples of such circumstances.

Existing legal standards, such as Article 20 of the International Covenant on Civil and Political Rights (ICCPR) and Article 10(2) of the European Convention on Human Rights (ECHR) protect freedom from religious discrimination by limiting free speech and hate speech and those who defend freedom of expression are not opposed to those restrictions when necessary. There is, however, a difference between hate speech laws and defamation of religion in that hate speech laws condemn incitement to racial hatred towards people, whereas defamation of religion condemns attacks against religion itself. There is no questioning that hate speech is damaging to freedom of religion, but 'protection, balanced against freedom of thought and expression . . . does not mean blanket immunity from criticism of beliefs'.[32]

Boyle spent most of his academic life advocating for the interconnection and interdependency of freedom of religion and freedom of expression. Boyle recalled that in international human rights treaties both freedoms are enumerated one after the other in addition to freedom of assembly and association which is vital for both freedom of religion and expression. Freedom of religion, indeed, cannot exist without freedom of expression and association. Boyle saw freedom of expression as the child of freedom of religion and recalled that the fight for religious liberty played an essential role in 'the emergence of the modern world'.[33] The mutually reinforcing nature of those two rights was reiterated by Andrew Smith on behalf of Article 19 at the 34th session of the UN Human Rights Council in March 2016:

> Recognition of the interdependence of these rights [freedom of religion and freedom of expression], together with the urgent need for action from States to secure their protection is essential.

Kevin Boyle's fight for the abolition of laws limiting freedom of expression is therefore still current and his work opened the way to more research and awareness of the issues at both national and international level.

As discussed above, Boyle advocated education as a potent tool for addressing discriminations. He was a proponent of using enlightenment and education in order to combat ignorance. He argued that individual prejudices are often the source of hate, violence and discrimination and that these prejudices can be the result of a strong commitment to one's own faith which may lead to ignorance of others, hence the need for education and dialogue to address those issues. Boyle denounced the lack of resources dedicated to education and mutual

32 Boyle, 'The Danish Cartoons' (2006) 24/2 *Netherlands Quarterly of Human Rights*,188.

33 Boyle and D'Souza, 'Striking a balance: Hate Speech, Freedom of Expression and Non-discrimination', 61.

understanding and called for a concerted effort to counter prejudice and ignorance.[34] This is still very much current, especially in light of growing prejudices against Muslim and Jewish minorities which are being articulated via social media.[35] In its report to the UN Human Rights Council the Special Rapporteur on Freedom of Religion and Belief advocated the promotion and advancement of literacy in relation to this right. He noted the complex nature of the right and denounced misperceptions and misconceptions about the content of the right itself. The Special Rapporteur highlighted that the right to freedom of religion and belief is not designed to protect the religion and beliefs themselves but rather individuals who are free to possess and manifest such beliefs. To that effect, the Special Rapporteur denounced anti-blasphemy laws which have a 'disproportionate impact on members of minority religious communities and non-believers'.

The legacy

Kevin Boyle's legacy in the field of Law and Religion is neglected, yet Boyle remains tightly associated with the field of international human rights law.[36] The reasons for this are twofold and relate in part to the timing of Boyle's work in the field of religious freedom and in part to external factors and socio-political influence on the discipline in the UK. As put by Ferrari, the field of Law and Religion comprises three main areas of research, namely the relationship between church and state; the right to religious freedom, and religion in the public sphere.[37] Initially the main focus of the discipline both in the United States and Western Europe was on the first aspect, as there was a need to manage the relationship between church and state following the establishment in many countries, such as France, Germany and Italy, of concordats and constitutions. While the human rights machinery developed in the aftermath of World War Two, religious human rights remained fairly ignored despite being identified by Boyle and others as the sources of many other human rights such as freedom of expression and freedom of assembly. John Noonan, a US Court of Appeal judge, even termed them 'a neglected stepchild of the human rights movement'.[38]

34 K Boyle 'Freedom of Religion in International Law' in Javaid Rehman and Susan Breau, *Religion, Human Rights and International Law: A Critical Examination of Islamic State Practices* (Martinus Nijhoff Publishers, 2007) 30.

35 O Rudgard, 'Rising anti-semitism in the UK fuelled by social media, report finds', *The Telegraph*, 23 April 2017. Available at http://www.telegraph.co.uk/news/2017/04/23/rising-anti-semitism-uk-fuelled-social-media-report-finds/, accessed 17 August 2018; I Awan, 'The social network of hate: Inside Facebook's walls of Islamophobia', *Middle East Eye* (26 July 2016), available at http://www.middleeasteye.net/columns/social-network-hate-inside-facebooks-walls-islamophobia-1723501542, accessed 17 August 2018.

36 N Rodley, 'Kevin Boyle Obituary' (Sunday 2 January 2011) *The Guardian*.

37 S Ferrari, *Routledge Handbook of Law and Religion* (Routledge, 2015).

38 AL Bogle and G Pyron, *When Law and Religion Meet: The Point of Convergence* (Eerdmans, 2007) 37.

It is events such as the international conference in 1994 on 'Religious Human Rights in the World Today' at Emory University in the US as well as publications such as Boyle's World Report which raised public awareness of religious human rights violations and inspired scholarship in the area of religious rights, which in the early 1990s had not been taken seriously.[39] In addition, world events such as the Iranian revolution of 1979 and the collapse of communism at the end of the 1980s meant that religion found itself at the forefront of world politics. Finally, challenges to the secularisation thesis and the resurgence of religion led scholars to also focus on religion in the public sphere.

However, Law and Religion in the UK developed at a slower pace than in its US and Western European counterparts and it is only in the past fifteen years that it has developed as a sub-discipline of law. Up until the beginning of the twenty-first century, the discipline of Law and Religion in the UK had mainly been associated with the laws of the Established Church of England. The absence of a codified constitution and the lack of formal separation between church and state did not require urgent consideration of the relationship between church and state as in the US and other European countries. The shift to religious freedom also occurred much later in the UK due to the late incorporation of the ECHR by the UK Parliament, which led to what Sandberg termed the 'juridification of religion'.[40] Publications on issues such as religious freedom, non-discrimination and manifestation of belief started to increase considerably leading to Law and Religion becoming an established sub-discipline of law in the UK. Law and Religion as a sub-discipline of law therefore emerged fairly recently in the UK and gained momentum only in the last fifteen years or so. This goes some way towards explaining why Boyle's work on religious freedom did not permeate the discipline in the UK.

In addition, boundaries of the discipline remain blurred with some academics pertaining more to human rights than Law and Religion. It is also fairly recently that specialist research clusters, journals and academics exclusively working in that area started to emerge. This is why those who have contributed to debates and academic literature on religious freedom have often placed themselves within the field of human rights rather than Law and Religion as such, arguably for strategic reasons related to funding bodies and publishers.[41]

Despite this, International Human Rights Law and religious freedom remain key aspects of the discipline as they pertain to the field of Religion Law. However, Boyle's work might have been less influential had it been confined to Law and Religion alone. Indeed, International Human Rights Law by its very nature has a wider geographical reach than Law and Religion since it purports to be universal and as such is relevant to most legal systems. Law and Religion, on

39 Lerner, *Religion, Secular Beliefs and Human Rights.*

40 Sandberg, *Law and Religion.*

41 Evans, *Freedom of Religion under the European Convention on Human Rights*, and Taylor, *Freedom of Religion: UN and European Human Rights Law and Practice.*

the other hand, tends to be confined to the national and regional levels as it is culturally relative and therefore varies with jurisdictions. To date, there is no 'International Law and Religion' as such which would have a more global reach and aim towards an international consensus on religious freedom. Some have called upon international lawyers to establish universal legal norms and processes which would draw from religious and cultural resources all over the world[42] but there is currently within the United Nations machinery no specific legally binding instrument to monitor and enforce religious freedom. Indeed, international law remains distant from religion and there is a tendency for liberal states to approach religion from a very secular perspective. In addition, religion is often seen as a cause of conflict and, as such, liberal states are reluctant to protect it further.[43] Given that aiming for an international law on religion is somewhat utopian, we can at least expect more cooperation between those working within the field of International Law and those working in the field of Law and Religion and as such the nominated work should be an inspiration to Law and Religion scholarship in the future as it is essentially international, religiously neutral and looks beyond purely legal solutions to the issues.

42 Mark W Janis and Carolyn Evans, *Religion and International Law* (Brill, 2004)
43 D Wehrenfennig, 'The Human Rights of Religious Freedom in International Law' (2006) 18:3 *Peace Review* 403–410. Available at http://dx.doi.org/10.1080/10402650600848498, accessed 17 August 2018.

3 *Religion and the Law*

An unconventional path maker

Anthony Bradney

The work

St John Robilliard, the author of *Religion and the Law*,[1] graduated with a first-class degree in Law from Emmanuel College, Cambridge in 1976. He was appointed as a lecturer in law at the University of Manchester in the United Kingdom in the same year, at the time that being the youngest ever such appointment.[2] In his early academic career Robilliard wrote a number of articles on Law and Religion,[3] whilst also contributing to the academic literature in various other areas of Law.[4] Robilliard published *Religion and the Law* in 1984. In 1987 Robilliard left academic life for a career in practice in the Channel Islands.[5] He became a senior partner at Mourant Ozannes.[6] He was also, amongst other things, an Academician of the International Academy of Estate and Trust Law and a member of the States of Guernsey Legislation Committee.[7] His subsequent prolific publications related to his life in practice.[8] On one occasion he contributed an article focusing on an area he had previously written about whilst an academic, the doctrine that

1 St John Robilliard, *Religion and the Law: Religious Liberty in Modern English Law* (Manchester University Press, 1984).
2 R Diggard, 'John Anthony Robilliard' (2015–2016) XCVIII *Emmanuel College Magazine* 279.
3 St John Robilliard, 'Religious Freedom as Part of a Bill of Rights' (1979) 60/61 *Law and Justice – Christian Law Review* 8. St John Robilliard, 'Discrimination and indirect discrimination: The religious dimension' (1980) 8 *New Community* 261; St John Robilliard, 'No crime on Sunday?' (1980) *Criminal Law Review* 496; St John Robilliard, 'Religion in prison' (1980) *New Law Journal* 800; St John Robilliard, 'Offences Against Religion and Public Worship' (1981) 44 *Modern Law Review* 556.
4 J McEwan and St John Robilliard, 'Recklessness: the House of Lords and Criminal Law' (1981) 1 *Legal Studies* 267.
5 Diggard, 'John Anthony Robilliard', 279–280.
6 'St John Robilliard, Mourant Ozannes' International Comparative Legal Guides. Available at https://iclg.com/firms/mourant-ozannes/st-john-robilliard accessed 17 August 2018.
7 Diggard, 'John Anthony Robilliard', 279, 280.
8 St John Robilliard, 'Security for costs in trust actions: and important Guernsey case' (2013) 19 *Trust and Trustees* 843.

one should not profit from one's own wrong, which had been central to a case he argued as a practitioner.[9] He died in 2015.[10]

Religion and the Law was neither first piece of work about religion and law to be published in the United Kingdom nor even the first monograph on the subject. The analysis of the intersection between law and religion was in the 1980s, and arguably still is, less developed in the United Kingdom than is the case in a number of other jurisdictions.[11] Indeed, Doe and Sandberg have suggested that 'the advent of a distinct academic literature' about Law and Religion in the United Kingdom begins only in 'the last quarter of the twentieth century'.[12] This may well be so, in the sense that the study of Law and Religion then begins to become an established sub-discipline within academic legal studies.[13] The sub-discipline, nonetheless, has lengthy antecedents. Thus, for example, Helmholz has analysed the work of a fourteenth-century canonist in the diocese of Hereford.[14] Pearce has written about the history of the law of religion in England.[15] Crowther published a monograph on religious trusts, the subject-matter of one chapter in Robilliard's book, as long ago as 1954, thirty years before Robilliard's book.[16] Many other examples of such work could be given. The study of Law and Religion has always been a feature, although usually a minor feature, of academic legal studies in the United Kingdom. Robilliard's book, when it was published, was only the latest in a long line of work in the area. It is, however, the sub-title to Robilliard's book, *Religious Liberty in Modern English Law*, that gives a clue to one matter that makes it a first and, in at least this sense, a leading work.

Robilliard begins the introduction to *Religion and the law* with an 1888 quotation from Maitland, '[r]eligious liberty and religious equality are complete'.[17] In many ways Robilliard's book is an attempt to assess the accuracy of this statement at the time when he was writing. Herman, in her analysis of the different categories of scholarship on Law and Religion in the United Kingdom, argues that such work 'tends to follow one of three paths' and places Robilliard in 'the

9 St John Robilliard, 'Spanish Manslaughter and Guernsey Assets' (1998) 136/137 *Law & Justice – Christian Law Review* 14.
10 Diggard, 'John Anthony Robilliard, 279.
11 F Cranmer et al, 'Preface' in F Cranmer et al (eds), *The Confluence of Law and Religion: Interdisciplinary Reflections on the Work of Norman Doe* (Cambridge University Press, 2016) 17.
12 N Doe and R Sandberg, 'Introduction', in N Doe and R Sandberg (eds) *Law and Religion: New Horizons* (Peeters, 2010) 9.
13 R Sandberg, *Law and Religion* (Cambridge University Press, 2011) 2–4.
14 R Helmholz, 'Legal authority in Canon Law: Cases from the Notebook of a Medieval English Ecclesiastical Lawyer' in F Cranmer et al (eds)*The Confluence of Law and Religion: Interdisciplinary Reflections on the Work of Norman Doe* (Cambridge University Press, 2016) 34.
15 A Pearce, 'England's Law of Religion – The History of a Discipline' in N Doe and R Sandberg (eds), *Law and Religion: New Horizons* (Peeters, 2010) 13.
16 CE Crowther, *Religious Trusts – Their Development, Scope and Meaning* (Oxford, 1954).
17 FW Maitland, *The Constitutional History of England* (Cambridge University Press, 1908) 520.

trajectory [that] focuses on the rights of minority religious groups to practise their faith'.[18] Many examples of such work, including contributions that Robilliard himself made, predate Robilliard's book and provide part of the foundation for his work. What makes the book unique for its time is the fact that it is the first general monograph in the United Kingdom in this subject area. The size and length of the work in this instance is important. The book is the first time that a legal academic in the United Kingdom has thought it worthwhile meditating, not just on a particular legal problem that has arisen in relation to the life of one religious believer or group, but instead looks at the general relationship that exists between religion and law in the United Kingdom from the perspective of both human rights arguments and theology.[19] Consideration of issues relating to Law and Religion is no longer just spread through various sub-disciplines within legal studies; it becomes something that matters both in itself and for itself.

The significance of *Religion and the Law*, however, lies not just in the subject area that it addresses. It was written at a time of transition in United Kingdom law schools. '[A]cademic law' in the United Kingdom was moving away from what had been 'by and large, a secure and somnolent infancy'.[20] Research, rather than teaching, was becoming much more central to the work of the law school. At the same time a dominant, doctrinal paradigm in the law school was beginning to give way to a sense of pluralism with an ever greater interest in socio-legal studies.[21] The fact that an academic in a United Kingdom law school was writing a monograph which analysed something that lay outside the mainstream undergraduate curriculum using, as will be seen, a method that was not purely doctrinal was itself noteworthy. The historical importance of the confluence of these two matters is easy to underestimate in the present day. Others had already written non-doctrinal monographs before the publication of *Religion and the Law*. Atiyah's *Accidents, Compensation and the Law*,[22] for example, had first been published in 1970. However, such books tended to have a clear relationship with things that were taught on existing undergraduate law curricula. They did not approach their subject-matter in the same way as had been done previously; *Accidents, Compensation and the Law* was a long way from being a traditional Tort Law textbook. Nevertheless, what was being done could be seen to be developing some aspect of existing curricula. *Religion and the Law* is not unique in not doing this. Tapper's *Computers and the Law*,[23] for example, also has no obvious

18 D Herman, *An Unfortunate Coincidence: Jew, Jewishness, and English Law* (Oxford University Press, 2011) 6.

19 St John Robilliard, *Religion and the law: Religious liberty in modern English law* (Manchester University Press, 1984) 10.

20 W Twining, 'Some Jobs for Jurisprudence' (1974) 1 *British Journal of Law and Society* 149.

21 A Bradney and F Cownie, 'An Examined Life: Research into University Legal Education in the United Kingdom and the Journal of Law and Society' (Forthcoming) *Journal of Law and Society*.

22 P Cane, *Atiyah's Accidents, Compensation and the Law* (Cambridge University Press, 1987).

23 C Tapper, *Computers and the Law* (Weidenfeld and Nicolson, 1973).

relationship with mainstream undergraduate curricula. Notwithstanding the existence of other examples of this kind of work, Robilliard's book was still at the time of its publication very unusual. Ideas were being pursued for reasons other than the possible better instruction of students. Whilst not the first example of a monograph looking outside of the undergraduate curricula, *Religion and the Law* was certainly a harbinger of things to come and in this way, too, a leading work.

The context

Robilliard's approach in *Religion and the Law* was to assess Maitland's contention about religious liberty and equality by reference to several different areas of law where religion figured heavily in legal rules or where the law was of particular significance to believers. The book has been described as 'comprehensive' in its coverage.[24]

Notwithstanding the novelty of Robilliard's book, he did have some previous work to build upon. There was, in the first instance, the history of specialist writing about Law and Religion noted above. There was also the fact that whilst the study of Law and Religion was not a subject in the undergraduate legal curriculum, it was touched on in some topics that were studied in that curriculum. Some areas that Robilliard chose to analyse, such as the Law of Charities, Family Law, Criminal Law, and Labour Law, were already part of the undergraduate curriculum at the time that his book was published, with established textbooks and a patina of scholarship devoted to them. However, even in these relatively mainstream subjects, there were variations in the quantity and value of previous work that was available to Robilliard.

Equity in general, and the Law of Charity in particular, had long been an area of mainstream academic interest. Thus, for example, Hanbury and Martin's *Modern Equity*, now a standard work on the subject, was first published in 1935. The practitioner text, *Tudor on Charities*, had first been published in 1854.[25] A number of other books on the subject had also been written with detailed consideration of religious trusts, the subject-matter of Robilliard's fourth chapter, in such works being standard practice. In addition to this, there was a considerable number of articles on the subject in both academic and practitioner journals. Robilliard, in his chapter on the subject, has numerous references to this literature, looking at both textbooks and other sources.[26] The law relating to religious charitable trusts was also something that had attracted regular official attention, by way of things such as reports of the Charity Commissioners. Here again, Robilliard has frequent references to such publications in his chapter.[27]

24 J Morison, 'Religion and The Law: Religious Liberty in Modern English Law by St A Robilliard' (1985) 36 *Northern Ireland Legal Quarterly* 64.

25 O Davies Tudor, J Warburton, D Morris et al, *Tudor on Charities* (Sweet & Maxwell, 2003).

26 St John Robilliard, *Religion and the Law: Religious Liberty in Modern English Law* (Manchester University Press, 1984) 78–83.

27 Ibid.

However, it is noticeable that Robilliard also makes use of a wider range of literature that was not used in the standard textbooks of the time. Thus, for example, Robilliard looked at *Thornton v Howe*,[28] which concerns whether or not the writings of a mystic, Joanna Southcott, could be the subject of a valid charitable trust. When he did so, Robilliard footnoted Balleine's historical account of Southcott and her writings.[29] By contrast to the Law of Charities, Family Law was a relatively new addition to the undergraduate curriculum at the time that *Religion and the Law* was written. The first undergraduate course was not offered until the academic year 1951/52.[30] Two leading Family Law textbooks existed by the time that Robilliard came to write *Religion and the Law*. The first edition of Bromley's *Family Law* had been published in 1957, whilst Cretney's *Principles of Family Law* was first published in 1974. However, in his chapter on Family Law Robilliard does not make any reference to Family Law textbooks, although he does refer to academic articles and official literature.[31] Examination of the Family Law textbooks available to Robilliard shows why he did not use them in his own book. Family Law's antecedents in Christianity refer to religion almost inevitably when it comes to academic analysis. However, religion itself did not have the same place in Family Law textbook analysis that it did when it came to the law of religious trusts. Cretney's first edition, for example, makes only limited references to religion. Religion does not figure as a category in the index. Cretney does, on at least one occasion, make particular reference to the theological basis for Family Law in England and Wales, observing that the origins of the prohibited degrees of marriage lie not just generally in canon law but specifically in Leviticus Chapter 18.[32] However, Cretney's analysis of the place of religion in Family Law is not developed. In his first edition, for example, Cretney has just one sentence on the place of religion in custody decisions.[33] By the third, 1979, edition, that was available to Robilliard when he was writing *Religion and the Law*, Cretney's discussion of religion and custody cases had only lengthened to two sentences.[34] Cretney's third edition makes no reference to any secondary literature on religion and child custody cases. As with Cretney, so with Bromley; Bromley's sixth 1981 edition of *Family Law*, the edition available to Robilliard when he was writing *Religion and the Law*, also has only a very limited analysis of the place of religion in child custody cases, although Bromley does make one reference to secondary

28 *Thornton v Howe* (1862) 54 ER 1042

29 Robilliard, *Religion and the Law: Religious Liberty in Modern English Law*, 78; G Reginald Balleine, *Past Finding Out: The Tragic Story of Joanna Southcott and Her Successors* (SPCK,1956).

30 SE Rowbotham, 'In the Matter of *Cretney v Bromley* (1974), Stephen Cretney's *Principles of Family Law*' in R Probert and C Barton (ed), *Fifty Years in Family Law: Essays for Stephen Cretney* (Intersentia, 2012) 40.

31 Robilliard, *Religion and the law: Religious liberty in modern English law*, 194–198.

32 SM Cretney, *Principles of Family Law* (Sweet and Maxwell, 1974) 100.

33 Ibid, 293.

34 Cretney, *Principles of Family Law*, 497.

literature on the matter.[35] For Robilliard, '[h]istorically family law disputes, especially those over the custody and religious upbringing of children, have been the major area where religious conflicts have had to be settled by law'.[36] In contrast to the treatment of religion and child custody disputes in Family Law textbooks, Robilliard's treatment in his Family Law chapter is very much more detailed and more scholarly, referring, for example, to seven pieces of secondary literature pertaining to child custody cases and religion.[37] Equally, whilst Family Law textbooks made only spasmodic references to religion, Robilliard followed his treatment of religion and child custody with an analysis of ' "Christian" marriage and polygamy', 'Forms of marriage and religion', 'Religious duress and marriage' and completed his chapter with a discussion of 'Divorce'. For Family Law Textbooks, religion was a very occasional matter for very limited reflection; for Robilliard, religion was the central matter for reflection and Family Law and religion are seen as being inextricably intertwined in Family Law. The chapter on Family Law in *Religion and the Law* does build on previous literature but that literature, unlike the case of religious trusts, largely lay outside the mainstream undergraduate curriculum.

Two of Robilliard's chapters focus on Criminal Law. Chapter 1 is concerned with the law of blasphemy. The other criminal law chapter, Chapter 7, discusses the law relating to witchcraft, 'false prophets and pious frauds', spiritual healing, exemption from the criminal law on the grounds of religious belief, and 'extreme religious belief'. All of these matters had been touched on in Criminal Law textbooks and in the secondary literature, but in most cases relatively little attention was given to them. In Chapter 2 the difference between Robilliard's approach and the approach in standard criminal law textbooks is that he gives blasphemy a much more extensive treatment, his chapter extending to twenty pages. Williams, in the second edition of his Criminal Law textbook, devotes a total of nine lines to blasphemy.[38] However, in Robilliard's general chapter on criminal law, Chapter 7, the difference between Robilliard's approach and standard treatments is not the depth of his analysis. Thus, for example, Robilliard gives over nearly two pages to the approach by the courts to spiritual healing in late nineteenth and early twentieth-century cases.[39] Robilliard cites Williams as using the same amount of space for analysis of the issue in Williams' 1978 textbook on Criminal Law as indeed Williams had in 1961.[40] Here, what Robilliard does in his chapter on Criminal Law that is different from previous textbook treatments is to link

35 P Bromley, *Family Law* (Butterworths, 1981) 296–297.

36 Robilliard, *Religion and the Law: Religious Liberty in Modern English Law*, 183.

37 Ibid, 183–190.

38 G Williams, *Criminal Law: The General Part* (Stevens and Sons Limited, 1961) 71–72 and 593.

39 Robilliard, *Religion and the law: Religious liberty in Modern English law*, 120–122.

40 Ibid, 129; G Williams, *Criminal law: The General Part* (Stevens and Sons Limited,1961) 145–146.

together different areas of Criminal Law in what then becomes a sustained analysis of religion's relationship with Criminal Law.

Whilst Robilliard was able to build, to some extent, on existing academic legal scholarship in some of his chapters, in others, which looked at matters that lay outside the purview of the undergraduate curriculum at the time that he was writing, there was much less work to provide him with a foundation. Given the focus of his book, it was natural, for example, for Robilliard to turn to the Sunday laws, designed to protect traditional Christian Sabbatarian beliefs, in one of his chapters. Yet, in this chapter Robilliard is only able to refer to three previous academic legal studies of the Sunday laws, one being by himself,[41] one being by an academic writing about law from the perspective of a political scientist[42] and one being by an academic writing about law from the perspective of a historian.[43] Robilliard's own previous work is the longest of the three, being six pages long, whilst Drewry's is the shortest, being only two pages long. The only other legal treatment of the Sunday trading laws that Robilliard was able to use in his chapter was a book by a barrister, Philip Skottowe, who wrote about a number of legal areas from a purely doctrinal perspective.[44] Other sources that Robilliard used in his chapter on Sunday laws included work by political scientists[45] and work from a historical perspective.[46] The paucity of academic literature, and in particular the lack of significant academic legal literature, that was available to Robilliard is to some degree a surprise. Robilliard himself notes both the controversy caused by such laws at the time that he was writing and the wealth of other reforms in the 1960s that had liberalised society.[47] Its absence serves to further underline the novelty of the work being done by Robilliard.

Robilliard's chapter on the Sunday laws is not the only chapter in the book where he finds a relative scarcity of academic literature to build on. In a similar fashion to his Sunday laws chapter, in Robilliard's chapter on prisons and the armed services five of Robilliard's references to the academic legal literature are to one previous work by himself, that work itself being only a one-page article.[48] Indeed, Robilliard's

41 St John Robilliard, 'No Crime on Sunday?'(1980) *Criminal Law Review* 496; Robilliard, *Religion and the Law: Religious Liberty in Modern English Law*, 46.

42 G Drewry, 'Sunday Laws' (1972) *New Law Journal* 501; Robilliard, *Religion and the Law: Religious Liberty in Modern English Law*, 47.

43 G Alderman, 'Jews and Sunday: The Use and Abuse of Delegated Legislation' (1982) LX *Public Administration* 99; Robilliard, *Religion and the Law: Religious Liberty in Modern English Law*, 52.

44 P Skottowe, *The Law Relating to the Blind* (Butterworth and Company, 1933); Robilliard, *Religion and the Law: Religious liberty in Modern English Law*, 46, 47.

45 P Richards, *Parliament and Conscience* (Allen and Unwin, 1970); Robilliard, *Religion and the Law: Religious liberty in Modern English Law*, 47.

46 AH Lewis, *A Critical History of Sunday Legislation from 321 to 1888 AD* (D Appleton and Company, 1888); St John Robilliard, *Religion and the Law: Religious liberty in Modern English Law* (Manchester University Press, 1984) 46.

47 Ibid, 47.

48 St John Robilliard, 'Religion in Prison'(1980) *New Law Journal* 800; Robilliard, *Religion and the Law: Religious liberty in Modern English Law*, 140–141.

chapter cites only one other piece of non-governmental work specifically devoted to religion and prisons, Horabin's *Problems of Asians in Penal Institutions: A Survey*,[49] this being a campaigning contribution rather than an academic study, published jointly by the Runnymede Trust and the Howard League for Penal Reform.

Even when successive governments had paid considerable attention to an area of law, this did not guarantee that there was any significant academic legal literature for Robilliard to build on. In Chapter 10 Robilliard turned to, as he styled it, 'public education'. Although the place of religion in schools had been regularly referred to in statute, debates in Parliament and government publications over many years, debate going back to the nineteenth century, Robilliard makes only one reference to the academic legal literature in his chapter, an article by Graham in the *Northern Ireland Legal Quarterly*.[50] In contrast to this, Robilliard makes copious use of a range of other literature including political memoirs,[51] historical analysis[52] and campaigning literature.[53] The paucity of academic legal literature that was available to Robilliard in many of his chapters underscores the novelty of his approach and thus the value of what he did in *Religion and the Law*.

One final matter that deserves analysis in terms of the context for *Religion and the Law* is the method that Robilliard used in his book. On first reading, to the modern eye the book seems to be a standard piece of doctrinal scholarship. At the end of the book there are tables of statutes, statutory instruments, 'international covenants' and cases. In the context of the subject-matter of the book, it is unsurprising that there is a more unusual table of Church of England measures, legislation specific to the Church of England as the established church in England, but this only seems to further underline the doctrinal nature of the work. Primary legal material, cases and legislation, are what seems to matter in the book. The footnotes at the end of most chapters are predominantly lists of cases and legislation that are referred to in the chapter. Yet, to describe *Religion and the Law* as a doctrinal work is to misread that character of the argument in the book. The book certainly does contain doctrinal analysis. Cases and legislation are examined with a view to ascertaining what legal rules have been created. Judgments are examined in scrupulous detail and, as for example, in the case of the treatment of child custody, cases that have escaped the attention of mainstream textbooks are analysed for what they can tell us about the way that the law has developed. However, none of this makes *Religion and the Law* a doctrinal book. In an era when we are told that in British university law schools, a doctrinal approach 'in its pure form is an approach [used] by only a minority of those working in English

49 Ibid, 136.

50 Ibid, 165.

51 Lord Butler, *The Art of the Possible* (Hamish Hamilton,1971); Robilliard, *Religion and the Law: Religious liberty in Modern English Law*, 153,158.

52 N Middleton and S Weitzman, *A Place for Everyone: A History of State Education from the End of the 18th Century to the 1970s* (Gollancz, 1976); Robilliard, *Religion and the Law: Religious liberty in Modern English Law*, 150, 151.

53 Religious Education Council (1975); Robilliard, *Religion and the Law: Religious liberty in Modern English Law*, 154, 155.

university law schools' when they do research;[54] when the law sub-panel for the last national external audit of research in university law schools has reported that 'there is a notable trend towards more broadly "contextual" approaches to the discussion of legal issues and the field of legal studies, as a whole, is increasingly influenced by socio-legal research methods and techniques'; and where debate is now about how pure socio-legal work has to be to be truly socio-legal,[55] it is easy to lose sight of what purely doctrinal work is and was. Doctrinal work is the explication of legal rules using only the internal evidence of primary legal materials, cases and legislation.[56] Only questions that can be asked and answered using this evidence are looked at. The question for the doctrinal lawyer is always, in essence, what precisely is the rule of law in this instance. Other questions, such as those about the impact of the rule or the value of the rule, cannot be addressed by doctrinal analysis. The doctrinal lawyer's proposition does not have to be that these other questions about law and legal rules are not valid or valuable; more simply, it can be that these questions do not fall within the domain of the academic doctrinal lawyer.[57] If this is what doctrinal work is, then, notwithstanding the space given over to primary legal material in *Religion and the Law*, the book is a long way from being a doctrinal book. Robilliard's final interest is always in the impact of legal rules on people within society; for him, questions about what the rules say matter only because of the effect that these rules can potentially have.

The significance

The fact that Robilliard was unable to use Family Law textbooks in *Religion and the Law* illustrates how the textbook tradition had limited the development of English legal scholarship. Textbooks were devoted to the perceived needs of practitioners or students rather than to the pursuit of knowledge. It is unsurprising that Becher's *Academic Tribes and Territories*, published in 1989 four years after *Religion and the Law* came out, reported that other academics thought that the work of academic lawyers was 'unexciting and uncreative, comprising a series intellectual puzzles among "large areas of description"'.[58] This was not just the perception of other academics. In a paper written in 1967, but published much later, Twining and Stevens had commented that 'the legal textbook symbolizes

54 F Cownie, *Legal Academics: Culture and Identities* (Hart Publishing, 2004) 58.

55 A Sanders, 'Poor Thinking, Poor Outcome? The Future of the Law degree after the Legal Education and Training Review and the Case for Socio-Legalism' in H Sommerlad, S Harris-Short, S Vaughan et al (eds), *The Futures of Legal Education and the Legal Profession* (Hart Publishing, 2015) 143–144.

56 R Posner, 'The Present Situation in Legal Scholarship' (1981) 90 *Yale Law Journal* 1114–1115.

57 Whether pure doctrinal analysis can ever result in valuable answers to significant questions about legal rules and whether it is intellectually coherent are issues that lies outside the scope of this essay.

58 T Becher, PR Trowler, *Academic Tribes and Territories: Intellectual enquiry and the culture of disciplines* (The Society for Research into Higher Education and Open University Press, 1980) 30.

for them [lay people] a general aridity, dullness, narrowness, and philistinism in the house of intellect of academic lawyers'.[59] Three years after the publication of *Religion and the Law*, Wilson, Professor of Law at the University of Warwick, was to write that 'the words "English legal scholarship", though high sounding, have a similar function to the words "disposable paper cup". Each adjective strengthens the message that one cannot expect much in terms of long term quality or utility from it'. [60] The intellectual malaise that pervaded British university law schools in the 1980s was not their only problem. Law schools were part of universities that were then experiencing considerable cutbacks in government finance.[61] In Cownie and Cocks' history of the professional association for legal academics, the Society of Legal Scholars, the only proxy there is for the history of British university legal education, the chapter on the 1980s is entitled 'A Difficult Decade'.[62] Robilliard's own law school, at the University of Manchester, was able to meet the university's target for reduction in numbers of academic staff only because of the retirement of one academic and the fact that three others moved into practice.[63] Yet, notwithstanding all the problems that British university law schools suffered from in the early 1980s, it would be wrong to suggest that the picture was one of unremitting gloom. Intellectually, there were signs that the hold that the doctrinal paradigm had on law schools was beginning to lessen and a wider range of scholarship was becoming more common. By the 1980s, socio-legal studies was not new to British university law schools. Harris, in an article published one year before *Religion and the Law*, surveyed the development of socio-legal studies in the United Kingdom over the previous decade.[64] Cownie and Cocks note the emergence of book series such as the 'Law in Context' series, which were devoted to such scholarship.[65] The *Journal of Law and Society*, originally the *British Journal of Law and Society*, had been founded in 1974, whilst the *International Journal of the Sociology of Law* had first been published in 1972. The Oxford Centre for Socio-Legal Studies had been set up in 1972.[66] Harris' early 1980s survey was of 'a thriving field'.[67]

59 W Twining, 'Reflections on "Law in Context"' in W Twining, *Law in Context: Enlarging a Discipline* (Clarendon Press,1997) 38, 39.
60 G Wilson, 'English Legal Scholarship' (1987) 50 *Modern Law Review* 819.
61 M Kogan and S Hanney, *Reforming Higher Education* (Jessica Kingsley Publishers, 2000) Ch. 4; M Tight, *The Development of Higher Education in the United Kingdom since 1945* (Open University Press, 2009) 75–81.
62 F Cownie and R Cocks, *'A Great and Noble Occupation!' The History of the Society of Legal Scholars* (Hart Publishing, 2009) 163.
63 B Pullan with M Abendstern, *A History of the University of Manchester 1973–90.* (Manchester University Press, 2004) 149.
64 D Harris, 'The development of socio-legal studies in the United Kingdom' (1983) 3 *Legal Studies* 315.
65 Cownie and Cocks, *'A Great and Noble Occupation!' The History of the Society of Legal Scholars*, 184; W Twining, *Law in Context: Enlarging a Discipline* (Clarendon Press,1997).
66 Harris, 'The development of socio-legal studies in the United Kingdom' (1983) 3 *Legal Studies* 319.
67 Cownie and Cocks, *'A Great and Noble Occupation!' The History of the Society of Legal Scholars*, 184.

Religion and the Law's claim to significance, like its claim to be a leading work, is twofold. First lies the place that the book had in the changing nature of legal scholarship in British university law schools. Robilliard's book was not limited by the perceived and ephemeral needs of either practitioners or students, and in it he was free to follow questions where they led him. Equally, he did not seem to be interested in 'producing research that will sell at a profit', as Wortley had once exhorted legal academics to do.[68] In the case of *Religion and the Law*, it can be argued that it is, in Weber's phrase, 'science for science's sake'.[69] Moreover, the book is socio-legal in the broad sense used by many to describe work about law that draws on academic disciplines other than law in its analysis.[70] However, whilst being socio-legal, *Religion and the Law* does not conform with the then model for socio-legal studies identified by Harris in his survey and use literature from one of a range of social sciences as its foundation.[71] Indeed, there are very few references to social science literature in the book. Instead, the non-legal academic literature that is used tends to come from history or political science. The book is thus, at the same time, both part of a challenge to what had been standard academic writing practice in British university law schools and is also a challenge to the new approaches that were being put forward.

Religion and the Law was unconventional, even in what was then an unconventional genre. This may in part account for the fact that the book received little by way of notice in academic law journals in the United Kingdom. Morison reviewed the book in the *Northern Ireland Legal Quarterly*,[72] whilst *Legal Studies* noted it as a 'book received'.[73] The book received some attention outside of the United Kingdom. In Ireland, for example, Hogan reviewed the book for the *Irish Jurist*, whilst the *American Journal of Comparative Law* listed it in its 'books noticed' section in 1985.[74] It would, however, be wrong to pretend that the book received a lot of publicity when it was published. Being significant and being widely noticed at the time of publication are two completely different things for a piece of academic work. The book's unconventional methodology and the fact that Law and Religion was then an area which attracted limited interest in university law schools in the United Kingdom, may be part of the reason for the lack of reviews. Morison's review of the book may also inadvertently identify

68 BA Wortley, 'Some Reflections on Legal Research after Thirty Years' (1965) 8 *Journal of Society of Public Teachers of Law* 258.

69 M Weber, 'Science as a Vocation' in H Heinrich Gerth and C Wright Mills, *From Max Weber: Essays in Sociology* (Routledge, 1988) 138.

70 F Cownie and An Bradney, 'Socio-Legal Studies: A Challenge to the Doctrinal Approach' in D Watkins and M Burton, *Research Methods in Law* (Routledge 2013) 35–36.

71 Harris, 'The Development of Socio-Legal Studies in the United Kingdom' (1983) 3 *Legal Studies*.

72 John Morison, 'Religion and the Law: Religious Liberty in Modern English Law by St A Robilliard' (1985) 36 *Northern Ireland Legal Quarterly* 64.

73 Harris, 'The Development of Socio-Legal Studies in the United Kingdom' (1983) 3 *Legal Studies* 240.

74 Gerard Hogan, 'St John A Robilliard, Religion and the Law' (1984) 19 *Irish Jurist* 366.

another reason for the book's lack of reviews. In his review, Morison opines that *Religion and the Law* might 'function as a handbook for civil libertarians'.[75] In fact, this seems likely to have been the case in only a very distant manner. Assessing whether religious liberty is complete in the United Kingdom at the time of the book's publication, as Robilliard intended to do,[76] does not, in any straightforward sense, necessarily assist in advising an individual whose own religious freedom might have been infringed or in propagating a political campaign about some issue relating to religious freedom. However, Morison's suggestion does lead to the question, who is the book intended for? Given that the book is neither a textbook nor even an obvious aid to a textbook, who is the book's reader? Abel had meditated on the distinction between books about law and law books in 1973, the former being 'a mode of *reflection* upon the legal system', whilst the latter was a work of 'legal doctrine',[77] in the context of legal scholarship in the USA. In the legal academy in the USA, Abel wrote that it had 'almost become de rigueur to claim allegiance to this new style in scholarship [and write books about law]'.[78] *Religion and the Law* was a book about law, rather than a law book, but in the mid-1980s in the United Kingdom, the place for such books in university law schools was still uncertain. Weber may have understood the importance of scholarship done for its own sake, but British university law schools in the mid-1980s were not so certain, hence Morison's suggestion and hence possibly the paucity of reviews.

Whilst it would be wrong to suggest that *Religion and the Law* was extensively reviewed upon publication, it would be equally wrong to say that it went unnoticed. In the year of its publication, Hadfield footnoted it in an article in the *Northern Ireland Legal Quarterly*.[79] In the same year, Weisbaum noted it in a list of selected readings about areas of foreign and international law.[80] Two years later, Larkin was to make extensive use of the book in an article in the *South African Journal of Human Rights*.[81] Early attention to the book was not limited to law journals. In 1987 Zellick referred to it in an article in the journal *Patterns of Prejudice*, a journal published by the Institute of Jewish Affairs.[82] These very early references to *Religion and the Law* established a pattern which was to continue to the present day.

75 J Morison, 'Religion and the Law: Religious Liberty in Modern English Law by St A Robilliard' (1985) 36 *Northern Ireland Legal Quarterly* 64, 65.

76 Robilliard, *Religion and the Law: Religious Liberty in Modern English Law*, 9.

77 R Abel, 'Law Books and Books about Law' (1973–74) 26 *Stanford Law Journal* 175, 176.

78 Ibid 175.

79 B Hadfield, 'The Prevention of Incitement to Religious Hatred – An Article of Faith?' (1984) 35 *Northern Ireland Legal Quarterly* 235.

80 Earl Weisbaum, 'Bibliography: Selected Readings in the Area of Foreign and International Law' (1984) 18 *International Lawyer* 481.

81 M Larkin, 'Promoting Peace and Harmony' (1986) 2 *South African Journal on Human Rights* 187, 182, 194 and 199.

82 G Zellick, 'Freedom of Religion and the Jewish Community in the United Kingdom' (1987) 21(2) *Patterns of Prejudice* 15.

The success of *Religion and the Law* is not surprising. For nearly a decade, until the publication of *Religion, Rights and Laws*,[83] it was to be the only monograph in its area in the United Kingdom and thus significant in a second sense. Other books, such as Poulter's *English Law and Ethnic Minority Customs*,[84] which were to follow *Religion and the Law*, had areas of overlap with Robilliard's book. Thus, for example, Zellick's article, 'Freedom of Religion and the Jewish Community in the United Kingdom', cites both *Religion and the Law* and *English Law and Ethnic Minority Customs* in the same footnote.[85] Nevertheless, until *Religions, Rights and Laws* no other book had precisely the same focus as *Religion and the Law*. To be, at first, the only monograph in a developing area of academic interest, then latterly, still one of only a small number of such books almost necessarily increases the significance of the work in question.

One thing that may have reduced the impact of Robilliard's book is his withdrawal from academic life comparatively soon after its publication. Why Robilliard chose to go into practice at the precise date that he did is a matter for conjecture. The financial situation of British universities in the 1980s adverted to above may well have motivated Robilliard's decision, although he was in any event keen to return to the Channel Islands.[86] However, whatever the reason for Robilliard's move, one consequence of it was that he did not develop his thoughts in *Religion and the Law* in further publications. This provides further testimony to the book's significance. In seeking to further their careers, some academics will attempt to persuade others of the value of the work they have done; successive works by them underscore the importance of that which they have before. Robilliard, having left academic life, was not in a position to do this. In the succeeding decades after its publication the book survived and thrived on its own merits, without any further help from the author.

The legacy

Exploring the legacy of academic work raises a number of complex problems which go the heart of academic culture. Every monograph, essay and article is in itself necessarily and immediately a legacy, bequeathing to the future what it has to say. It would then seem that the only question to ask is: what is the quality of that legacy?

In his memoir, *Errata*, Steiner reflected regretfully that he thought there would be no movement to follow on from him after his death.[87] Some, perhaps many, academics worry about the legacy of their work in this sense. Sartre and Foucault's relationship was notoriously fraught as they both sought intellectual

83 A Bradney, *Religion, Rights and Laws* (Leicester University Press, 1993).

84 S Poulter, *English Law and Ethnic Minority Customs* (Butterworths, 1986).

85 Zellick, 'Freedom of Religion and the Jewish Community in the United Kingdom' (1987) 21(2) *Patterns of Prejudice* 15.

86 Diggard, 'John Anthony Robilliard', 279, 280.

87 G Steiner, *Errata: An examined life* (Weidenfeld and Nicolson, 1997) 155.

dominance.[88] What was at stake was both their reputation during their lifetime and also the quality of the legacy of they left behind them. This may seem both understandable and unproblematic. A concern with reputation or legacy can, however, carry with it serious dangers. If, as Weber argues, academic work should be done for its own sake, there are limits to how much the opinions of others about our work ought to matter; one should be 'devoted *solely* to the work at hand'.[89] Russell, in his book on academic freedom, cautions against academics concerning themselves with what others think of their work. 'The moment one suggestive quote is tailored for fear Professor So-and-so may not like it, the quality of the whole [academic] undertaking is called in question'.[90] What academics should not do is to alter their work, so as to make others more receptive to it. Close attention needs to be paid to suggestions by others of inaccuracy or incoherence in what we have said. Apart from that Eliot's suggestion about the writing of poetry,

> '. . . there is no competition . . .
> . . .
> For us there is only the trying. The rest is not our business',[91]

applies to all academic writing. Academics are right to attend to the quality of the legacy of their work but wrong to worry about what others will make of that legacy.

This does not mean that the quality of a legacy should not be considered. Academic scholarship is often precisely about the consideration and reconsideration of the legacy that we work with. Yet, the inanities of successive research assessment exercises over the past few decades in the United Kingdom, which latterly have sought to attach ordinal numbers to individual pieces of research, underline the caution with which any such enterprise ought to be undertaken.[92] All judgements about legacy are provisional and are made in conditions of uncertainty.

It is clear that *Religion and the Law* has a continuing legacy. The legacy lies in part in the 29 academic libraries in the United Kingdom and Ireland that the non-comprehensive COPAC database says continue to hold the book.[93] It also lies in the citations that the book has had and continues to have in the United Kingdom and elsewhere, both in the academic legal literature and in the literature of other academic disciplines. A legacy of this nature is objective and quantifiable. The legacy that the book had and has on the development of an academic sub-discipline, Law and Religion, is more nebulous. Had the book not been

88 J Miller, *The Passion of Michel Foucault* (HarperCollins 1993) 44–45.
89 Weber, 'Science as a Vocation', 138 and 137.
90 C Russell, *Academic Freedom* (Routledge, 1993) 28.
91 TS Eliot, *Four Quartets* (Faber and Faber, 1959) 31.
92 D Sayer, *Rank Hypocrisies: The Insult of the REF* (Sage Publications, 2015).
93 COPAC database. Available at copac.jisc.ac.uk/search?&author=Robilliard&title=%22Religion+and+the+law%22, accessed 18 August 2018.

published, Law and Religion would still have come into being as a sub-discipline in academic legal studies in the United Kingdom. Moreover, it would probably have taken much the same fractured form that Herman has described.[94] This, however, does not disqualify *Religion and the Law* from being a leading work, nor does it diminish the quality of the book or the significance of what Robilliard did. *Religion and the Law* was published at a time when research in law schools in the United Kingdom was limited and a narrowly conceived undergraduate curriculum dominated horizons within law schools. As one of the books that took law schools in a very different direction, *Religion and the Law* justly deserves the label 'leading work'.

94 Herman, *An Unfortunate Coincidence: Jew, Jewishness, and English Law*, 6–7.

4 *Of Presbyters and Kings*

A Scottish trail-blazer

Frank Cranmer

The work

When I was training to be a reader in the Church of England in the 1990s, one of the tasks we were set by our doctrine tutor was to write an essay on a 'current problem' in the Church. None of the choices on offer looked particularly appealing, so I picked what I thought was the least boring option: 'Establishment'. Contemporary critics of the establishment of the Church of England tended to point to the Church of Scotland as the obvious alternative model, so I started investigating the Scottish version – only to find that in order even to begin to understand the legal and constitutional position of the Kirk I had to read at least some of the decided cases. So, not without a certain degree of misgiving, I opened a law report for the first time in about 30 years.

Fortunately, as it turned out, reading cases is a bit like riding a bike: once you have the knack you never quite lose it. The byways both of church–state relations and of Scots Public Law proved to be fascinating, however, and I started getting seriously interested in the subject: so much so that after I finished my training I signed up for the Archbishop of Canterbury's Diploma in Theology and started writing a comparative study of the history of ecclesiastical establishment in England, Scotland and Sweden since 1800.

It was at that point, rummaging one afternoon through a pile of second-hand books about Scotland in Armadale Castle, in Skye, that I stumbled upon *Of Presbyters and Kings*[1] – and as I started leafing through it I realised that my knowledge of the subject was even sketchier than I had imagined. Any English lawyer who has the temerity to tangle with the Scottish aspects of Law and Religion needs constantly to bear in mind that, like 'the past', legal Scotland 'is a foreign country: they do things differently there'.[2] So I bought the book and, that evening, began reading it carefully. And the result was that I more or less rewrote the Scottish section of my dissertation.

1 F Lyall, *Of Presbyters and Kings: Church and State in the Law of Scotland* (Aberdeen University Press, 1980).
2 The opening line of LP Hartley, *The Go-Between* (Hamish Hamilton, 1953).

Of Presbyters and Kings begins with some very basic theoretical concepts about the relationship between civil and ecclesiastical authority, then sketches a brief history of religion in Scotland from the Scots Reformation in 1560 to the Union of the Parliaments in 1707. Next come discussions of the Disruption – about which more below – and the post-Disruption period, followed by an analysis of the events leading up to the passing of the Church of Scotland Act 1921 and the Articles Declaratory appended to it in the Schedule, which made it possible for the Kirk and the greater part of the United Free Church to reunite in 1929.

Lyall then turns to 'The Church outside Establishment'. In doing so, he looks at the legal existence and nature of Churches other than the Church of Scotland and details some of the pitfalls in their advance to full toleration and legal personality, culminating in *McDonald v Burns*,[3] in which Lord Justice Clerk Aitchison laid down the limits that the Court of Session would observe in reviewing (or declining to review) the decisions of 'dissenting religious associations'. He pays particular attention to disputes over church property, the most famous of which is the Free Church case of 1904,[4] in which the House of Lords held that the majority of the Free Church that had joined with the United Presbyterian Church to form the United Free Church had departed from the 'original principles' of the Free Church and therefore had forfeited any rights to its property and endowments – with the result that the dissident minority who had opposed the scheme of union were entitled to all of it.[5]

Finally, the main part of the book concludes with a broader survey of 'The Interaction of Religion and Law', covering such matters as education, broadcasting, charity law, marriage and divorce, medical practice, oaths, Sunday observance and religious discrimination – the first time, so far as I am aware, that anyone had attempted that kind of systematic analysis within the framework of Scots law.

The context

Lyall is now Emeritus Professor of Public Law at Aberdeen University and his principal interest during a long academic career has been in Air and Space Law. But his PhD thesis was about relations between church and state[6] – and it was that thesis which provided the basis both for his inaugural lecture at Aberdeen[7] and for *Of Presbyters and Kings*. As he notes in its preface, Scots law and the Presbyterian government of the Church of Scotland were 'the two elements preserved in the Treaty of Union with England in 1707'.[8] The context, however, was

3 1940 SC 376.

4 *General Assembly of the Free Church of Scotland* v *Lord Overtoun*: *MacAlister v Young* (1904) 1 F (HL) 1, [1904] AC 515.

5 A decision which was unsustainable in practice and resulted in the establishment of a Commission under the Churches (Scotland) Act 1905 to make an equitable redistribution of the property.

6 F Lyall, *Church and State in Scotland*: Thesis submitted in candidature for the Degree of Doctor of Philosophy (Faculty of Law, University of Aberdeen 1972).

7 Published as F Lyall, 'Religion and law' (1976) *Juridical Review* 21, 58.

8 Lyall, *Of Presbyters and Kings: Church and State in the Law of Scotland*, ix.

this: at the time he was writing, the modern church history of Scotland had been widely documented – perhaps most notably by Alexander Drummond and James Bulloch[9] and by John Burleigh[10] – but there had been relatively little objective analysis of the way in which the secular law of Scotland had interacted with the events that the historians had described.

The classic early commentary on the wider issues of religion in Scots law is still Alexander Taylor Innes's *The Law of Creeds in Scotland*,[11] first published in 1867, with a second edition in 1902. The first edition remains an important source for the state of the law in the mid-nineteenth century; but the second had the misfortune of being published in 1902, two years before the decision of the House of Lords in the Free Church case. The result was that Taylor Innes was unable to take account of what was possibly the most important twentieth-century judgment about the powers of Churches to order their own affairs – and as much for England and Wales as for Scotland.

Christopher Johnston, Procurator of the Church of Scotland from 1907 to 1918 and later a Senator of the College of Justice with the judicial title of Lord Sands, wrote a retrospective assessment of the Free Church judgment in 1910;[12] but though various manuals of Scottish church practice and procedure were published during the intervening period – most notably *Cox*,[13] – there appeared to be very little academic comment on the more general interactions between religion and secular law for the next 50 years or so, apart from a few isolated articles such as those by Thomas Taylor in 1957[14] and Ronald King Murray in 1958.[15] Rolf Sjölinder published *Presbyterian Reunion in Scotland*[16] in 1962; but, important though it is as a work of closely-observed and detailed church history, it concentrates primarily on the negotiations surrounding the Church of Scotland Act 1921 and the 1929 reunion of the Church of Scotland and the United Free Church, rather than on the technical history of the legal battles that preceded it.[17]

9 AL Drummond and J Bulloch, *The Scottish Church, 1688–1843* (St Andrew Press, 1973), *The Church in Victorian Scotland, 1843–1874* (St Andrew Press 1975) and *The Church in Late Victorian Scotland, 1874–1900* (St Andrew Press 1975). A promised fourth volume on the twentieth century was never published.

10 JHS Burleigh, *A Church History of Scotland* (OUP, 1960).

11 A Taylor Innes, *The Law of Creeds in Scotland* (William Blackwood & Sons, 1867).

12 CN Johnston, 'Doctrinal Subscription in the Church of Scotland', (1910) *Juridical Review* XVII, 201.

13 JT Cox, *Practice and Procedure in the Church of Scotland* (William Blackwood & Sons 1934). The last edition was the sixth, edited by DFM Macdonald (Committee on General Administration of the Church of Scotland 1976).

14 TM Taylor, 'Church and State in Scotland' (1957) *Juridical Review* 23, 121.

15 R King Murray, 'The Constitutional Position of the Church of Scotland' [1958] *Public Law* 158. He later became a Senator of the College of Justice with the judicial title of Lord Murray.

16 R Sjölinder, *Presbyterian Reunion in Scotland, 1907–1921: Its Background and Development* (*Acta Universitatis Upsaliensis*, Almqvist &Wiksell 1962, T & T Clark 1962).

17 For example, he deals with the Free Church case itself in three pages: 112–114.

Lyall, however, was primarily concerned with the case law; and his account of what is commonly known as the 'Ten Years' Conflict' leading up to the Disruption of 1843 is a meticulous discussion of disputes that arose as a result of two Acts of the General Assembly passed in 1934: the Veto Act and the Chapel Act,[18] both of which provoked bitter controversy. Section I of the Veto Act provided that:

> if, at the moderating in a call to a vacant pastoral charge, the major part of the male heads of families, members of the vacant congregation, and in full communion with the Church, shall disapprove of the person in whose favour the call is proposed to be moderated in, such disapproval shall be deemed sufficient ground for the Presbytery rejecting such person, and he shall be rejected accordingly.

In short, it gave congregations the right to override the nominations of patrons. Evangelical congregations were now free to reject nominations of ministers from the Moderate party in the Church and they did so in increasing numbers – and to the increasing fury of the Moderates.

The immediate effect of the two Acts was ten years of legal disputes, beginning with the *Auchterarder* cases[19] and ending with the Stewarton case,[20] all of which Lyall analyses in some detail. The outcome of the litigation was that the Court of Session declared the Veto Act *ultra vires*. In the Lethendy case, Lord President Hope summed up the position like this:

> If the Church can prevail upon Parliament to repeal or modify the law of patronage, as shall be most agreeable to their views, good and well; but while patronage is the law of the land, it is also the law of the church and must be obeyed – *bona fide* and honestly obeyed . . . If any man chooses to remain a lay subject of the kingdom, he is bound by his allegiance to the Sovereign: if he cannot submit to that allegiance, he must retire to another country where that allegiance is not binding. In the same way, *if a minister cannot conscientiously submit to the law of the Established Church, it is impossible that he should remain a minister of the Established Church.*[21]

18 Act XII of 1834 (Overtures and Interim Acts on the Calling of Ministers) and Act IX of 1834 (Declaration Enactment as to Chapels of Ease), reproduced in *Acts of the General Assembly of the Church of Scotland, 1638–1842* (Edinburgh Printing & Publishing Co 1843)1037, available at: http://www.british-history.ac.uk/church-scotland-records/acts/1638-1842/pp1028-1042#h3-0010, accessed 21 August 2018.

19 *Earl of Kinnoull and Rev R Young v Presbytery of Auchterarder* (1838) 16 S 661, affirmed (1839) McL& Rob 220 and *Earl of Kinnoull and Rev R Young v Rev John Ferguson and others (a majority of the Presbytery of Auchterarder)* (1841) 3 D 778, affirmed (1842) 1 Bell 662.

20 *Cuninghame v Presbytery of Irvine* (1843) 5 D 427.

21 *Clark v Stirling* (1839) 1 D 955 [emphasis added]: the quotation is from CG Robertson, *Report of Proceedings in the Court of Session in the Lethendy Case* (Blackwood 1839).

Given the circumstances, the Evangelical party in the Church despaired of any prospect of change and finally lost patience. The consequence was that at the General Assembly of 1843, Thomas Chalmers made a marathon speech, laid a Protest on the Table and led the retiring Moderator, David Welsh, and some 200 of their ministerial colleagues out of St Andrew's Church down to Tanfield Hall in Canonmills, to establish what was first known as 'The Church of Scotland Free' – and to trigger a schism that was not resolved until 1929.[22]

Quite apart from the cataclysmic effect on the Church of Scotland itself, the importance of the Disruption for the subsequent history of Scotland was considerable, not least because it was no longer feasible to leave the operation of the Poor Law to a Church of Scotland that had been depleted in numbers. Perhaps more important, however, were the less tangible effects on Scottish society more generally of the loss of a major unifying institution.[23]

The significance

I would suggest that *Of Presbyters and Kings* is significant for three reasons. First, it is – so far as I am aware – the first detailed study in modern times of the *legal* aspects of the Disruption and its consequences, as opposed to analyses of its socio-historical or theological implications. There was much written around the time of the Disruption itself and, later, after the Free Church case in 1904; but most of the discussion was from various partisan points of view and, from then on, the subject appears to have been largely ignored by academic lawyers. Secondly, it is – again to the best of my knowledge – the first systematic attempt in modern times to survey the interactions between secular law and religious observance in Scotland. Thirdly, it helped to trigger a modest revival in interest in the subject.

Prior to its publication, the intricacies of Scots secular law in relation to religion appear to have been largely neglected; after it, interest appeared to grow, most notably in the work of scholars such as the late Alan Rodger,[24] Marjory MacLean,[25] and Chloë Kennedy.[26] And even then, Lord Rodger noted that the decision of the House of Lords in *Percy*[27] – which was of enormous importance to

22 And not totally even then: a group within the United Free Church who remained opposed to Establishment and who supported voluntaryism refused to enter the union of 1929 and constituted themselves as the United Free Church (Continuing) – dropping '(Continuing)' after five years.

23 O Checkland, *Industry and Ethos: Scotland 1832–1914* (Edinburgh UP 1989) 122.

24 Lord Rodger of Earlsferry, *The Courts, the Church and the Constitution: Aspects of the Disruption of 1843* (Edinburgh University Press, 2008).

25 MA MacLean, *The Crown Rights of the Redeemer: The Spiritual Freedom of the Church of Scotland* (St Andrew Press 2009) and MA MacLean (ed), *Legal Systems of Scottish Churches* (Edinburgh University Press, 2009) – but the latter is primarily about the internal law of the Churches rather than their interactions with the secular legal system.

26 C Kennedy, 'Criminal Law and Religion in Post-Reformation Scotland' (2012) 16 *Edinburgh Law Review* 178.

27 *Percy v Board of National Mission of the Church of Scotland* [2005] UKHL 73, 2006 SC (HL) 1, in which the House of Lords held that an associate minister of the Church was 'employed'

the Church of Scotland – appeared 'to have prompted no comment at all in the ordinary British legal journals and there seem to be only two discussions of the jurisdiction point'.[28] In fact there were three: Lyall himself published an article on the judgment in the *Edinburgh Law Review*[29] – but it no doubt appeared in print after Lord Rodger's own submission deadline.

Recently, however, there have been two important developments. Lyall has published a major update of his earlier book[30] – in effect, a complete rewrite to bring the story up to the end of 2014, in the course of which he deals at some length with *Percy* –while, at the same time, Callum Brown, Thomas Green and Jane Mair have produced an extremely comprehensive analysis of the present state of Law and Religion in Scotland.[31] You wait ages for an up-to-date analysis of Law and Religion in Scotland and two come along at once. Nevertheless, the topic still remains a fairly specialist one with relatively few practitioners.

The legacy

Brown and his co-authors observe that in Scotland:

> there has been little detailed exploration or analysis of the place of religion in contemporary law and, in the absence of explicit conflict in the courts between secular and religious values . . . there has been little need to consider the interaction between law and religion.[32]

A careful reading of the footnote references in their own work and in Lyall's update confirms that view: King Murray and Thomas apart, there are very few references in either work to any kind of academic legal comment between the early 1930s and the 1980s. They attribute what they describe as 'a natural and

---

for the purposes of the Sex Discrimination Act 1975 and that the events surrounding her departure from her post did not fall within 'the separate and independent government and jurisdiction of this Church in matters spiritual' as contemplated by Article IV of the Articles Declaratory annexed to the Church of Scotland Act 1921. The case was ultimately settled.

28 Lord Rodger of Earlsferry, *The Courts, the Church and the Constitution: Aspects of the Disruption of 1843* (Edinburgh University Press, 2008) 93. As it happens, I contributed to both of them: see F Cranmer and S Peterson, 'Employment, Sex Discrimination and the Churches' (2006) *Ecc LJ* 392 and MA MacLean, F Cranmer and S Peterson, 'Recent Developments in Church-State Relations in Scotland' in R M Morris (ed), *Church and State in 21st Century Britain* (Palgrave Macmillan, 2009).

29 F Lyall, 'Church Ministers as Employees: *Percy v Church of Scotland Board of National Mission* (2006) 10 *Edinburgh Law Review* 446.

30 F Lyall, *Church and State in Scotland: Developing Law* (Routledge 2016).

31 CG Brown, T Green and J Mair, *Religion in Scots Law: Report of an Audit at the University of Glasgow* (Humanist Society Scotland 2016) Available at: https://www.humanism.scot/wp-content/uploads/2016/02/Religion-in-Scots-Law-Final-Report-22-Feb-16.pdf, accessed 21 August 2018.

32 Ibid, 17.

precipitous decline' in academic interest since the late 1920s to the consequences of the Church of Scotland (Property and Endowments) Act 1925:

> As a result of the 1925 Act all historical financial links between the Church of Scotland, heritors, and teinds have been broken, as a result of which ecclesiastical parochial law has effectively ceased to be a unique branch of Scots civil law relating to the financial affairs of the Church of Scotland.[33]

But, at the same time, they observe that: 'Recently . . . there has been a remarkable revival of interest in religion and law.'[34] They also note that:

> In 1980, one of the leading experts on the law of church and state in Scotland, Francis Lyall, wrote that: 'It seems inevitable that there will be further change in the Law of Scotland on Church and State. The decline of institutional Christianity, the polarisation of divergences within the denominations, the spread of the smaller and more cohesive churches, and the trend towards individualism and "liberty" in civil life, in short the emergence of the so called "secular society", will make that change and development necessary'.[35]

Subsequent events proved Lyall right.[36] Nor has he changed his view: he begins the Conclusions to his recent book like this:

> This Chapter is mis-titled, but deliberately. It has been thirty-five years since my last book-length venture into these waters. Much has changed. And there are no indications that change has ceased.[37]

He then goes on to argue, for example, that on the general issue of religious manifestation as a human right there needs to be a rebalancing exercise, citing Lady Hale in support of 'reasonable accommodation' between competing interests and convictions. He also suggests that this will require restraint on the part of those in authority who hold strong views, whether religious or not:

> Profound conviction or dogmatism can tempt into action, but it does not confer immunity from seeking the general good through argument and discussion rather than by fiat.[38]

I cannot disagree: if anything, as the pace of change in matters of law and religious manifestation has accelerated, the need both for restraint by all parties

33 Ibid.
34 Ibid, 17–18.
35 Ibid, 23.
36 Who in 1980, for example, could have imagined the Civil Partnership Act 2004 or the Equality Act 2010 – still less same-sex marriage?
37 Lyall, *Church and State in Scotland: Developing Law*, 225.
38 Ibid, 228.

to potential disputes and for rational and unprejudiced academic analysis of the underlying legal principles involved has become greater than ever before. In conclusion, the text of *Of Presbyters and Kings* has long since been superseded – not least by Lyall's own recent book – simply because so much has changed since 1980. Nevertheless, *Of Presbyters and Kings* is where it all started. Lyall's book ensured that the interaction of Law and Religion in Scotland received separate attention and its integration of a historically informed yet still distinctively legal analysis of matters concerning Church and State with a wider exploration of ways in which religious conscience interacted with the law sets a standard rarely met elsewhere in the Law and Religion literature. *Of Presbyters and Kings* remains the trail-blazer on Law and Religion in the Scottish context and must still, on that account alone, be reckoned a 'leading work'.

5 The European Convention on Human Rights

A living leading work

Frank Cranmer[1]

The work

One of the Rumpole adventures includes the following exchange:

> 'So we're off to The Hague, are we?'
> 'You may be, Mr Rumpole, but the Court of Human Rights sits in Strasbourg.'
> 'Of course! That's the one I meant.'[2]

When I learned from a casual email that this book was at the planning stage, my instant, unreflecting suggestion for the Leading Work was, 'by a country mile the European Convention on Human Rights, and not just Article 9'. But is it a 'work'? And does it have an author? Every reader will be familiar with the Convention, and especially with Article 9 (Freedom of thought, conscience and religion). And if the definition of 'work' as 'a thing or things done or made; the result of action',[3] is a reliable guide, it must undoubtedly be a 'work' of some kind. Its authorship, however, is rather more complicated.

Enter David Maxwell Fyfe. An Edinburgh Scot, he spent too much time on Conservative undergraduate politics at Oxford and took a Third in Greats. Once called to the English Bar, however, he was extremely assiduous: he took silk in 1934 and entered Parliament as Member for Liverpool West Derby in the following year, aged 35. He maintained a busy legal practice as an MP and served as the wartime Solicitor General then, briefly, as Attorney. Home Secretary under Churchill from 1951 to 1954, he was at the same time Minister for Welsh Affairs, earning him the unkind soubriquet 'Dai Bananas'.[4] Ennobled as the Earl of

1 I should like to thank Russell Sandberg for his careful editing which, as always, has been both extremely helpful and thought-provoking, Celia Kenny for commenting on a very early draft, and the colleagues, too numerous to list by name, with whom I have tested some of the ideas in this chapter in various conferences, seminars and casual conversations.

2 JC Mortimer, *Rumpole and the Angel of Death* (Viking, 1996) 178.

3 C Soanes and S Hawker, *Compact Oxford English Dictionary* (Oxford University Press, 2008) 1196.

4 P Williams, *The Psychology of Distance: Wales: One Nation* (Welsh Academic Press, 2003) 35.

Kilmuir, he was Lord Chancellor from 1954 until July 1962, when Harold Macmillan sacked him in the 'Night of the Long Knives'.[5]

But Maxwell Fyfe is remembered neither for his time as Home Secretary, nor even for his judgments as Lord Chancellor.[6] Perhaps ironically, what assures his place in legal history is not his ministerial career but his extra-Parliamentary activities while in Opposition: as deputy prosecutor at Nuremberg to his successor as Attorney, Sir Hartley Shawcross, as chairman of the Committee on Legal and Administrative Questions of the Consultative Assembly of the Council of Europe[7] and – crucially for what follows – as one of the draftsmen of the European Convention on Human Rights (ECHR).

The context

The UN General Assembly adopted the Universal Declaration of Human Rights (UDHR) on 10 December 1948; however, though critically important as a statement of principles, it is no more than its name suggests: a declaration. To say that, is by no means to underestimate the seminal importance of the UDHR for the development of human rights jurisprudence. It enumerates the right to life, liberty and security of person and condemns slavery and servitude, torture and cruel, inhuman or degrading treatment. It recognises the right to recognition as a person before the law; it declares that all are equal before the law and entitled to equal protection and an effective remedy before an independent and impartial tribunal without discrimination. It condemns arbitrary arrest, detention or exile; it upholds the presumption of innocence, it envisages protection of privacy, family life, home and private correspondence; it upholds the right to freedom of movement, residence, nationality and asylum; it protects the right to marry and to found a family – and so on. Specifically, in relation to religion, Article 18 UDHR declares the right to freedom of thought, conscience and religion very much in the same terms as Article 9(1) ECHR.[8] It also recognises the right to own property (Article 17) and the right to education (Article 26) – subjects that were not addressed by the ECHR until the First Protocol added them in March 1952.

5 Lord Kilmuir David Maxwell Fyfe, *Political Adventure: The Memoirs of the Earl of Kilmuir* (Weidenfeld and Nicolson, 1964) 323.
6 He sat in only 25 cases, five of which were Privy Council appeals in which he did not deliver the opinion. N Duxbury, *Lord Kilmuir: A Vignette* (Hart Publishing Ltd, 2015) 1. What *did* survive him were the 'Kilmuir Rules' of 1955, which severely limited the public expression of extrajudicial opinions by judges in England and Wales. Another Scottish Conservative Lord Chancellor, Lord Mackay of Clashfern, scrapped them in 1987.
7 Now the 'Parliamentary Assembly'.
8 The qualifier in Article 9(2) ECHR is paralleled by the overall qualifier in Article 29(2) UDHR: 'In the exercise of his rights and freedoms, everyone shall be subject only to such limitations as are determined by law solely for the purpose of securing due recognition and respect for the rights and freedoms of others and of meeting the just requirements of morality, public order and the general welfare in a democratic society'.

However, at the time when the UDHR was adopted, there was at least a tenable argument – if not an uncontested one – that not even strict adherence to the law was an absolute guarantee of respect for human rights. Hitler had been careful to observe the Weimar Constitution to the letter during his rise to power – even if he had then subverted it.[9] Maxwell Fyfe believed that legislation, such as the *Ermächtigungsgesetz* of 1933,[10] demonstrated that not even strict adherence to constitutional legality was an absolute guarantee of the integrity of democratic institutions. Moreover, because he had shouldered day-to-day responsibility for the British contribution to the Nuremberg prosecutions – while Shawcross's principal involvement had been the opening and closing speeches[11] – he had read the detailed accounts of Nazi atrocities. He was in no doubt that the accused

> in carrying out the criminal programme of Nazi Germany had thoroughly 'corrupted the human conscience'. Nor, he insisted, should anyone doubt that such events could occur again. The fundamental question facing Europe in 1946 was: how might its recurrence be prevented?[12]

Maxwell Fyfe was convinced that the only answer to his fundamental question was to reassert the primacy of the rule of law and human rights in such a way as to put their integrity well beyond the reach of sticky-fingered national politicians – though presumably, like others in post-War Western Europe, *Realpolitik* compelled him modestly to avert his gaze from the activities of Josef Stalin. In short, he shared the view of his close adviser Hersch Lauterpacht that any European Convention to enshrine human rights in international law would be effective only if the signatory states were prepared fully to integrate it into their domestic laws and to surrender at least a limited degree of national sovereignty.[13]

In 1947, Churchill appointed Maxwell Fyfe the Opposition's representative on the Committee of the European Movement, which by 1948 became responsible for making recommendations on European integration to national governments.[14] The Council of Europe was established in May 1949; and in July the European Movement sent its Council of Ministers a draft proposal for a Convention on Human Rights.[15] Its authors were Maxwell Fyfe, Pierre-Henri Teitgen,

9 E Feuchtwanger, 'The Transition from Weimar to the Third Reich' in Panikos Panayi (ed) *Weimar and Nazi Germany: Continuities and Discontinuities* (Longman, 2001) 107ff.

10 The 'Enabling' or 'Authorisation' Act, which had given the Executive – in effect, Hitler himself as *Reichskanzler* – the power to make laws without the approval of the *Reichstag*.

11 Duxbury, *Lord Kilmuir: A Vignette*, 14.

12 Ibid, 103.

13 Duxbury, *Lord Kilmuir: A Vignette*, 114–115, 117.

14 Ibid, 106.

15 Ibid.

French Minister of Justice from 1945 to 1946,[16] and Fernand Dehousse, former Belgian Minister of Labour and representative to the UN.[17]

Their draft was greatly influenced by the text of the UDHR but, crucially, they went one step further, proposing a Convention with teeth and overseen by a Court. Teitgen argued that only a justiciable Convention would prevent a repetition of Germany's experience of dictatorship by stealth:

> Democracies do not become Nazi countries in one day. Evil progresses cunningly . . . one by one, freedoms are suppressed in one sphere after another. Public opinion and the entire national conscience are asphyxiated. And then, when everything is in order, the '*Führer*' is installed and the evolution continues even to the oven of the crematorium. It is necessary to intervene before it is too late. . . . An international Court, within the Council of Europe, and a system of supervision and guarantees, could be the conscience of which we all have need.[18]

Maxwell Fyfe agreed. For a Convention to be effective and – unlike the UDHR – enforceable, each signatory would have to make a firm commitment to make it part of its domestic law.[19] Like Teitgen, he believed that a Court, with its jurisdiction accepted by formal agreement, should be established before which complaints against any member State of falling below the standard should be examined.[20] But not everyone was convinced. Moreover, though the Council of Ministers finally agreed a Convention with provision for a supervisory European Court of Human Rights (ECtHR), the Court attracted considerable opposition, not least from the UK Government: Lord Chancellor Jowitt described it as a 'half-baked scheme to be administered by some unknown court'.[21]

The Court was not established until 21 January 1959, sitting for the first time on 23 February and delivering its first judgment in November 1960.[22] Initially, however, acceptance both of the Court's jurisdiction and of the right of individual petition were optional: the United Kingdom did not accept them until 1966,

16 He became a judge of the ECtHR in 1976: D Johnson, 'Obituary: Pierre-Henri Teitgen' *The Independent*, 10 April 1997.

17 E Bates, 'The Birth of the European Convention of Human Rights – and the European Court of Human Rights' in Jonas Christoffersen and Mikael Rask Madsen, *The European Court of Human Rights between Law and Politics* (Oxford University Press, 2011) 20.

18 W Schwimmer, 'Statement at the Commemorative Ceremony' in *Proceedings: European Ministerial Conference on Human Rights and Commemorative Ceremony of the 50th anniversary of the European Convention* (2000) Council of Europe, 146.

19 Duxbury, *Lord Kilmuir: A Vignette*, 108–109.

20 D Maxwell Fyfe [The Earl of Kilmuir], 'Next Steps for "United Europe"' (1947–48) 38 *Round Table* 747.

21 Anthony P Lester, 'Fundamental Rights: The United Kingdom Isolated?' (1984) 46 *Public Law* 51–52.

22 *Lawless v Ireland* [1960] ECHR 1.

Italy until 1973 and France until 1981.[23] Furthermore, at the outset individuals did not have direct access to the Court but had to apply first to the European *Commission* of Human Rights: a sifting body that decided on admissibility and reported on merits.[24]

So, it was a very long haul indeed from Maxwell Fyfe's and Teitgen's initial conception to the establishment of the modern Court; nevertheless, 'Maxwell Fyfe's involvement in the process of drafting the ECHR was key';[25] and I would argue that the two have a strong claim to be regarded as the 'authors' of the ECHR as we know it today. That was evidently Maxwell Fyfe's own view; some 25 years on he wrote that he and his colleagues:

> had succeeded in doing what the United Nations had failed to do, namely, to create an enforceable convention guaranteeing democratic rights . . . I do not want to be a boring 'proud father', but I think I am entitled to be glad that I have done something positive as well as negative in regard to tyranny, which so many of my generation in the twentieth century have accepted without a murmur.[26]

Briefly, the Court in its modern format, subsequent to the reforms of 1998, normally sits to hear applications in 'Chambers' or 'Sections' of seven judges, in each case including the President of the Section and the judge elected in respect of any State Party concerned – who, if not already a member of the Section to which the application has been assigned, sits *ex officio*.[27] Where a pending case raises 'a serious question affecting the interpretation of the Convention or Protocols thereto', the Chamber may relinquish jurisdiction in favour of the Grand Chamber, consisting of seventeen judges,[28] unless one of the parties has objected within one month of being informed of the decision to relinquish.[29] The Grand Chamber includes the President and the Vice-Presidents of the Court, the Presidents of the Sections, the judge elected in respect of the Contracting Party concerned *ex officio* and, where a Chamber has relinquished jurisdiction, the members of that Chamber.[30] The other function of the Grand Chamber is to hear appeals under Article 43 of the Convention – in which case, the judges who

23 A Donald, J Gordon and P Leach, *The UK and the European Court of Human Rights* (Equality and Human Rights Commission, 2012) 9.
24 Abolished in 1998, when Protocol 11 created a single, full-time, permanent Court.
25 F Klug, *A Magna Carta for All Humanity: Homing in on Human Rights* (Routledge, 2015) 151.
26 Lord Kilmuir D Maxwell Fyfe, *Political Adventure: The Memoirs of the Earl of Kilmuir* (Weidenfeld and Nicolson,1964) 184.
27 *Rules of Court*, Rule 26.
28 *Rules of Court*, Rule 24.1.
29 *Rules of Court*, Rule 72.1.
30 *Rules of Court*, Rule 24.2(a), (b) and (c).

sat at first instance are excluded, apart from the President of the Chamber, the judge who sat in respect of the State Party concerned and any judge who ruled on the admissibility of the application.[31]

I would suggest that it is because of Maxwell Fyfe's influence that the Court bears the distinct imprint of the common law rather than being purely a civilian institution. For example, Rule 74.2 allows for separate concurring and dissenting opinions.[32] No lawyer from the United Kingdom would regard that as anything other than commonplace, whereas in France, not only does the judicial system not allow dissenting opinions, its judges must swear an oath of confidentiality: *le secret du délibéré*.[33] Perhaps because it began life uninfluenced by the common law, the Court of Justice of the European Union (CJEU) by contrast follows French practice and issues a single determination.[34] More generally, Lord Neuberger PSC quotes the former President of the ECtHR, Dean Spielmann, to the effect that the UK and Strasbourg 'have developed a jurisprudential dialogue of the highest standard, as well as an informal dialogue through regular meetings' and that '[c]ertain important principles, entrenched for centuries in the British legal culture' have strongly influenced its case law.[35]

I also have the impression – though I should emphasise that it is *only* an impression – that the ECtHR is usually more ready than the CJEU to quote its previous judgments as authority. The CJEU is by no means averse to doing so;[36] but its focus tends to be on detailed analysis of the facts before it set against the text of the Regulation or Directive at issue. In contrast, because the ECtHR works from little more than a statement of very general principles, it tends as a regular

31 *Rules of Court*, Rule 24.2(d).

32 *Károly Nagy v Hungary* [2015] ECHR 1051 – a claim for unfair dismissal by a Reformed Church minister – is a recent example of very complex concurrence and dissent. It was decided by four votes to three: Lemmens J was the only member of the Court who agreed unequivocally with the majority opinion, Raimondi P, Keller and Kjølbro JJ concurred in part and dissented in part, while Sajó, Vučinić and Kūris JJ dissented completely. At the time of writing there had been a rehearing before the Grand Chamber.

33 Personal communication from Marie-Luce Cavrois, *conseiller à la Cour de cassation*.

34 Whether the CJEU should change its position on unanimity has been the subject of debate within the EU itself. Rosa Rafaelli, *Dissenting opinions in the Supreme Courts of the Member States* (Directorate-General for Internal Policies, European Parliament, 2012).

35 DE Neuberger, DE [Baron Neuberger of Abbotsbury], 'Has the identity of the English Common Law been eroded by EU Laws and the European Convention on Human Rights?' (Lecture at the Faculty of Law, National University of Singapore, 18 August 2016) https://www.supremecourt.uk/docs/speech-160818-01.pdf quoting D Spielman 'Graduation Ceremony' (University College London, 6 July 2016). Available at https://www.laws.ucl.ac.uk/wp-content/uploads/2016/07/spielmann_dean_graduation-ceremony_speech_2016.pdf, accessed 21 August 2018.

36 See, for example, the two recent *hijab* cases: in *G4S Secure Solutions* [2017] EUECJ C-157/15 the Court cited three of its earlier judgments, while in *Bougnaoui and ADDH* [2017] EUECJ C-188/15 it cited five. In *S.A.S. v France* [2014] ECHR 695, a case about the *niqab* veil referred to below, the majority cited more than sixty of its own opinions – though, admittedly, in a much longer judgment.

practice to look beyond the Convention to its own previous decisions for guidance. Moreover, while Strasbourg is willing to concede a margin of appreciation to Member States, Luxembourg reserves the margin of appreciation to the European Commission:

> Where the evaluation of a complex economic situation is involved, the Administration enjoys a wide measure of discretion. In reviewing the legality of the exercise of such discretion, the court must confine itself to examining whether it contains a manifest error or constitutes a misuse of power or whether the authority did not clearly exceed the bounds of its discretion.[37]

Otherwise, notes Mark Hill, its function is to apply EU law to the instant case:

> The ECtHR consistently defers to national legislators in relation to political, social, cultural and other considerations. Whilst the ECJ openly acknowledges and applies the principle of subsidiarity, no such elasticity is afforded the ECJ in the enforcement of EU Directives.[38]

Or, as Baroness Hale DPSC put it in a lecture, there is no margin of appreciation for parties in Luxembourg.[39] David Feldman concludes that 'There is no doctrine of *stare decisis* in the Strasbourg institutions, which treat the ECHR as a dynamic instrument, not a static one'.[40] True: but nevertheless, the ECtHR seems slow to depart without good cause from a well-established line of reasoning relevant to the case before it, 'in the interests of legal certainty, foreseeability and equality before the law'.[41] As its then President explained in 2006, the Court

> has continued to offer guidance to national courts on the development and evolution of human rights protection. Yet at the same time it has followed precedent, except where cogent reasons impelled it to adjust the interpretation of the Convention to changes in societal values or in present-day conditions, . . . not only in judgments concerning particular respondent States but also in recognising that the same European minimal standards should be observed in all member States.[42]

37 *A Racke v Hauptzollamt Mainz* [1978] EUECJ R-136/77, 1.
38 M Hill, 'Freedom of religion: Strasbourg and Luxembourg compared' in Cole Durham and Donlu Thayer (eds), *Religion and Equality: Law in Conflict* (Routledge, 2016) 30.
39 BM Hale [Baroness Hale of Richmond], 'Freedom of and Freedom from Religion.' Lecture at the annual conference of the Ecclesiastical Law Society, St Bride's Institute, 12 March 2016.
40 D Feldman, 'Standard of Review and Human Rights in English Law' in David Feldman, *English Public Law* (Oxford University Press, 2009) 328.
41 *Christine Goodwin v United Kingdom* [2002] ECHR 588 [74].
42 L Wildhaber, 'Speech given by Mr Luzius Wildhaber, President of the European Court of Human Rights, on the occasion of the Opening of the Judicial Year, 20 January 2006' (*European Court of Human Rights Annual Report 2005*) 21.

That is by no means a doctrine of *stare decisis* – Murdoch describes it as a 'moderated doctrine of precedent' which 'for lawyers from a continental legal tradition . . . may need some further explanation' – but it is certainly some distance from the civilian assumption that a judicial decision does no more than decide the dispute between the parties.[43]

Francesca Klug believes that the Convention is 'as British as custard',[44] while former Director of Public Prosecutions Ken Macdonald has claimed that 'the Strasbourg Court has played an estimable part in the spread of English common law values across the continent of Europe, just as Winston Churchill and the English common lawyers who drafted the European Convention on Human Rights intended'.[45] One of Maxwell Fyfe's recent successors as Attorney, Dominic Grieve QC, shares that view:

> Much of substance of the Convention reflects the rights and freedoms hard won in this country over the centuries. The prohibition of torture, right to liberty and right to a fair trial in the Convention all reflect the development of British common and statute law from *Magna Carta*, *habeas corpus* to the Bill of Rights. British politicians from Winston Churchill to David Maxwell Fyfe were instrumental in the development of the Convention. I am proud of that legacy.[46]

And, for what it is worth, so am I.

The significance

I would contend that the overall domestic significance of the ECHR for human rights generally cannot be overestimated. As we shall see, it was directly because of the ECtHR's ruling in *Dudgeon*[47] that gay sex was decriminalised in Northern Ireland. It was primarily because of our adherence to the ECHR that, in *A & Ors*,[48] the House of Lords concluded that the indefinite imprisonment without trial of foreign nationals suspected of terrorist sympathies was unreasonably

43 J Murdoch, '*Protecting the right to freedom of thought, conscience and religion under the European Convention on Human Rights*' (2012) Directorate General of Human Rights and Rule of Law, Council of Europe, 7.

44 F Klug, 'The Universal Declaration of Human Rights: Sixty years on' (Lecture at Chatham House, 8 December 2008), 14. Available at http://www.lse.ac.uk/humanRights/aboutUs/articlesAndTranscripts/ChathamHouseDec08.pdf, accessed 21 August 2018. By which I assume she means that nasty yellow stuff that comes out of a packet.

45 Director of Public Prosecutions Ken Macdonald has claimed (2016).

46 D Grieve ' European Convention on Human Rights: Current Challenges' (Attorney General's Office, The Rt Hon Dominic Grieve QC, 24 October 2011). Available at https://www.gov.uk/government/speeches/european-convention-on-human-rights-current-challenges, accessed 21 August 2018.

47 *Dudgeon v United Kingdom* [1981] ECHR 5.

48 *A & Ors v Secretary of State for the Home Department* [2004] UKHL 56.

disproportionate and discriminatory and made a quashing order in respect of the Human Rights Act 1998 (Designated Derogation) Order 2001, declaring section 23 of the Anti-terrorism, Crime and Security Act 2001 incompatible with Articles 5 and 14 ECHR – with Lady Hale JSC asserting that 'Executive detention is the antithesis of the right to liberty and security of person'.[49] The importance of the Convention for religious manifestation in the UK may not have been quite so profound; but I would argue that it has had a far-reaching influence both on practice and on academic discourse.

The overall significance of the ECHR for Law and Religion depends, at least in part, on how one defines a sub-discipline that is still relatively new and evolving. Norman Doe has observed that 'Academic discussion of religious freedom in Europe has been dominated by the jurisprudence of the European Court of Human Rights on religious freedom under Article 9'.[50] True enough: but even a cursory examination of the leading cases suggests that, though it is the key provision, disputes over manifestation of religion and belief have ranged well beyond Article 9: Articles 6, 8, 10, 11, 12 and 14 and Articles 1 and 2 to the First Protocol have all been cited in cases involving religious rights.

The result has been either that what would appear to be a 'Law and Religion' case, broadly defined, has sometimes been argued under an Article other than Article 9, or that the Court has decided that it is unnecessary to examine a complaint under Article 9 because another Article has been violated. So, for example, in *Darby*[51] the Court held that the refusal to grant a temporary resident the reduction in church tax given to permanently resident non-members of the Church of Sweden breached Article 14 taken with Article 1 of Protocol 1 and did not pursue the Article 9 point.

Perhaps unsurprisingly, in family cases involving religious disputes the Court has tended to give more weight to Article 8 than to Article 9. In *Hoffmann*[52] and *Ismailova*[53] for example, both involving child custody disputes after divorce where the mother was a Jehovah's Witness, the Court decided the cases on Article 8 grounds and, though part of the problem was religious differences between the estranged parents, concluded that no separate issue arose under Article 9. Subsequently, in *Gineitienė*,[54] in which the mother was a member of an unregistered 'new religious movement', an application under Articles 8 and 14 was judged admissible – though rejected on the facts – while the application under Article 9

49 At [222] – though it should also be noted that Lord Hoffmann pointed out at [88] that the liberty of the individual was also a classic right under the common law: 'Freedom from arbitrary arrest and detention is a quintessentially British liberty, enjoyed by the inhabitants of this country when most of the population of Europe could be thrown into prison at the whim of their rulers.'

50 N Doe, *Law and Religion in Europe* (Oxford University Press, 2011) 40.

51 *Darby v Sweden* [1990] ECHR 24.

52 *Hoffmann v Austria* [1993] ECHR 25.

53 *Ismailova v Russia* [2007] ECHR 1003.

54 *Gineitienė v Lithuania* [2010] ECHR 1204.

was judged inadmissible. In *Vojnity*[55] the Court held that removing a divorced man's access rights to his son, essentially on grounds of his eccentric religious convictions, violated Article 14 taken together with Article 8 and 'amounted to a complete disregard of the principle of proportionality, requisite in this field and inherent in the spirit of the Convention';[56] however, as in *Hoffmann* and *Ismailova*, no separate issue arose under Article 9. Finally, on this point, *Obst*[57] and *Schüth*,[58] both of which related to the dismissal of Church employees for adultery, were decided on the basis of the Article 8 rights of the applicants; only passing reference was made to the putative Article 9 rights of the two denominations involved to secure their employees' adherence to their discipline and doctrines.

Similar considerations apply to freedom of expression and freedom of assembly and association under Articles 10 and 11. In *Wingrove*,[59] the Court upheld the British Board of Film Classification's refusal to certify the video of *Visions of Ecstasy*, a vaguely pornographic and rather tedious art-house film about Theresa of Avila. Though the case undoubtedly had a strong religious dimension, it was incidental to the main issue because the applicant could hardly plead Article 9 when, in effect, he was arguing against the United Kingdom's blasphemy laws. The Court decided the matter under Article 10, holding that because the film was deemed to be blasphemous, the Board's refusal was both prescribed by law and pursued the legitimate aim of protecting the rights of others. In *Glas Nadezhda EOOD*,[60]about the authorities' refusal without adequate reason to license a religious radio station, there was certainly a potential issue about the applicants' right to manifest; however, the Court ruled that because Article 10 had been violated it was unnecessary to examine the complaint under Article 9. In *NF*[61] and *Maestri*,[62] both of which involved judges disciplined because they were Freemasons, the Court found a violation of their right to association under Article 11 and, again, did not find it necessary to examine the complaints under Article 9.

That said, however, the ECtHR has not always been entirely consistent in its judgment as to what an Article 9 case is and what it is not. In *Folgerø*,[63] *Zengin*[64] and *Appel-Irrgang*,[65] all of which involved disputes over obligatory education in religion and ethics, the Court chose to examine the complaints under Article 2

55 *Vojnity v Hungary* [2013] ECHR 131.
56 Ibid, [42].
57 *Obst v Germany* [2010] ECHR (No. 425/03).
58 *Schüth v Germany* [2010] ECHR (No. 1620/03).
59 *Wingrove v United Kingdom* [1996] ECHR 60.
60 *Glas Nadezhda EOOD & Elenkov v Bulgaria* [2007] ECHR 804.
61 *NF v Italy* [2001] ECHR 501.
62 *Maestri v Italy* [2004] ECHR 77.
63 *Folgerø & Ors v Norway* [2007] ECHR 546.
64 *Hasan and Eylem Zengin v Turkey* [2007] ECHR 787.
65 *Appel-Irrgang & Ors v Germany* [2009] ECHR 783.

of Protocol No. 1. In *Grzelak*,[66] however, the Court held that failing to provide a primary-school child with a course in ethics as an alternative to religious education breached the *child*'s rights under Articles 14 and 9 but that the content of the religion and ethics curriculum fell within the Polish Government's margin of appreciation and did not, therefore, violate the rights of the child's parents under Article 2 of Protocol No. 1 –so the parents' complaint under Article 9 fell away. Similarly, in *Dojan*[67] the Court was prepared to examine a complaint that compelling children to attend the *Lütke Fastnacht* – which the applicant parents regarded as an immoral Roman Catholic festivity – and a school theatre workshop aimed at raising awareness about sexual abuse violated Article 2 of Protocol No. 1, Article 8 and Article 9, both separately and in conjunction with Article 14. As in *Grzelak*, however, it did so primarily under Article 2 of Protocol No. 1 and, having done so, concluded that any interference with the applicants' rights under the individual Articles was justified and that no separate issue arose in conjunction with Article 14.

Finally, on this point, there have been cases in which the non-appearance of Article 9 has been inexplicable. *Hämäläinen*[68] was about the authorities' refusal to change the identity number of a male-to-female transsexual to show her acquired gender in her official documents unless her wife agreed to convert their marriage into a civil partnership or the couple divorced. Divorce was against the couple's religious convictions and they felt that a civil partnership would not provide them and their child with the same degree of security as marriage. *Hämäläinen* was twice argued unsuccessfully under Articles 8 and 12, separately and in conjunction with Article 14. Article 9 is not mentioned in either judgment; but for the couple themselves the bottom line seems to have been that, as devout Lutherans, they did not wish to divorce as a precondition of registering Ms Hämäläinen's new gender. In October 2013, Ms Hämäläinen's wife had explained to the Court that, 'I have entered into holy matrimony and [any] other arrangement is against my religious conviction and puts me in an unequal position *vis-à-vis* . . . other wives having a spouse with a treatable disease'[69] – the 'treatable disease' in this instance being gender dysphoria. What was that, if not a religious claim? Why was Article 9 not argued? Did Ms Hämäläinen's legal team feel that to do so would be fruitless, or was it merely an unfortunate oversight?

A similar pattern can be found in terms of the influence of Article 9 upon UK domestic law. In 1970, four years after the UK had accepted the jurisdiction of the ECtHR and the right of individual petition, the Court of Appeal in *Segerdal*[70] upheld the Registrar General's refusal to register a chapel of the

66 *Grzelak v Poland* [2010] ECHR 904.

67 *Dojan & Ors v Germany* [2011] ECHR 1420.

68 *H v Finland* [2012] ECHR 1916, *Hämäläinen v Finland* [2014] ECHR 787.

69 Anon, 'Defending our faith and marriage' in Heli Hämäläinen *Ihmisen kokoisia ihmisoikeuksia* (2013). Available at http://helihamalainen.puheenvuoro.uusisuomi.fi/152795-defending-our-faith-and-marriage, accessed 23 August 2018.

70 *R v Registrar General R ex p Segerdal & Anor* [1970] 3 All ER.

Church of Scientology under the Places of Worship Registration Act 1855 without any reference to Convention rights whatsoever. The domestic impact of the Convention began slowly; at first, the ECtHR and the Commission took a fairly restrictive view of the right to manifest in cases to which the UK was a party. In *Arrowsmith*,[71] in which the applicant claimed that her conviction for distributing leaflets intended to dissuade members of the armed forces from serving in Northern Ireland had violated her Article 9 right to manifest her pacifism, the Commission considered that the term 'practise 'in Article 9(1) did not cover every act motivated or influenced by a religion or belief: 'when the actions of individuals do not actually express the belief concerned they cannot be considered to be . . . protected by Article 9(1), even when motivated or influenced by it'.[72] In *Ahmad*,[73] the Commission held that refusing a Muslim teacher time off for Friday prayers had not violated his Article 9 rights. Freedom of religion was not absolute and 'it may as regards the modality of a particular religious manifestation, be influenced by the situation of the person claiming that freedom'[74]: in short, the 'specific situation rule' later elaborated in *Kalaç*.[75]

In *Campbell and Cosans*,[76] however, the balance appeared to be shifting. The Court declared that philosophical convictions that attained 'a certain level of cogency, seriousness, cohesion and importance' engaged the provisions of the ECHR [36] and upheld the applicants' objection to corporal punishment at their children's schools: nor could the duty to respect those convictions be overridden by the alleged necessity of striking a balance between the conflicting views involved. Though the Court agreed unanimously that there had been no violation of Article 3 (inhuman or degrading treatment), it found a violation of Article 2 of Protocol No. 1 by 6 votes to 1. So, in *Williamson*,[77] though the House of Lords agreed that the appellants' claim of a parental right to allow their children's teachers to administer what they described rather creepily as 'loving corporal correction' in accordance with their religious beliefs engaged Article 9(1), they concluded that the statutory ban on corporal punishment in schools satisfied the test in Article 9(2).

71 *Arrowsmith v United Kingdom* (1978) 3 EHRR 218, Cm.
72 Ibid, [71].
73 *Ahmad v United Kingdom* (1981) 4 EHRR 126, Cm.
74 Ibid, [11].
75 *Kalaç v Turkey* [1997] ECHR 37 [27], about the dismissal of the Legal Director of the Air Force because of his religious activities.
76 *Campbell and Cosans v United Kingdom*[1983] ECHR 3.
77 *R v Secretary of State for Education and Employment & Ors ex p Williamson* [2002] EWCA Civ 1926: *R (Williamson & Ors) v Secretary of State for Education and Employment & Ors* [2005] UKHL 15. For analyses, see S Langlaude, 'Flogging Children with Religion: A Comment on the House of Lords' Decision in *Williamson*' (2006) 8 *Ecclesiastical Law Journal*, 339 and F Cranmer, 'Beating People is Wrong: *Campbell and Cosans, Williamson* and their Aftermath' in M Hunter-Henin (ed), *Law, Religious Freedoms and Education in Europe* (Ashgate, 2012).

The test in *Campbell and Cosans* has become increasingly influential, particularly where Article 9 has been pleaded. In *Suryananda*,[78] the Administrative Court held that Article 9 was engaged by two decisions of the Welsh Assembly Government to slaughter the temple bullock at the Hindu Monastery and Temple at Skanda Vale, Llanpumsaint, and quashed them – though that decision was subsequently overturned by the Court of Appeal, which held that a proper balancing exercise had been carried out in terms of Article 9(2).[79] In *Power*,[80] though the claimant ultimately lost on the merits, Clark J upheld the findings of a Pre-hearing Review in August 2009 that Mr Power's belief in spiritualism and the philosophical belief in life after death and psychic powers were capable of being a 'belief' for the purposes of the Employment Equality (Religion or Belief) Regulations 2003 because it met the criteria of the jurisprudence of Article 9 ECHR. In two cases on very similar facts – *Goldstein*[81] and *Rotsztein*[82] – the Court noted in both instances that there was a conflict between the duty of the coroner to determine the cause of death by means of an invasive autopsy if necessary and the demands of Jewish religious law that corpses should be buried promptly and not be desecrated. The Court accepted in both cases that Article 9 was engaged; and in *Rotsztein* Mitting J set out very precise guidance for coroners where the relatives of the deceased had a religious objection to invasive post-mortem procedures.[83]

The ECHR's influence on matters of religion and belief and on moral issues more generally has had a considerable effect on the domestic law of Member States and has gone far beyond the confines of Article 9, as the following examples illustrate.

To take Article 9 first: a long-running battle was fought at Strasbourg over the provisions of the Greek Code of Criminal Procedure obliging advocates and witnesses who wanted to make a solemn declaration instead of swearing an oath to declare that they were not Orthodox Christians and/or that they did not wish to reveal their religious beliefs. In a series of cases,[84] the Court found violations of Articles 9 and 13.[85] The complaint in *Dimitras* had related to a trial in 2009; by the time it came before the ECtHR in 2014 Greece had got the message and

78 *R (Suryananda) v Welsh Ministers* [2007] EWHC 1736 (Admin).

79 *Surayanda v Welsh Ministers* [2007] EWCA Civ 893. For some unaccountable reason, the spelling of the claimant's name was different in the two cases.

80 *Greater Manchester Police Authority v Power* [2009] UKEAT/0434/09/DA.

81 *R (Goldstein) v HM Coroner for Inner London District* [2014] EWHC 3889 (Admin).

82 *Rotsztein v HM Senior Coroner for Inner London* [2015] EWHC (Admin) (28 July) [unreported]: my thanks to Robert Cohen of 5 Essex Court for supplying me with a copy of the approved transcript.

83 *Rotsztein* [27–29].

84 Beginning with *Alexandridis v Greece* [2008] ECHR (No. 19516/06) and culminating in *Dimitras and Gilbert v Greece* [2014] ECHR 1023.

85 F Cranmer, 'Oaths, the Greek judicial system and Article 9 – again' (2014) *Law & Religion UK*. Available at http://www.lawandreligionuk.com/2014/10/18/oaths-the-greek-judicial-system-and-article-9-again/, accessed 23 August 2018.

removed the offending requirement from the Code, providing instead a simple choice between a religious oath and a solemn declaration.

In Belgium, the Constitutional Court held that parents had a fundamental right under Article 2 Protocol 1 to ensure that their children were educated in accordance with their own religious and philosophical convictions and that there was no reason to distinguish between religious instruction and other subjects. The Court held that even non-denominational ethics classes could be subjective because the teacher could show support for a particular philosophical system. Classes in ethics or religion could not be regarded as objective, critical and pluralistic in accordance with ECtHR case law and it should therefore be possible for pupils to be exempted from them.[86]

Even before the Human Rights Act 1998, the Westminster Government had felt obliged to amend the law in Northern Ireland after the ECtHR had held in *Dudgeon*[87] that criminalising homosexual acts breached the applicant's rights under Article 8 (respect for private and family life). Westminster enacted the Homosexual Offences (Northern Ireland) Order 1982 in the face of considerable local opposition, not least from eight Northern Ireland MPs. Subsequently, the ECtHR has slowly developed a more supportive stance towards legal recognition of same-sex relationships. In *Schalk*,[88] the First Section held that though Article 8 protected the family life of same-sex couples,[89] it did not impose a requirement on States Parties to institute same-sex marriage[90] – a position reiterated in *Hämäläinen*.[91] However, the Court held unanimously in *Oliari*,[92] that Italy's failure to provide same-sex couples with any kind of legally recognised civil union whatsoever violated Article 8; and in 2016 the Italian Parliament legislated to remedy the position.[93]

Finally, on this point, in *O'Donoghue*,[94] in a purported attempt to prevent sham marriages, from 2005 onwards a Home Office scheme required most immigrants without settled status to apply for a Certificate of Approval to marry – the exceptions being EEA nationals and those who were to marry according to the rites of the Church of England. The applicants, Roman Catholics, lived in Northern Ireland where, as the Court rather drily observed, 'There is no Church of England'.[95] The ECtHR found a violation of Article 12 (right to marry) and of

86 *De Pascale et de Thier c. Ville de Bruxelles et la Communauté* française [2015] Constitutional Court of Belgium 34/2015: for an official summary in English see http://www.const-court.be/cgi/arrets_popup.php?lang=en&ArrestID=3863, accessed 23 August 2018.
87 *Dudgeon v United Kingdom* [1981] ECHR 5.
88 *Schalk and Kopf v Austria* [2010] ECHR 995.
89 Ibid, [94].
90 Ibid, [108].
91 *Hämäläinen v Finland* [2014] ECHR 787 [71].
92 *Oliari & Ors v Italy* [2015] ECHR 716.
93 *Legge 20 maggio 2016, n. 76: Regolamentazione delle unioni civili tra persone dello stesso sesso e disciplina delle convivenze* (16G00082).
94 *O'Donoghue & Ors v United Kingdom* [2008] ECHR 1574.
95 Ibid, [2].

Article 14 taken with Articles 12 and 9: the UK Government subsequently abolished the scheme.

The ECHR has also been of wider significance in terms of international law. The influence of one document on another is always impossible to determine; however, some of the later human rights codes bear more than a passing conceptual resemblance to the ECHR. The Canadian Constitution Act 1982, for example, begins by declaring that the Charter of Rights and Freedoms 'guarantees the rights and freedoms set out in it subject only to such reasonable limits prescribed by law as can be demonstrably justified in a free and democratic society', while it goes on to guarantees four 'fundamental freedoms: conscience and religion; thought, belief, opinion and expression, including freedom of the press and other media of communication; peaceful assembly; and association'.

Similarly – and unsurprisingly – the EU Charter of Fundamental Rights builds on the ECHR rather than attempting to supplant it. The EU Charter is much more comprehensive than the ECHR but the Treaty of Lisbon nevertheless declares that fundamental rights, as guaranteed by the ECHR and as they result from the constitutional traditions common to Member States, 'shall constitute general principles of the Union's law'[96] – though the issue of institutional accession by the EU to the ECHR has been somewhat derailed by the opinion of the CJEU on the incompatibility of the accession agreement with Article 6(2) of the Treaty on European Union.[97]

The legacy

The gradual shift after *Campbell and Cosans* has resulted in the integration of Article 9 into domestic law almost by osmosis – a process accelerated by the Human Rights Act 1998. More than forty years on from *Segerdal*, in *Hodkin*[98] the Supreme Court had to revisit the issue of refusal to register a Scientologist chapel. By then, the right to manifest under Article 9 had simply become a given – not least because of the impact of the Human Rights Act 1998. The wheel had turned full circle and the Court did not find it necessary to address the issue of manifestation at all. The 'description'[99] of religion offered by Lord Toulson was so wide that the Court was able to decide the matter simply on the basis of the inherent injustice in a narrow interpretation of section 26(1)(bb) of the Marriage Act 1949.[100]

96 2007/C 306/01 para 8.

97 *Re: accession of the European Union to the Convention for the Protection of Human Rights and Fundamental Freedoms* [2014] EUECJ Avis-2/13.

98 *R (Hodkin & Anor) v Registrar-General of Births, Deaths and Marriages* [2013] UKSC 77.

99 Ibid, [57].

100 Ibid, [65]. For a recent discussion of the two cases see CG Kenny, 'Law, Religion and the Curve of Reason' in F Cranmer et al (eds) *The Confluence of Law and Religion* (Cambridge University Press, 2016) 19.

On some issues of principle, the ECtHR has been resolute. On conscientious objection to military service, the Grand Chamber declared in *Bayatyan*[101] that 'opposition to military service, where it is motivated by a serious and insurmountable conflict between the obligation to serve in the army and a person's conscience or his deeply and genuinely held religious or other beliefs'[102] attracted the guarantees of Article 9. The Court has also taken a firm line on artificial impediments to the recognition and registration of religious groups.[103] It has not, however, been so ready to intervene in some other controversies.

A brief detour in 2010 aside,[104] one area on which the Court has had very little impact is religious dress. In *Eweida*[105] the Fourth Section somewhat blunted the effect of *Arrowsmith* and *Kalaç* by holding that whether there was a sufficiently close and direct nexus between an act and its underlying belief was sensitive to the facts of the individual case.[106] Accordingly, it upheld Ms Eweida's right to wear a visible cross with her British Airways uniform but dismissed Mrs Chaplin's claim about wearing her crucifix and neck-chain because they were a legitimate health and safety concern for her NHS Trust. In *S.A.S.*,[107] however, the Grand Chamber held by a majority that the French law prohibiting the concealment of one's face in public places did not violate Articles 8 or 9, contending that:

> under certain conditions the "respect for the minimum requirements of life in society" . . . or of "living together", as stated in the explanatory memorandum accompanying the Bill, . . . can be linked to the legitimate aim of the "protection of the rights and freedoms of others".[108]

The dissenters, Nussberger and Jäderblom JJ, argued that criminalising the full-face veil was disproportionate to the aim of protecting the idea of 'living together' which, in any case, could not be readily reconciled with the Convention's restrictive catalogue of grounds for interference with basic human rights. Similarly, in *Ebrahimian*,[109] the Fifth Section upheld the non-renewal of a psychiatric social worker's contract at a public hospital for refusing to remove her *hijab*: a decision that attracted a withering dissent from De Gaetano J, who concluded in paragraph 3 of his opinion that 'what is prohibited under French law

101 *Bayatyan v Armenia* [2011] ECHR 1095.
102 Ibid, [110].
103 Most recently, *Magyar Keresztény Mennonita Egyház & Ors v Hungary* [2014] ECHR 552, *Church of Scientology of St Petersburg & Ors v Russia* [2014] ECHR 1019 and *İzzetin Doğan & Ors v Turkey* [2016] ECHR 387.
104 *Ahmet Arslan & Ors v Turkey* [2010] ECHR 2260, in which the criminal convictions of members of a Muslim group for wearing their religious dress in public other than for religious ceremonies were held to violate Article 9.
105 *Eweida & Ors v United Kingdom* [2013] ECHR 37.
106 Ibid, [82].
107 *S.A.S. v France* [2014] ECHR 695.
108 Ibid, [121].
109 *Ebrahimian v France* [2015] ECHR 1041.

with regard to public officials is the subjective manifestation of one's religious belief and not the objective wearing of a particular piece of clothing or other symbol'. At about the same time in a French domestic case, *Baby-Loup*,[110] the *Cour de Cassation* was rejecting a wrongful dismissal claim by an employee of a private nursery that had required her to remove her *hijab* and long *jilbab* dress[111] and it was reported that she intended to take her claim to Strasbourg.[112] It was thought that the matter might be resolved by two *hijab* cases before the CJEU – *G4S Secure Solutions*[113] and *Bougnaoui*[114] – in which the two Advocates General, Kokott and Sharpston, had issued rather conflicting opinions.[115] In the end, however, the Grand Chamber leaned towards the employer in *G4S* but towards the employee in *Bougnaoui* – reflecting the opinions of the two Advocates General and, it appears, satisfying hardly anyone.

S.A.S., *Ebrahimian* and the Grand Chamber rulings in *Lautsi*,[116] on the display of crucifixes in state schools, and *Fernández Martínez*,[117] about the effective sacking of a former Roman Catholic priest from his teaching post in a *state* secondary school after a newspaper had published a photograph of him and his family at a meeting of the Movement for Optional Celibacy, all suggest that the legacy might be a mixed one. In some judgments, the Court seems to have been suffering from an excess of *Realpolitik* – even if in *Fernández Martínez* the applicant lost by a single vote.

In *Kokkinakis*,[118] the first case to be decided under Article 9, the Grand Chamber asserted that the margin of appreciation for States Parties was 'subject to European supervision, embracing both the legislation and the decisions applying it, even those given by an independent court'[119] and that its task was 'to determine whether the measures taken at national level were justified in principle and proportionate'. It remains an open question, however, as to whether the Court has moved sufficiently far from mere toleration of religion to its protection as of right.

110 *X & Y c. Association Baby-Loup* [2014] *Cour de Cassation: Assemblée Plénière Arrêt n° 612 du 25 juin*.
111 M Hunter-Henin, 'Religion, Children and Employment: The *Baby Loup* Case' (2015) 64 *International & Comparative Law Quarterly* 717.
112 Al Boudet, 'La CEDH, de Vincent Lambert à l'affaire *Baby-Loup*, présentation d'une institution européenne', *Huffington Post Edition Française* (6 June 2015). Available at http://www.huffingtonpost.fr/2014/06/25/cedh-vincent-lambert-affaire-baby-loup-presentation-institution-europenne_n_5526082.html, accessed 23 August 2018.
113 *G4S Secure Solutions* [2017] EUECJ C-157/15, perhaps more widely known as *Achbita*.
114 *Bougnaoui and ADDH* [2017] EUECJ C-188/15.
115 S Benedi Lahuerta, 'Wearing the veil at work: *Achbita* and *Bougnaoui* – Can a duty to reasonable accommodation be derived from the EU concept of indirect discrimination?' (2016) *EU Law Analysis*.
116 *Lautsi and Others v Italy* [2011] ECHR 2412.
117 *Fernández Martínez v Spain* [2014] ECHR 615.
118 *Kokkinakis v Greece* [1993] ECHR 20.
119 Ibid, [47].

Javier Martínez-Torron has argued, with some justification, that decisions such as *Kjeldsen*,[120] *Efstratiou*,[121] *Kalaç* and *Cha'are Shalom*[122] are 'unrealistic and bound to end up legitimizing unjustified limitations on freedom of conscience'.[123] Part of the problem is that the Court has been much less ready to defend the *forum internum* than the *forum externum*. Taylor, for example, cites the historic confusion in the Commission and the Court between compulsion and restriction on manifestation and suggests that in *Buscarini*,[124] in which the Grand Chamber held that the obligation on members of the San Marino Parliament to swear an oath 'on the Holy Gospels' was a violation of Article 9, the decision had been correct but the reasoning had been wrong:

> There could not be a clearer case of compulsion in the obligation to swear in accordance with religious beliefs that are not personally held, yet the . . . Court was treating that obligation as a restriction on manifestation.[125]

It can, of course, be argued that the *forum internum* is, almost by definition, unfathomable and that the aphorism attributed to Elizabeth I that she would not 'make windows into men's souls'[126] merely recognises an obvious truth. De Gaetano J suggests in paragraph 3 of his dissent in *Ebrahimian*, however, that it is much more complex than that:

> A woman may wear a headscarf not to manifest a religious belief, or any belief for that matter, but for a variety of other reasons. The same can be said of a man wearing a full beard, or a person wearing a cross with a necklace.

In his view, therefore, obliging public officials to disclose that a particular item *is*, in fact, a manifestation of religious belief trespasses on the *forum internum*. The same might be said of the facts in *Alexandridis* and *Dimitras*; but the Court appears to be drawing a not entirely defensible distinction between different disclosure obligations.

I would go even further than Martínez-Torron: judgments such as *Lautsi*, *S.A.S.*, *Ebrahimian* and *Fernández Martínez* suggest to me, at least, that Strasbourg might be losing its nerve in the face of sustained and often inaccurate

120 *Kjeldsen, Busk Madsen and Pedersen v Denmark* [1976] ECHR 6, on compulsory sex education in state schools.

121 *Efstratiou v Greece*[1996] ECHR 69, on the refusal of two Jehovah's Witness schoolchildren to take part in a school parade: *Valsamis v Greece* [1996] ECHR 72 is almost identical.

122 *Cha'are Shalom Ve Tsedek v France* [2000] ECHR 351, about banning religious slaughter for *glatt kosher* meat.

123 J Martínez-Torron, 'The case of the European Court of Human Rights' in F Requejo and C Ungureanu, *Democracy, Law and Religious Pluralism in Europe* (Routledge, 2014) 130.

124 *Buscarini & Ors v San Marino* [1997] ECHR 188.

125 P Taylor, *Freedom of Religion: UN and European Human Rights Law and Practice* (CUP, 2005) 130.

126 Most probably the words of Francis Bacon.

criticism from increasingly hostile media and the kind of political posturing that promises, on minimal evidence, to 'reverse the mission creep that has meant human rights law being used for more and more purposes, and often with little regard for the rights of wider society'.[127]

Theresa May appeared to have dropped that commitment when she launched her successful campaign for the Conservative leadership in June 2016 and said that she would not campaign to leave the ECHR.[128] It resurfaced, however, when the Secretary of State for Justice, Elizabeth Truss, told the House of Commons Justice Committee that Government had not abandoned its plans to repeal the Human Rights Act but did intend to remain a signatory to the ECHR.[129] But she did not rule out ending the right to plead the Convention before the UK courts;[130] and that uncertainty was increased by a press report[131] that the Prime Minister supported a proposal to include withdrawal from the ECtHR's jurisdiction in the Conservatives' 2020 General Election manifesto.

As it turned out, Parliament was dissolved in 2017 and the Conservative Manifesto said that a Conservative Government would not seek to repeal or replace the Human Rights Act while the process of departure from the European Union was underway; however, the legal framework of human rights would be considered when the process of leaving the EU had been concluded: 'We will remain signatories to the European Convention on Human Rights for the duration of the next parliament.'[132] What that might mean in practice remains to be seen – and perhaps the beneficial effect of the Brighton Declaration[133] on the work of the Court will help redress the balance – but I am not holding my breath.

To conclude: I would claim that the ECHR is one of the 'leading works' of the last hundred years on law and religion and possibly, from a purely European perspective, *the* leading work – though whether it is the common interpretation of the text rather than the text itself that has been the more influential remains an open question. I have already referred to Norman Doe's conclusion on the extent to which the Convention,[134] and Article 9 in particular, have dominated academic discussion; and the work of scholars such as Sir Malcolm Evans, Jean-François

127 Conservative Party (2015) Conservative Election Manifesto 2015, 73. Available at https://www.bond.org.uk/data/files/Blog/ConservativeManifesto2015.pdf, accessed 23 August 2018.
128 J Elgot and R Mason, 'Theresa May launches Tory leadership bid with pledge to unite country' (20 June 2016) *The Guardian*.
129 Oral evidence: 'The work of the Secretary of State' (HC 620, Wednesday 7 September 2016) QQ 81–82.
130 Ibid, Q 85.
131 Christopher Hope, 'Theresa May to fight 2020 election on plans to take Britain out of European Convention on Human Rights after Brexit is completed' (28 December 2016) *The Telegraph*.
132 Conservative Party (2017), Conservative Election Manifesto 2017, 37. Available at https://www.conservatives.com/manifesto, accessed 23 August 2018.
133 The Brighton Declaration (ECtHR, 2012).
134 N Doe, *Law and Religion in Europe* (Oxford University Press, 2011) 40.

Renucci and Paul Taylor [135] lends strong support to that view – as does a string of book chapters and journal articles far too numerous to cite. Even critics such as Andrew Williams,[136] who would like to see the Convention replaced wholesale, cannot avoid engaging with it, if only in the attempt to rebut its presumptions. But perhaps the most telling point in support of the ECHR's influence on the academic study of Law and Religion is to ask oneself this: love it or loathe it, what would domestic law look like without it?

In one sense, that question is incapable of an answer: things are as they are. However, without the ECHR we would still be entirely dependent on a common law, freedom-based approach to religious manifestation instead of the rights-based model that is gradually supplanting it. While it may be true that the rights-based and freedom-based models 'are not binary alternatives; rather, they describe points on a continuum',[137] without the Convention, the Human Rights Act 1998 and the culture change that flowed from them, would the Royal Navy have allowed a rating to register as a Satanist and perform rituals aboard Her Majesty's ships?[138] Could a Wiccan have pleaded unfair dismissal successfully when her employers rubbished her religion and sacked her after she had changed shifts to celebrate a feast day?[139] Would belief in man-made climate change[140] or life after death and psychic powers have been recognised as worthy of protection? Could the Church of Scientology have registered its Central London chapel as a place of worship? I may be wrong, but I very much doubt it. But perhaps the last word about the current debate on withdrawal should be left to Maxwell Fyfe's grandson, Tom Blackmore:

> I don't think people do realise what's happening – we've had an extraordinary period of change. I just feel guilty for my generation making such an arse of it.[141]

135 MD Evans, *Religious Liberty and International Law*(Cambridge University Press,1997); C Evans, *Freedom of Religion under the European Convention of Human Rights* (Oxford University Press, 2001); J Renucci, *Article 9 of the European Convention on Human Rights: Freedom of thought, Conscience and Religion* (Council of Europe, 2005); and Taylor, *Freedom of Religion: UN and European Human Rights Law and Practice.*).

136 A Williams, 'The European Convention on Human Rights, the EU and the UK: Confronting a Heresy' (2013) 24(4) *European Journal of International Law*, 1157.

137 M Elliott and R Thomas, *Public Law* (OUP, 2011) 726.

138 Helen Carter, 'The Devil and the Deep Blue Sea: Navy gives blessing to Sailor Satanist' *The Guardian* (25 October 2004).

139 *Holland v Angel Supermarket Ltd & Anor* [2013] ET/3301005/2013.

140 *Grainger Plc & Ors v Nicholson* [2009] UKEAT/0219/090/311.

141 Patrick Smith, 'How a Tory Barrister who Prosecuted the Nazis made the Human Rights Laws the Government wants to Scrap' (22 October 2016) *Buzzfeed*, available at https://www.buzzfeed.com/patricksmith/how-a-tory-barrister-who-prosecuted-the-nazis-made-the-human?utm_term=.drY89G0n02#.rpE8D3pKpx, accessed 23 August 2018.

6 *Republican Fundamentalism Against Laïcité*

Tempering the appropriation of a constitutional doctrine

Eoin Daly

The work

It might seem odd, at first glance, to classify a book by a French sociologist and historian as a leading work on Law and Religion. Jean Baubérot, sociologist of religions, professor emeritus and formerly chair of the *École pratique des hautes études* in Paris, is arguably France's leading intellectual authority on *laïcité* – the French doctrine of constitutional secularism, and the overarching legal and political doctrine relating to the role of religions in the French State and society. While Baubérot has produced an impressive corpus of work comprising both popular-market books along with more 'academic' pieces, in this chapter I will focus on his landmark 2006 book – translatable as *Republican Fundamentalism Against Laïcité*[1] – in part because it marks a reaction against an increasingly illiberal interpretation of the *laïcité* doctrine in recent decades. While in France and elsewhere, it is often assumed that *laïcité* is a distinctive, or even unique – and therefore, a somewhat singular model of State secularism – Baubérot has helped show the diverse meanings and origins of the doctrine and has therefore illuminated ways in which it might be rescued from the regressive and often illiberal interpretations that have prevailed in recent French developments. Hopefully, this overview of Baubérot's work will give English-speaking readers an insight into the evolving intellectual discourse on the interplay between religions, law and the state in contemporary France.

The context

French law relating to religions is dominated by a single, overarching doctrine – *laïcité*, which can be roughly, although not uncontroversially, translated as 'constitutional secularism'. Within France itself and sometimes overseas, *laïcité* is often understood as a French specificity. While generally understood as referring

1 J Baubérot, L'intégrisme républicain contre la laïcité *(Editions de l'Aube, 2006)*. The book is not translated into English. The title translates as *Republican Fundamentalism Against Laïcité*. Note that all French-English translations in this chapter are my own and that I assume responsibility for any errors.

to a separation of churches and state along with strict state neutrality both between and towards religions, the supposed distinctiveness or uniqueness of *laïcité* is undermined by the very diverse and often contradictory uses that have been made of it in French politics and law in recent decades. In reality, it is quite an amorphous principle that can mask a number of different, quite diverse ideologies concerning the role of religion in the state and society. Indeed, Baubérot himself has described this understanding of *laïcité* as itself uniquely distinctive as reflecting an insular mythology of French exceptionalism – an '*Astérix* complex'.[2] So pure is the doctrine of *laïcité*, quips Baubérot, that it is 'the only noun of the French language to which it is taboo to add an adjective'.[3] Yet *laïcité*, now more than ever, is the subject of disparate and diverse claims, 'liberal', 'republican' and even 'communitarian' in varying shades and degrees.

The term *laïcité* is a relatively recent neologism dating from the late-nineteenth century, during the early decades of the Third French Republic. Specifically, it arose amidst a fraught, protracted battle between the Roman Catholic Church and largely anti-clerical republican elites, concerning control of public schools in particular, as well as the wider issue of the public status or privileges of the established churches.[4]

Initially, French republicans embraced secularism as part of a wider programme of social and political emancipation, aimed at ridding society of supposedly backward religious influences, and in progressing science and reason as the official ideologies of the new regime. In this spirit, the intellectual elites of the Third Republic sought to dislodge 'unexamined beliefs of any kind', and prevent 'authoritarian imposition of dogmatic beliefs' by the clergy in particular.[5] The aim, then, was to privatise religion not only legally and institutionally, but sociologically as well. The Roman Catholic Church, in particular, was associated with monarchist reaction and the old regime, and so lessening its influence across all spheres came to be seen a matter of political stability, or even existentially, of survival for the new and relatively fragile republic. According to this muscular and emancipatory strand of the republican tradition, the state should not merely protect formal liberties, but should assume a more activist role in uprooting servility and domination in social relationships[6] – both in order to promote human flourishing and in order to secure the stability of the republican constitution, in a spirit that is something akin to what we now call 'militant democracy'.

However, radical and anti-clericalist republicanism waned with the turn of the century. A landmark law – the 1905 law of separation of churches and

2 Ibid, 35.

3 Ibid, 33.

4 J Baubérot, *Laïcité 1905–2005:entre passion et raison* (Seuil, 2004), 13.

5 L Dobuzinskis, 'Defenders of Liberal Individualism, Republican Virtues and Solidarity' The Forgotten Intellectual Founding Fathers of the French Third Republic' (2008) 7 *European Journal of Political Theory* 287.

6 See generally C Laborde, *Critical Republicanism: the Hijab Controversy and Political Philosophy* (Oxford University Press, 2008).

state – provided an enduring settlement to the church–state conflagration in France and unstable legislative template for institutional state–religion relations. Ultimately, this reflected a more liberal understanding of constitutional secularism, which emphasised state neutrality over emancipation, gave fuller acknowledgment to religious freedom and placed greater weight on the institutional disentanglement of churches and state. Thus despite an initial republican radicalism concerning religious matters, *laïcité*, for much of the twentieth century, referred to the institutional separation of churches and state while recognising the freedom of religious denominations in the private sphere. Indeed, the much-venerated 1905 law – whose centenary was marked with some fanfare in 2005[7] – is taken as one of the crowning legislative achievements of the Third French Republic, which consolidated and stabilised the republican form of government following a relatively chaotic period.

However, this 'liberal' view of *laïcité* began to change towards the end of the twentieth century, particularly with the emergence of controversies relating to the integration of Islamic communities in French society. In particular, a number of 'headscarf affairs' erupted in French public schools from the late 1980s, placing the concept of *laïcité* centre stage.[8] And increasingly, in particular, *laïcité* was invoked to problematise certain kinds of religious practices – almost always Muslim practices – that were understood as insufficiently private or discreet. Thus, increasingly, *laïcité* was again understood as excluding religion not only from the institutional space of the state, but also from public space in a much broader sense. It was increasingly interpreted not only as imposing duties of neutrality on the state, but also, duties of discretion on private citizens, while manifesting their faiths.[9] Crucially, this seemed to harken back to an older sense of secularism inspired, at least ostensibly, by perfectionist Enlightenment philosophy – not least because legislative measures, including the 2004 ban on religious attire in schools, were justified with reference to an aim of emancipating Muslim women and girls from supposedly oppressive or patriarchal religious practices.[10] Such practices were also portrayed as threats to the social cohesion of French republican society and as undermining the virtues required of republican citizens.

This increasingly illiberal interpretation of *laïcité* may be viewed in part as a response to an alleged phenomenon of 'incivilities' motivated by ethnic and religious resentment, and particularly of increasing claims for accommodation by religious and cultural minority groups. It became a catchphrase, in short, with which to push back against the public visibility and standing of minority religious identities in particular. Indeed, the concept of '*vivre-ensemble*' – literally 'living together' – became a common refrain in the debate on the banning of the *burqa*

7 See Baubérot, *Laïcité 1905–2005: entre passion et raison*.

8 See generally J Bowen, *Why the French Don't Like Headscarves* (Princeton University Press, 2008).

9 E Daly, 'Ostentation and republican civility: Notes from the French face-veiling debates' (2015) 14 *European Journal of Political Theory* 297.

10 See generally Laborde, *Critical Republicanism: the Hijab Controversy and Political Philosophy*.

and *niqab*. The *Gerin* parliamentary commission report on the 'full veil' argued that 'refusing to engage others with an uncovered face is a sign of defiance, rejection, and even as a threat' – and therefore, that the republic 'must confront those movements whose aim is to destabilise its foundations'.[11] The feminist intellectual Elisabeth Badinter argued, in testimony to the commission, that the 'full veil' could not be seen merely as an item of clothing – it signified a 'rupture of the social pact'.[12] And the European Court of Human Rights, in its judgment on the face-veiling ban in *SAS v France*,[13] accepted 'vivre ensemble' – understood roughly speaking as a goal of democratic sociability – as a legitimate ground for restricting the manifestation of religious beliefs under Article 9 of the European Convention on Human Rights.

Thus, *laïcité* has been understood, in recent years, not only as an instrument of republican liberty and equality, but of *fraternity* as well – and as a valid mechanism for promoting dispositions of fraternity amongst citizens. One the one hand, this is consistent with what Laborde describes as a distinctive 'communitarian' strand of French republicanism, which holds that 'a nation founded on abstract, disembodied principles [of] individuality, neutrality or autonomy . . . would be inherently fragile'.[14] This underlies, she says, the need for 'feelings of fraternity' to give life and reality to the juristic abstractions of liberty and equality. On the other hand, *laïcité* understood in this particular sense – as an instrument of communal cohesion – seems intrinsically incompatible with its alternative conception as a principle of state neutrality, because it involves the state assuming a more proactive role in regulating and checking religious practices.

More generally, for practical purposes at least, *laïcité* began to appear in effect as a mechanism for checking and limiting the public visibility of Islam in French society, and in regulating socially unacceptable manifestations of Islamic beliefs or identity in public space. This trend, which had started with the first headscarf controversies in the 1980s, culminated in the 2010 law prohibiting the wearing of the *burqa* and *niqab* in public spaces.[15] Increasingly, as outlined, *laïcité* was no longer applied as a duty of neutrality upon the state and its agents, but rather was invoked against ostentatious expressions of religiosity which were perceived as negating the virtues of civility and fraternity that underpin the social cohesion of republican society.

Most critically, *laïcité* is now often taken as imposing a 'duty of discretion' in the exercise of religious belief. Former President Sarkozy, indeed, had called on French Muslims to 'refrain from any ostentation or provocation . . . practising

11 National Assembly, 'Rapport d'information au nom de la mission d'information sur la pratique du port du voile intégral sur le territoire national' (2010) Paris, 21.

12 Ibid, 46.

13 (2014) (Application no. 43835/11).

14 C Laborde, 'On Republican Toleration' (2002) 9 *Constellations* 167, 176.

15 Bowen, *Why the French Don't Like Headscarves*; Daly, 'Ostentation and Republican Civility: Notes from the French Face-Veiling Debates' (2015) 14 *European Journal of Political Theory* 297.

their faith in a humility borne . . . out of fraternal respect'.[16] Parallel with the political instrumentalisation of *laïcité* by the centre right and far right, some intellectuals have, however, challenged this ascendant understanding of the ideal. For Durand, for example, the re-conceptualisation of *laïcité* as requiring religious 'discretion' is historically and conceptually bogus: she suggests it arises from a 'bourgeois habitus' of 'obliged discretion' in relation to religion and belief), which has 'no real legal or constitutional foundation'.[17]

The significance

As outlined, there has been a growing understanding of *laïcité* as privatising religion beyond the narrow institutional sense – as requiring not merely a secular state, but a secular *public space* that is to remain free of assertive, conspicuous markers of religious identity. And *laïcité*, then, is conceptualised as an instrument of social cohesion rather than an abstract ideal of state neutrality and so, in turn, as a limitation upon religious freedom rather than its bedrock. It is against this backdrop I have outlined – in particular, that of *laïcité* being invoked to check minority religious claims – that we must evaluate the significance of Jean Baubérot's work.

Baubérot's starting point is to observe that *laïcité* has been used primarily, in recent years, as a means to problematise Muslim religious practices and to resist their public visibility, and as a constitutional and ideological justification for restrictive legislative responses. His book begins with an insistence that 'another way of discussing *laïcité* is possible'.[18] He notes the formation, in recent years, of a 'secular republican catechism' which has promoted a number of dogmas concerning the permissible extent of religious expression in public life. For Baubérot, then, 'republican fundamentalism' refers largely to the appropriation of the republican idiom, in France, by right-wing political forces bent on manipulating concepts of liberty, equality, fraternity – and indeed, increasingly, of *laïcité* – to support increasingly illiberal and xenophobic policies.

Much of the book is then devoted to demonstrating how this illiberal 'republican' account of *laïcité* is incoherent historically as well as conceptually. Critically, one of its main contributions is to undermine any understanding of *laïcité* as a distinctively French and thus, indeed, as a necessarily *singular* concept. In particular, referring to the debates around the drafting of the 1905 law, Baubérot describes how French discourse has oscillated between a radical *laïcité* of social transformation (*laïcité intégrale*, or *'comprehensive'* laïcité) – aimed at emancipating society from religion – and, on the other hand, a more modest model which eschews any emancipatory secularist ambition and emphasises state neutrality

16 N Sarkozy, 'Respecter Ceux Qui Arrivent, Respecter Ceux Qui Accueillent' (2009) *Le Monde*.
17 B Durand, *La Nouvelle Idéologie Française* (Editions Stock, 2010) 40.
18 J Baubérot, L'intégrisme républicain contre la laïcité *(Editions de l'Aube, 2006)* 12.

towards religion as a component of political legitimacy and a corollary of religious equality.

Needless to say, these contrasting visions underpin very different conceptions concerning the role of religion in public life. In contemporary discourse, as I have outlined, it is often assumed that *laïcité* requires religion to remain a 'private' affair in rather a broad sense – and specifically, that religious practices should not be publicly conspicuous or even publicly visible. In short, it is interpreted as meaning that religious practitioners are obliged to exercise discretion in publicly manifesting their beliefs.

On the one hand, this has a certain resonance, Baubérot points out, with the religious politics of the Third French Republic – the period in the late-nineteenth century during which radical republicans sought not only to disestablish the Catholic Church, but also to exclude Catholicism from public life in the fullest sense, to diminish its social influence in the name of a much wider politics of social transformation.[19] This is what Baubérot describes as *laïcité intégrale,* a model whose aim is to promote a 'comprehensive doctrine' of secular liberalism, based on ideals of reason and Enlightenment.[20] For example, the reaction against practices such as street prayers in contemporary France has echoes in a history of republican hostility to Catholic processions during the nineteenth century, which were interpreted as ostentatious and provocative. Indeed, in a 1905 debate in the Chamber of Deputies, one proposed (albeit failed) amendment to the church–state law sought to prohibit priests from wearing the soutane in public. Using language that has again become familiar, some republicans argued that the clerical garb was not freely chosen but imposed and that it attempted to impose 'an impermeable barrier with secular society'.[21] Equally, it was alleged to be a *foreign* practice, imposed by Rome, and an affront to human dignity. Thus, while Baubérot describes the journey from an anti-clericalist to a politically liberal *laïcité*, the recent measures against Muslim dress arguably evoke, at least distantly, *laïcité*'s overzealous and authoritarian ancestry.

Yet crucially, this is not the version of *laïcité* that ultimately prevailed in French law. The landmark 1905 law of separation of churches and state, while initially opposed rather fiercely by Catholics, actually reflected a very liberal solution to the church–state problem in France. While the established religions were privatised and state remuneration discontinued – making France one of the first European states without an established or endowed religion – proposals that were more restrictive of religious freedom (including the aforementioned soutane ban) were rejected. The moderate vision of Jaurès and Briand prevailed over that of the anti-clericalist Emile Combes. This was an important rupture in large part because, under France's 'Gallican' tradition, consolidated under Napoleon's Concordat and after his fall, religions were tolerated but subject to

19 Ibid, chapter 2.
20 Ibid.
21 Ibid, 181–2.

a large degree of state administration and supervision, treated in some senses as a quasi-public utility. The law, while privatising public religions, also recognised liberty of conscience and largely ended the anti-congregational excesses of the late-nineteenth century, thus reflecting the ascendancy of a liberal republicanism. *Laïcité*'s prior association with anti-clericalism was jettisoned: for Aristide Briand, the chief political architect of the 1905 law, *laïcité* meant the state was to be 'neither religious nor anti-religious, but a-religious'.[22] Similarly, Jean Jaurès was insistent that 'no dogma may be at the basis of social order . . . *laïcité* is not a State ideology'.[23] In a circular to school teachers, he warned 'you are in no way the apostles of a new religion of secularism'.[24]

This 'liberal' *laïcité* is given expression mainly as a principle of state neutrality, preventing the establishment or endowment of religions while protecting religious liberty and equality. Crucially, it has no role in secularising society per se, or in checking public expressions of religious belief. Indeed, in a 2004 report, the *Conseil d'Etat* affirmed that the framers of the 1905 law had not understood *laïcité* as 'banishing religions and religious expression from public spaces and confining it to the private sphere', but rather 'as ensuring that State and society should not be dominated by religion or vice-versa'.[25] *Laïcité*, it said, must 'recognise the religious diversity of society and accommodate the coexistence of different religious sensibilities in public spaces'.[26]

Thus, insofar as *laïcité* received a definitive legal expression, it was focused on the institutional relation between churches and state and eschewed any ambition of secularising society as such, or even of regulating the public visibility of religious practices. And many of the residual church–state controversies over the twentieth century related to residual institutional questions, and particularly the status and funding of private religious schools. Against this wider historical backdrop, *Baubérot* argues that the 2004 law – which banned conspicuous religious attire in public schools – can be viewed as something of an aberration, as historically incongruous.[27] Indeed, even the *Gerin* parliamentary commission report on the *burqa* and *niqab* conceded, based on expert testimony, that *burqa*-wearing by private individuals offended *laïcité* only in its 'philosophical', but not its 'juridical' sense.[28] Yet simultaneously, the commission described *laïcité* as a principle which 'creates obligations for citizens as well as the state'[29] – illustrating considerable dissensus as to the import of the principle, even at elite levels. Tellingly,

22 X Ternisien, *Etat et Religion* (Odile, 2007), 16.
23 See J Jaurès, 'L'enseignement laïque' (1904) *L'Humanité*.
24 C Laborde, 'Secular Philosophy and Muslim Headscarves in Schools' (2005) 13 *The Journal of Political Philosophy* 305, 324.
25 Conseil d'Etat, *Un siècle de laïcité* (2004) 263.
26 Ibid, 276.
27 Baubérot,L'intégrisme républicain contre la laïcité, 186.
28 National Assembly, 'Rapport d'information au nom de la mission d'information sur la pratique du port du voile intégral sur le territoire national' (2010) Paris 93.
29 Ibid, 88.

while many politicians invoked *laïcité* against religious face-coverings, eventually the official narrative declined to the principle as a justification for the law. This partial retreat stemmed in part from the pressure of liberal jurists who, in their testimony to the parliamentary commission on face-veiling, and in the broader public debate, rejected any understanding of *laïcité* as incurring obligations for persons other than public servants and public institutions.[30] Furthermore, the *Conseil d'Etat*, in its capacity as an advisory body to the Government, stated in its report on the face-veiling issue that *laïcité* could not serve as a justification for prohibiting religious expression on the part of private individuals. As a legal principle, it said, *laïcité* 'cannot be applied directly to society or to individuals.'[31]

Therefore, through the lens of Baubérot's work we can see that the appropriation of *laïcité* as a means to discipline or marginalise Muslim practices is, alternatively, either a return to the emancipatory perfectionist philosophy of nineteenth-century French republicanism – albeit directed against a new target – or at least an opportunistic political manipulation of a rather elastic, amorphous concept by reactionary and nationalist tendencies in contemporary French politics.

Baubérot's treatment of *laïcité* also connects with the wider paradoxes of republicanism, understood as France's official public philosophy. More specifically, he takes aim at the understanding of *laïcité* as a 'universalist' principle – that is, a principle that is derived from universal political principles and that transcends cultural, religious or ethnic 'particularisms'. Put differently, it is thought that *laïcité* itself is culturally neutral and thus cannot be thought of as an unjust imposition on any particular cultural or religious group. This view, it should be noted, stems from a wider tradition of universalism in French public law. For Bui-Xuan, this 'universalist foundation suggests that individuals enjoy the same rights and duties; they have a veritable "right to indifference" with regard to their origins'.[32]Accordingly, this universalist doctrine leans against any specific accommodation of religious and cultural difference, based partly on a rather strict and abstract notion of equality before the law. Thus minorities cannot constitutionally be recognised qua minorities, nor can the state recognise infra-national communities as such – a doctrine reflected, for example, in the invalidation by the *Conseil Constitutionnel* (French Constitutional Court) of a legislative accord recognising a Corsican 'people' and its cultural distinctiveness.[33] Indeed, reflecting this peculiar tradition, the *Conseil*, in a different ruling, interpreted *laïcité* itself as precluding 'the use of religious beliefs as a criterion with which to gain

30 Ibid.

31 Conseil d'Etat, *Etude relative aux possibilités juridiques d'interdiction du port du voile intégral* (2010) Paris.

32 O Bui-Xuan, *Le Droit Public Français entre Universalisme et Différencialisme* (Economica, 2004) 15.

33 Conseil Constitutionnel, *Decision n° 91–290 DC, May 9, 1991 and n° 2001–454 DC,* (17 January 2002).

exemption from the rules governing the relationship between private individuals and public entities'.[34]

On the one hand, *laïcité*, like other republican principles, has never been universally or evenly applied in France and is subject to sometimes chaotic and anomalous exceptions. In particular, the regime of separation instituted in 1905 was never extended to three eastern *départements* in Alsace-Moselle – where certain features of the pre-1905 Concordat[35] regime remain in place – while religious 'establishments' remain in place in certain overseas territories such as French Guyane.[36] A version of sharia law was even applied in the Indian Ocean territory of Mayotte.[37] More broadly, while the official doctrine of *laïcité* suggests a strict hands-off stance – even indifference – on the part of public bodies, in reality the state has adopted various measures to positively accommodate religious practice, albeit inconsistently and unevenly. In its 2004 report on *laïcité*, the *Conseil d'Etat* said: 'while the State recognises no religion, it must ignore none'.[38] It even cited Rivero's claim that, along with its negative aspect encompassing non-recognition, *laïcité* 'obliges the State to make religious exercise possible'.[39] For example, provision is made for chaplaincies in public services, in the Education Code as well as the legislative provisions relating to prisons.[40] And even the non-subvention or non-endowment principle contained in the 1905 legislation – the cornerstone of the law – has been applied by the administrative courts in a markedly relaxed way.[41]

Aside from historical and regional anomalies, more fundamentally, *laïcité* will inevitably be interpreted and applied in a way that fails to transcend cultural and religious factors. Genuine religious neutrality is impossible, Baubérot points out, not least because the background public culture is at least tacitly influenced by the dominant religious tradition. This is seen, for example, in the recognition of Catholic feast days and, correspondingly, the hypocritical reaction against minority demands for recognition of alternative religious feasts – demands which are incoherently portrayed as an illicit kind of communal specificity, or as claims for special treatment. Such measures, aimed at remedying historical biases, should

34 Conseil Constitutionnel, *Decision N° 2004–505DC*, (10 September, 2008).

35 Under the Concordat concluded between Napoleon and the Roman Catholic Church in 1801, the latter was recognised as the majority Church, whereas the State reserved the power to nominate bishops. It also paid clerical salaries until the passage of the 1905 law of separation. Protestant, Catholic and Jewish clergy are still remunerated by the State in Alsace-Moselle. See generally Baubérot, L'intégrisme républicain contre la laïcité.

36 Ibid, 64–5.

37 Ibid.

38 Conseil d'Etat *Un Siècle delaïcité* (2004), 277.

39 Ibid, 278.

40 See Code de L'Education, R 141–6; alinéa 2 de l'article D. 433 du code de procédure pénale. The provision for chaplains is often depicted an 'exception' to *laïcité*.

41 See E Daly, 'Public Funding of Religions in French Law: The Role of the Council of State in the Politics of Constitutional Secularism' (2014) 3 *Oxford Journal of Law and Religion* 103.

be understood as giving effect to the principles of republican universalism, but instead are derided in the political sphere as precisely the opposite, as deviations from a supposedly neutral public sphere.[42] More generally, religious or cultural claims to 'special' accommodation – for example, requests for gender-specific swimming sessions in municipal swimming pools, or for female patients not to be treated by male doctors – are fiercely resisted as 'communitarian' threats to the universalism of the republican laws and state, when in fact they should, as Baubérot argues, be understood as requests for accommodation within social practices that are culturally particularist. Minority claims to exemption are castigated as aggressively 'particularist' demands even where the standard or law from which the exemption is claimed is itself based on a dominant cultural identity. One commentator opined: 'the majority of French citizens believe that . . . only the Other remains impermeable to secularisation. So, Christmas and Easter are part of the common culture of all the French, while feasts associated with Islam are seen as particularist expression of "communitarian" rebellion'.[43] Yet this logic is ignored by the mainstream of the French republican ideology, which typically castigates 'normative multiculturalism'– associated with countries such as Canada and the UK – as a form of ethnic essentialism and as a recipe for communalist Balkanisation.[44]

This is what Baubérot coins a '*Catho-laïque*' false universalism (a word play on *Catholique* and *laïque*, the adjective for *laïcité*).[45] A genuine, 'concrete' version of republican universalism would, he argues, take account of, rather than ignoring religious differences, so as to integrate citizens equally within a common public sphere.[46] In a wider perspective, the rejection of religious accommodation seems increasingly anomalous given that the tenets of traditional 'universalism' have progressively been relaxed or abandoned – as evidenced, for example, in the introduction of a gender parity law for political candidates.[47] More generally, Baubérot also argues that the neutrality claims of *laïcité* are problematic because far from secularising the public sphere, the function of *laïcité* historically has been in part to sacralise the state and public institutions, particularly the public schools, as alternative sites of religiosity.[48] Equally, Baubérot points out, the internal logic of *laïcité*, predicated on state neutrality, is undermined by the desire of public authorities to 'instrumentalise' favoured elites within Islam, in order to create a 'French Islam' or more generally to maintain a kind of stewardship of

42 Baubérot, L'intégrisme républicain contre la laïcité, 127.
43 D Bouzar, 'Ce que veulent les musulmans? La loi de 1905, c'est tout' (2011) *Le Monde*, 1.
44 J Jennings, *Revolution and the Republic: A History of Political Thought in France since the Eighteenth Century* (Oxford University Press, 2011) 587.
45 Baubérot, L'intégrisme républicain contre la laïcité, 129.
46 Ibid, 127.
47 J Wallach Scott, *Parité: Sexual Equality and the Crisis of French Universalism* (Chicago University Press, 2008).
48 Baubérot, L'intégrisme républicain contre la laïcité, 97.

tutelage over Muslim communities in France.[49] Indeed, Baubérot has described Sarkozy's politics on religion, in particular, as 'neo-Gallican', seeking to restore a degree of state supervision. Indeed, while Minister of the Interior, Sarkozy played a pivotal role in the establishment of the *Conseil Français du Culte Musulman*, a representative body for French Muslims.[50] Such hypocrisies of French secularism were also reflected, for example, in the government's insistence that the *burqa* fell outside the scope of religious freedom, based on the understanding that it was not a genuine or mandatory requirement of Islam. This reflected an implicit understanding of the state as having a legitimate role in interpreting the substance of religious beliefs – contradicting any pretence of strict neutrality.

In summary then, *laïcité* tends to problematise and exclude minority forms of religious expression, and thus, indirectly, to reinforce the dominance of the majority culture. Using the rhetoric of republican universalism, it then becomes an insidious mask of majoritarian domination.[51] In this guise, *laïcité* is conceptualised not as a principle of state neutrality towards religions and indeed competing conceptions of the good, but rather the reverse – an instrument for maintaining a dominant non-political culture, based on commonalities of language, religion and ethnicity. Reflecting this conception, former President Sarkozy, while appealing to Muslims to exercise 'discretion' in their faith, sketched the idea of a France that is '*laïque*' but affirms its 'Christian roots'.[52] More generally, this reflects a wider view that 'rationalist universalism, rooted in the philosophy of the eighteenth-century Enlightenment, now looks more and more like a form of European ethnocentrism'.[53]

Laïcité, then, is routinely invoked against the dreaded spectre of *communautarisme* (roughly 'communalism') – the phenomenon of ethnic and religious balkanisation, and the alleged tendency of minority groups to affiliate with subnational identities. Yet paradoxically, Baubérot points out, it ends up itself as a form of 'majoritarian communalism' that imposes and exalts the dominant culture, albeit insidiously.[54] Ignoring its own cultural and historical biases, this 'republican' ideology 'conceives itself as universal relative to itself'.[55] Historically, Baubérot notes, outsiders or Others have consistently been portrayed as 'threats to the Republic' – a role previously occupied at various points by the Catholic congregations, the Jesuits and the clergy.[56] Secularism, then, becomes

49 Ibid, 86.
50 Ibid. See also M Zeghal, 'La constitution du Conseil Français du Culte Musulman: reconnaissance politique d'un Islam Français?' (2005) 129 *Archives de sciences sociales des religions* 1.
51 Baubérot, L'intégrisme républicain contre la laïcité, 115.
52 Sarkozy, 'Respecter ceux qui arrivent, respecter ceux qui accueillent' (2009) *Le Monde*.
53 Jennings, *Revolution and the Republic: A History of Political Thought in France since the Eighteenth Century*, 579.
54 Baubérot, L'intégrisme républicain contre la laïcité, 86.
55 Ibid.
56 Ibid, 99.

a means of delineating outsiders by problematising particular kinds of religiosity and religious expression. This undermines, in turn, the universalist pretensions of French-republican discourse, in which citizenship is supposed to transcend racial, religious or cultural particularisms.[57] Thus the politics of *laïcité* helps to illustrate the hypocrisies of republican nationalism and its universalist pretensions.

The legacy

Baubérot's work – which has reached a wider public as well as an academic audience – has helped temper the intellectual expropriation of *laïcité*, as a legal and constitutional doctrine, by Islamophobic and reactionary political forces. In particular, he has used historical insights to expose how a chauvinistic majoritarian nationalism has opportunistically adapted the doctrine, while clothing itself in 'universalist' and 'republican' vocabularies. And this is set within a wider, compelling critique of the degeneration of republican discourses in contemporary French society. Moreover, one of Baubérot's main contributions has been to point out the inconsistencies and the hypocrisies in the interpretation and implementation of *laïcité* in practice, both historically and in contemporary French society.

The polemic around *laïcité* and Islam only intensified after the publication of Baubérot's 2006 book – particularly after the onset of the global economic crisis and the beginning of a debate on the *burqa* and *niqab*. And indeed, Baubérot continued to disseminate a measured and nuanced account of *laïcité* in subsequent books, particularly *La laïcité falsifiée* ('Secularism Falsified') in 2012.[58] In an updated account, Baubérot argues that what he labels 'false' *laïcité* or '*laïcité falsifiée*' has shifted the focus of secularism away from institutional church–state issues towards a more sinister and illiberal project of regulating expressions of religious identity in public space. Thus, in practice it is instrumentalised as a means with which to regulate expressions of Muslim identity in the public sphere. As Wolmark observes, 'the *laïcité* principle has been instrumentalised to the point where we have forgotten it originally applied only to the State.'[59] Similarly, in *Les Sept Laïcités françaises*,[60] ('Seven French Secularisms'), Baubérot sketches a more elaborate typology of various models of *laïcité*. Of particular interest is his account of an emergent *laïcité identitaire* ('identitarian' *laïcité*), that understands secularism as an instrument with which to regulate favoured types of sociability and social identity.

In this light, Baubérot's work forms part of a wider intellectual resistance to the illiberal instrumentalisation of *laïcité*. Reflecting many of Baubérot's arguments, the *Conseil d'Etat*, France's supreme administrative court, has pushed

57 Ibid, 111.

58 J Baubérot, *La laïcité falsifiée* (La Découverte, 2012).

59 C Wolmark and P Waquet, 'Convient-il d'interdire le port de signes religieuses dans l'entreprise' (2009) 18 *Revue de droit du travail* 488, 488.

60 J Baubérot, *Les sept laïcités françaises* (Éditions de la Maison des Sciences de l'Homme, 2015).

back against any understanding of *laïcité* as having a regulatory role for private religious practices, even where exercised in public spaces.[61] As a leading public intellectual, Baubérot has helped push back against this illiberal trend, effectively illuminating the republican history of republican thought so to challenge its contemporary abuse.

61 Daly, 'Public Funding of Religions in French Law: The Role of the Council of State in the Politics of Constitutional Secularism' (2014) 3 *Oxford Journal of Law and Religion* 103.

7 *Freedom of Religion under the European Convention on Human Rights*

Foreshadowing interpretative dilemmas

Peter W. Edge and Lucy Vickers

The work

Carolyn Evans studied at Melbourne University before undertaking DPhil study at Oxford University as a Rhodes Scholar, initially under the supervision of Professor Mark Janis, and later Professor Guy Goodwin-Gill. She returned to Melbourne in 2000, and is currently Dean of Melbourne Law School.

The monograph *Freedom of Religion under the European Convention on Human Rights*[1] focuses on those provisions of the European Convention on Human Rights most clearly relevant to freedom of religion: Article 9, and Article 2 of the First Protocol. These provisions are placed in context, both in terms of the development of freedom of religion at the international level, and in terms of the history of the drafting of the provisions. Evans then moves on to sustained consideration of the key legal issues: defining religion or belief (Chapter 4), freedom of religion or belief simpliciter (Chapter 5), manifestation of religion or belief (Chapter 6), and, justifiably, limitations on the manifestation of religion or belief (Chapter 7). The text concludes with a focus on a particular problem – how to deal with neutral and generally applicable laws which impact on religion (Chapter 8), and a brief conclusion (Chapter 9).

The text is a revised version of Evans' DPhil thesis. As would be expected of such a work, it was far from Evans' final word on Law and Religion. She has continued to write on Law and Religion with a particular emphasis on Australian law, and comparative law projects involving Australia.[2] This has, however, run alongside continued work in the interaction of Law and Religion at the theoretical level,[3] and a sustained contribution to the literature on the

1 C Evans, *Freedom of Religion under the European Convention on Human Rights* (Oxford University Press, 2011).

2 C Evans, 'Corporations and Freedom of Religion: Australia and the United States Compared' (2015) *Sydney Law Review* 37; C Maree Evans, *Legal protection of religious freedom in Australia*. (Federation Press, 2012).

3 C Evans, 'Principles and Compromises: Religious freedom in a Time of Transition' in L Lazarus, C McCrudden and N Bowles (eds), *Reasoning Rights: Comparative Judicial*

European Convention on Human Rights (ECHR).[4] She has also helped to frame the scholarship of others, for instance through editorship of significant collections.[5]

The context

Carolyn Evans' *Freedom of Religion under the European Convention on Human Rights* was the first monograph published in the Oxford ECHR Series. The aim of the series was to provide 'enough practical detail to be used by practitioners . . . as well as taking a critical approach to past practice'.[6] The series has since closed, but the focus fits well with Evans' combination of assured, thoughtful exposition of the primary legal sources of the ECHR, and her critical consideration of how the jurisprudence of the ECHR was developing.

The exposition function was particularly important in a text on freedom of religion or belief. It was the first full-length text providing a sustained consideration of freedom of religion under the ECHR, as opposed to in international law more generally. In focusing so tightly on the ECHR and religion, she was developing the scholarly agenda from Malcolm Evans' *Religious Liberty and International Law in Europe*,[7] as well as the generalist ECHR texts of the day. The text appeared less than a decade after the Court had finally given a full decision on Article 9, in *Kokkinakis v Greece*,[8] and before 9/11 with its consequences for religion cases globally. Evans was writing at a time when not only was there comparatively little commentary on the ECHR and religion, but the primary legal sources upon which to draw were also comparatively small. This led to her placing weight on decisions of the Commission, as well as principles derived more broadly from international law, and from a principled approach to religious liberty. The theoretical basis for religious freedom is, to Evans, central to the development of the Convention: '[u]nless a coherent philosophical justification underlies all the cases dealing with Article 9, then the result is likely to be inconsistency and unfairness

Engagement (Hart Publishing, 2014); C Evans and T Baker, 'Religion and Human Rights: Principles and Practice' in F Cranmer, M Hill, C Kenny and R Sandberg (eds), *The Confluence of Law and Religion: Interdisciplinary Reflections on the Work of Norman Doe* (Cambridge University Press, 2016).

4 C Evans, 'Religious Autonomy and Labour Law: A comparison of the jurisprudence of the United States and the European Court of Human Rights' (2012) *Oxford Journal of Law and Religion* 1; C Evans, 'The Islamic scarf in the European Court of Human Rights' (2006) *Melbourne Journal of International Law* 7.

5 C Evans (ed), *Religion and International Law* (Kluwer, 1999); C Evans (ed), *Law and Religion in Historical and Theoretical Perspective* (Cambridge University Press, 2008); Carolyn Evans, *Mixed Blessings: Laws, Religions and Women's Rights in the Asia-Pacific Region* (Martinus Nijhoff, 2006).

6 Evans, *Freedom of Religion under the European Convention on Human Rights.*

7 MD Evans, *Religious liberty and international law in Europe* (Cambridge University Press, 1997).

8 *Kokkinakis v Greece* [1993] ECHR 20.

as the judges move from one rationale to another to justify their intuitions about the right outcomes for a particular factual situation'.[9] She takes some time over the theoretical foundations, devoting a wide-ranging chapter to the theoretical rationale for religious freedom, before concluding that arguments from autonomy, emphasising dignity and freedom in decision-making, represent the best approach for the Court in developing the ECHR.

The significance

The text was well received on publication, being described as 'a clear, sensible and appropriately critical account of an important part of Strasbourg human rights jurisprudence',[10] 'a careful and thorough analysis'[11] and 'replete with insightful observations and sound judgment and sensible suggestions and it is surely destined to become a standard point of reference on the subject'.[12] In this chapter, we argue that the insights, judgment, and in particular suggestions make this monograph particularly important, more than its use as a standard point of reference.

That is not to say that the text has not had an obvious impact on scholars and judges as evidenced by citation. Within specialist work on Law and Religion, this can be seen in texts as diverse as PM Taylor's consideration of UN and European law and practice on freedom of religion,[13] Trigg's consideration of the privatisation of religion,[14] McCrea's study of religion in the EU,[15] and Temperman's consideration of religious neutrality.[16] Outside of this core audience, the text has been important to two scholarly audiences which do not necessarily identify as Law and Religion specialists. Firstly, scholars who work on the topic of religion, but who do not work within a legal frame, and who seek to engage with legal ideas of religious rights under the European Convention on Human Rights.[17] Secondly, scholars of human rights, and human rights law, who do not have a particular focus on religious rights and religious human rights, especially those

9 Evans, *Freedom of Religion under the European Convention on Human Rights*, 33.

10 J Rivers, 'Publication Review: Freedom of Religion under the European Convention on Human Rights' (2003) 52(2) *International and Comparative Law Quarterly* 540.

11 G Moon, 'Publication Review: Freedom of Religion under the European Convention on Human Rights' (2002) 1 *European Human Rights Law Review* 126.

12 MD Evans, 'Publication Review: Freedom of Religion under the European Convention on Human Rights' (2001) 7(4) *European Public Law* 705.

13 PM Taylor, *Freedom of Religion: UN and European Human Rights Law and Practice* (Cambridge University Press,2005).

14 R Trigg, *Religion in Public Life: Must Faith be Privatized?* (Oxford University Press,2007).

15 R McCrea, *Religion and the Public Order of the European Union* (OUP,2010).

16 J Temperman, *State-religion Relationships and Human Rights Law: Towards a Right to Religiously Neutral Governance* (Brill, 2010).

17 A Marinovic and D Marinovic Jerolimov, 'What About our Rights? The State and Minority Religious Communities in Croatia: A Case Study' (2012) 5(1) *Religion and Society in Central and Eastern Europe* 39; J Ipgrave, 'Religious Diversity: Models of Inclusion for Schools in England' (2011) 40(2) *Contemporary Issues in Diversity and Education* 7.

writing on the UK situation.[18] The text has also been cited by national courts, for instance by the UK Supreme Court in *RT (Zimbabwe) v Secretary of State of the Home Department*;[19] the Court of Appeal in Northern Ireland in *Re Parsons*;[20] and the Federal Court of Australia in *Iliafi v Church of Jesus Christ of the Latter Day Saints*.[21]

The greater significance of the text, however, is in Evans' prefiguring of concerns in the way in which the jurisprudence of the European Court of Human Rights (ECtHR), then in its very early days in relation to freedom of religion, could take the wrong turn. In the current century, the Court has returned to these issues repeatedly, gradually overcoming the tremendous reluctance of the Court to engage with religious liberty cases as religious liberty cases, and a pattern of closing down discussion of religious liberty as quickly as possible even in such cases. In four areas in particular Evans identified significant problems with the way in which the jurisprudence may develop – areas in which her concerns were, for at least some of the cases decided since her text, fully justified by later events.

1 The religion or belief rights of atheists and Lautsi

An ongoing concern in the text is that under-theorising by the judges means that Article 9 in particular lacks an explicit foundation: 'unless a coherent philosophical justification underlies all the cases dealing with Article 9, then the result is likely to be inconsistency and unfairness as the judges move from one rationale to another to justify their intuitions about the right outcomes for a particular factual situation'.[22] It may be argued that one area where the Court has not properly thought through the issues is in relation to the Article 9 rights of atheists and agnostics. Evans was concerned that the jurisprudence on education in particular was 'less sympathetic to atheists/agnostics who claim the need to be exempted from religious instruction than to members of other religious faiths'.[23]

A lack of sympathy, or perhaps better put, a failure of judicial imagination when considering the position of atheists within a religious rights regime, materialised in *Lautsi v Italy*.[24] In that case an atheist parent and children complained at the display of a crucifix in the classrooms of the state school attended by the children. Initially, the Chamber found that the mandatory display was a violation of Article 2 of the First Protocol taken together with Article 9. The Chamber found that the State had an obligation to refrain from imposing beliefs, even

18 D Feldman, *Civil liberties and human rights in England and Wales* (Oxford University Press, 2002).
19 *RT (Zimbabwe) v Secretary of State of the Home Department* [2012] UKSC 38.
20 *Re Parsons* [2003] NICA 20.
21 *Iliafi v Church of Jesus Christ of the Latter Day Saints* [2014] FCAFC 26.
22 Evans, *Freedom of Religion under the European Convention on Human Rights*, 33.
23 Ibid, 95.
24 *Lautsi v Italy* (App no 30814/06 (ECtHR 18 March 2011) [2011] ECHR 2412).

indirectly, in places such as schools where persons were particularly vulnerable. The crucifix, although a complex symbol, had a predominantly religious meaning, so that compulsory display of the crucifix not only clashed with the secular convictions of the family, but was also emotionally disturbing for non-Christian children. The finding by the Chamber was controversial, and as the case proceeded to the Grand Chamber a significant number of third-party interveners, including national governments, joined the case. The Grand Chamber took quite a different view of the crucifix: there was no evidence that the display of the religious symbol 'may have an influence on pupils',[25] and the crucifix was 'an essentially passive symbol . . . it cannot be deemed to have an influence on pupils comparable to that of didactic speech or participation in religious activities'.[26] The Grand Chamber noted in particular that 'Italy opens up the school environment in parallel to other religions',[27] giving examples of non-majority religious practices including Islamic practices. While the Grand Chamber could see why 'pupils who are in favour of secularism may see in the presence of crucifixes in the classrooms of the State school they attend an infringement of [their] rights',[28] the Grand Chamber did not agree. The Grand Chamber failed, as Evans feared, to be fully sympathetic towards the atheist's family.

2 *The nature of manifestation of religion, individual belief, and* Eweida

A second area of concern identified by Evans relates to the nature of manifestation and the extent to which individually held beliefs are protected. She notes that the relatively liberal approach to the definition of religion by the Court and Commission was subtly undermined at the manifestation stage with the requirement that, in order to be protected, a practice must be necessary to the religion or belief, as opposed to merely being inspired by that belief.[29] The requirement can be found in *Arrowsmith v UK*,[30] where a pacifist was prevented from distributing pacifist leaflets to soldiers: the Court's view was that distributing leaflets was not an expression of her beliefs, and so was not a manifestation of her beliefs; thus her right to manifest religion or belief was not infringed.

The *Arrowsmith* approach led to a narrowing of the protection potentially offered by Article 9, with the result that even serious burdens on religious practice, such as limiting public employment, could go unprotected. In effect, questions of proportionality were never reached as cases were disposed of at an earlier stage of analysis. As a result, the proper parameters for the protection of religion were not fully explored. Evans identified this as a particular problem for those

25 Ibid, 66.
26 Ibid,72.
27 Ibid,74.
28 Ibid,78.
29 Evans, *Freedom of Religion under the European Convention on Human Rights*, 132.
30 *Arrowsmith v UK* [1978] 3 EHRR 218.

with individual beliefs that are informal and non-hierarchical,[31] as well as for individuals from more formal religions who do not accept all the teachings of the religion, or who believe that the religion puts additional demands on them.[32] Evans suggested that the Court could deal more respectfully with the subjective claims of individuals[33] to avoid undermining the importance of religion or belief, and to allow individuals to create their self-identity and to live autonomously.[34]

Others have echoed this concern,[35] and have noted that, since Evans was writing, the Court has somewhat softened its approach to the link between religious practice and religious requirements and allowed a manifestation to be seen where there is an intimate link between the practice and the belief.[36] The Court went further in *Eweida et al v UK*,[37] where a flexible approach was taken to the issue of manifestation of religion, saying that there is no requirement on applicants to establish that they were fulfilling a duty mandated by the religion in question; instead there could be a manifestation of religion where there existed a sufficiently close and direct nexus between the act and the underlying belief. This acceptance by the Court that the manifestation of religion can include a much wider range of activities than those strictly required by religion is very welcome, and avoids some of the problems identified by Evans in 2001.

In addition, the more flexible approach in *Eweida* also means that a religious practice can potentially be protected (e.g. wearing a cross visibly over a uniform) even though the claimant has not identified others who share her view that this is essential to the witness of her religion. Thus, to a large extent, Evans' major concerns regarding the narrow interpretation of manifestation of religion in *Arrowsmith* have been allayed by the 2013 decision in *Eweida*. As a result, a significant preliminary barrier to claims under Article 9 has been removed and many more religious practices can be viewed as manifestations of religion. This does not lead to automatic protection, of course: a manifestation will not be protected, under Article 9(2), if a restriction is necessary and proportionate to the achievement of a legitimate aim. However, by removing the prior barrier, religion and belief are better protected, as cases no longer fall at the first hurdle, and the proportionality of any restrictions on religion can be assessed.

3 *Article 9(2), the margin of appreciation and* SAS v France

Although *Eweida* removed the initial hurdle in making a religion or belief claim, a second hurdle is immediately encountered: the margin of appreciation. Evans also noted the use of a wide margin of appreciation in religion or belief cases as

31 C Evans, *Freedom of Religion under the European Convention on Human Rights*, 57.
32 Ibid, 122.
33 Ibid, 205.
34 Ibid, 201.
35 R Sandberg, *Law and Religion* (Cambridge University Press, 2011) 84.
36 S Knights, *Freedom of Religion, Minorities, and the Law* (Oxford University Press, 2007).
37 *Eweida et al v UK* [2013] ECHR 37.

an area of concern.[38] Moreover, she noted that the Court and Commission had been too willing to accept reasonably trivial reasons for interfering with religious freedom, as well as giving considerable weight to State claims involving public order and administrative convenience.[39] These concerns seem especially prescient in the light of the decision in *S.A.S. v France*[40] in 2014, and discussed by Evans in 2016.

In *S.A.S. v France* the 'rights of others' was defined even more broadly than in the earlier cases noted by Evans. The case involved a significant and far-reaching restriction on religion and belief by imposing a criminal sanction on the wearing of face coverings or veils in public spaces. The ECtHR discounted several legitimate aims that the ban could potentially serve, such as to uphold human dignity or gender equality, or to maintain security. However, it concluded that the aim of 'living together' (*le 'vivre ensemble'*) could potentially justify the ban. The decision typifies the concern identified by Evans, as it creates space for very broad aims for any restriction on religion or belief.

Of course, even if the legitimate aim is relatively easy to establish, any restriction must also be necessary in a democratic society; however, with a wide margin of appreciation in religion and belief cases, any protection from the Court may be rather weak. Again, *S.A.S. v France* is illustrative of the problem predicted by Evans and discussed again in her later work,[41] having noted the need for careful consideration of the proportionality given the broad nature of the legitimate aim of 'living together', the Court relied on the margin of appreciation to decide that the ban was proportionate, despite having noted earlier that the face veil ban was inconsistent with international human right norms and European values and that it was necessary neither to uphold human dignity nor gender equality.

S.A.S. v France serves as a useful illustration of the flexibility of the notion of the margin of appreciation and the way in which it can undermine the protection available in the ECHR for religion and belief. However, the broad use of the margin of appreciation is not only a creation of the jurisprudence of the ECtHR. Since Evans was writing, ideas of subsidiarity and the margin of appreciation have been put on a more formal basis within the Convention itself, which now explicitly refers to the margin of appreciation in Article 1 of Protocol 15 to the Convention. The formalisation of the role of the margin of appreciation in the Convention reflects the sensitivity of religion and belief matters to member states, and their preference for leaving the setting of the parameters for legal protection to national courts, taking into account the national context. The effect on the

38 Evans, *Freedom of Religion under the European Convention on Human Rights*, 143.
39 Ibid, 207.
40 *S.A.S. v France* (App. 43835/11).
41 Evans and Baker, 'Religion and Human Rights: Principles and Practice' in Cranmer, Hill, Kenny and Sandberg (eds), *The Confluence of Law and Religion: Interdisciplinary Reflections on the Work of Norman Doe.*

scope of European supervision for human rights remains, as Evans noted,[42] with the risk that religious vitality and tolerance are undermined.

4 The definition of religion or belief

Evans devoted an entire chapter to definitional issues, and in particular identified the complexity of the relationship between 'religion or belief' and 'thought and conscience' with a clarity which has not always been followed through in later discussions of the issue.[43] More specifically, she identified concerns that individualised beliefs were not always protected because of difficulties of proof.[44] There has been some solidification of the Courts' understanding of religion or belief since. In *Eweida*, for instance, the court cited a line of post-Evans cases to show that 'the right to freedom of thought, conscience and religion denotes views that attain a certain level of cogency, seriousness, cohesion and importance'.[45] The same decision stressed the significance of Article 9 as an individual right. The importance for individualised beliefs is brought out most clearly by the partly dissenting opinion of Bratza and Björgvinsson: 'to require evidence of group disadvantage will often impose on an applicant an excessive burden of demonstrating that persons of the same religion or belief are put at a particular disadvantage. This may be especially difficult, as the applicant argues, in the case of a religion such as Christianity, which is not prescriptive and which allows for many different ways of manifesting commitment to the religion'.[46] The ramifications of this for individualised religion have still to be worked out.

The legacy

The political climate regarding religion and belief has changed dramatically since Evans was writing in 2001, meaning that it is more important than ever that clarity is achieved in relation to the scope of Article 9. At the time that Evans was writing, the case law was just emerging, and the issue that was expected to develop in terms of religion or belief in Europe was the role of religion in emerging Eastern European countries as they negotiated religious freedom after an era of religious oppression. Since 2001 the political context has entirely changed and the range of issues with which the Court is concerned has grown ever wider. One focus is on Islam in an era of heightened security concerns; another focus is on social concerns such as abortion, embryo screening, same-sex civil partnership, and religion-related refugee rights, all in a context of an increased polarisation of opinion. In the UK context, questions have also emerged regarding the State's

42 Evans, *Freedom of Religion under the European Convention on Human Rights*, 208.
43 Ibid, ch. 4.
44 Ibid, 57.
45 *Eweida et al v UK* [2013] ECHR 37, 81.
46 Ibid, 9.

commitment to accepting the jurisdiction of the ECHR and its replacement with a British Bill of Rights. All this suggests that, long after the publication of *Freedom of Religion under the ECHR*, the concerns it raised remain subjects of serious interest to legal scholars.

The text also had a significant impact on how we developed our own work on Law and Religion.[47] In particular, while the text would not claim to be methodologically innovative, it is methodologically sensitive. It would not have been unusual if the text had taken methodological issues around data collection and data analysis as implicitly understood by author and reader, simply a given within doctrinal international legal scholarship. Evans did not do this, instead taking time to outline a robust and explicit methodology around data collection – even when the data she draws upon are public domain sources of law. This thoughtfulness had a strong influence on Edge, particularly as it highlighted to him that doctrinal legal scholarship needed to think through methodology in the same way as other forms of legal scholarship. Similarly, her subtle multi-method, drawing on other forms of scholarship and other types of argument to aid her doctrinal project, has influenced us in our later work – the centre of gravity for the text is clearly doctrinal international law, but arguments are enriched by her consideration of, for instance, the historical context of the provisions drafting.

47 PW Edge, *Religion and Law: An Introduction* (Ashgate, 2006); L Vickers, *Religious Freedom, Religious Discrimination and the Workplace* (2nd edn, Hart Publishing, 2016).

8 *The Impossibility of Religious Freedom*

'Legal religion' and its discontents

Méadhbh McIvor

The work

Winnifred Fallers Sullivan published *The Impossibility of Religious Freedom*[1] while an Associate Professor of Law at the University of Buffalo, the State University of New York. In addition to this leading work, she has written and taught on religious discourse in the US Supreme Court; the regulation of religious practice in US prisons; chaplaincy and the 'naturalisation' of religion; the legal establishment of religion; and the politics of religious freedom in a global context.[2] She is currently Professor and Chair of Religious Studies at the University of Indiana, Bloomington, where she is also Affiliate Professor at the Maurer School of Law.

Sullivan trained in the academic study of both Law and Religion at the University of Chicago, from which she holds a JD and a PhD in Religious Studies. Chicago is an institution with which she has a long-standing relationship. Both parents had studied and worked at the University, where her mother, Margaret Fallers, served as associate provost and affirmative action officer, and her father, Lloyd Ashton 'Tom' Fallers, had been Distinguished Service Professor of Anthropology and Sociology. Margaret, too, was an anthropologist. While Tom focused on East Africa and later Turkey, Margaret had done fieldwork on the Marshall Islands.

Sullivan's early years were shaped by her parents' academic careers and anthropological interests. She was born in 1950 in London, where Tom was studying at the London School of Economics as part of the first Fulbright Scholars programme. Six weeks later, the family travelled by ship through the Suez Canal to Mombasa, Kenya, before continuing by train to Kampala, Uganda. It was in Uganda that Tom would carry out much of his most important field research,

1 WF Sullivan, *The Impossibility of Religious Freedom* (Princeton University Press, 2005).

2 WF Sullivan, *Paying the Words Extra: Religious Discourse in the Supreme Court of the United States* (Harvard University Press, 1994); WF Sullivan, 'We are all Religious Now. Again' (2009) 76 *Social Research* 1181; WF Sullivan, *A Ministry of Presence: Chaplaincy, Spiritual Care, and the Law* (University of Chicago Press, 2014); WF Sullivan and L Beaman, *Varieties of Religious Establishment* (Ashgate, 2013); WF Sullivan, S Hurd, S Mahmood et al, *Politics of Religious Freedom* (University of Chicago Press, 2015).

resulting in the publication of what are now classic texts in the anthropology of colonial East Africa. These monographs, including *Bantu Bureaucracy*[3] and *Law without Precedent*,[4] made a significant contribution to the emerging sub-disciplines of political and legal anthropology. The Fallers were based in Uganda until 1957, when they returned to the United States.

Given this early exposure to legal anthropology as a field (and cultural diversity in practice), Sullivan was always likely to take a socio-culturally informed view of legislation and legal institutions. But while her father's ethnography raised the classic definitional question of what, exactly, should be taken to constitute Law – a debate that has never quite been settled in ethnographic studies of social order – Sullivan's work has focused on a category that has proved equally hard to define: that of religion, particularly in the context of the courts. It is the question whether or not it is possible or desirable to delineate the boundaries of legally protectable 'religion' that motivates the leading work in question; a question to which, as the title suggests, Sullivan ultimately answers with a firmly argued 'no'.

Relying on the extended case method, *The Impossibility of Religious Freedom* presents an ethnographic account of the application of laws guaranteeing religious liberty in the contemporary United States. The case method, which has a long pedigree in legal anthropology,[5] assumes that one will learn more about a legal norm by examining its application in practice than its rationale in theory. It is for this reason that Sullivan focuses on a case in which the boundaries of religion, legally defined, were in dispute. The case in question, *Warner v City of Boca Raton*,[6] concerned a number of 'nonconforming' ornaments, statues and memorials that had been erected on graves in a municipal cemetery in Boca Raton, Florida, throughout the 1980s and 1990s. These ornaments and decorations, many of which were homemade, included images of the Virgin Mary, Jesus and the Sacred Heart; Stars of David; freestanding crosses; a bench; statues of children playing; and various forms of grave markers, including ropes and stones, which were used to demarcate the boundaries of burial plots so as to prevent their being walked upon.[7] Although technically in violation of the cemetery regulations, these decorations had long been tolerated by the sexton and his assistants, who were unwilling to harass the grieving friends and family of the deceased about the letter of the cemetery law.

All this changed, however, in 1991. Whether for economic, health and safety, or cemetery upkeep reasons – or, as was alleged by the nonconforming grave

3 LA Fallers, *Bantu Bureaucracy: A Century of Political Evolution Among the Busoga of Uganda* (University of Chicago Press,1965).

4 LA Fallers, *Law without Precedent: Legal Ideas in Action in the Courts of Colonial Busoga* (University of Chicago Press,1969).

5 M Gluckman, 'Ethnographic Data in British Social Anthropology' (1961) 9 *Sociological Review* 5; JM Conley and WM O'Barr, 'Legal Anthropology Comes Home: a Brief History of the Ethnographic Study of Law' (1993) 27 *Loyola Law Review* 41.

6 *Warner v City of Boca Raton*, 64 F. Supp. 2d 1272 (S.D. Fla. 1999).

7 Sullivan, *The Impossibility of Religious Freedom.*

owners, because of the unspoken, but incredibly powerful, influence of class-based aesthetics – the City began to enforce the rules. Freestanding decorations would no longer be tolerated. In accordance with industry standards, grave markers were to be flush to the ground, allowing cemetery gardeners to mow over them with ease. Grave owners protested. Over the next half decade, a number of attempts at resolution failed.

Finally, in January 1998, the American Civil Liberties Union (ACLU) brought an action on behalf of the group of plot owners who would become known as the *Warner* plaintiffs. The plaintiffs claimed that their decorations were an expression of religion, and were, therefore, protected under the First Amendment of the US Constitution, the Florida Constitution, and the Florida Religious Freedom Restoration Act, all of which safeguard the 'free exercise' of religion. City officials countered that the ornaments were simply decorating choices. They also alleged that these choices violated the cemetery regulations – regulations to which the grave owners had signed up when purchasing the plots in which their loved ones were buried. The case turned on whether or not the memorials constituted a constitutionally protectable form of religious practice. It was an argument that the plaintiffs, despite their best efforts to translate their self-identified religious acts into a legally legible form, were unable to win.

By charting the *Warner* plaintiffs' unsuccessful experience at a Florida state court, Sullivan's book tells two stories. The first is an account of what has been called 'lived religion' – that is, the kind of religion that 'takes place beneath the radar of religious officials and institutions' – as evidenced by the burial practices of a 'motley group of ordinary Americans'[8] in the last decades of the twentieth century. From Sullivan's perspective, it is the sheer normalcy of the *Warner* plaintiffs and their religious lives that marks them as a useful site for exploration. These were, she argues, 'ordinary Americans' attending to the deaths of their parents, spouses and children in 'modest' and 'typically American mainstream' ways.[9] True, the monuments they erected did not reflect the religion of the imam, minister, priest or rabbi. They sometimes lacked scriptural or creedal grounding. The rationale behind the ornaments was often difficult to put into words. They didn't always fit with the dominant middle-class aesthetics of what was, by then, a wealthy Florida town. But if we accept that care of the dead and questions of mortality are central to those practices we typically frame as being 'religious', then surely these modest memorials constitute the very 'heart' of religious life.[10]

Sullivan's second point, however, is more contentious. This is the story of the law's incapacity to protect this form of religious life, despite (or perhaps even because of) the United States' oft-stated commitment to religious liberty. By analysing the testimony and cross examination of the plaintiffs, defendants and expert witnesses, as well as the resulting judgment, Sullivan suggests that

8 Ibid, 2.
9 Ibid, 5.
10 Ibid, 11.

Warner is proof of the problematic nature of legislation aimed at protecting freedom of religion. Protectable religion, she argues, requires definable religion; but as anthropologists and scholars of religion have long argued, there is no neutral means by which to distinguish legitimate from illegitimate manifestations of religiosity. Freedom of religion cases, then, often end up turning on quasi-theological grounds, with secular courts ultimately adjudicating not between religion and non-religion, but between orthodoxy and heresy. That the courts are involved in theological debates raises doubts as to the efficacy of legal efforts to protect religious freedom in any meaningful way. After all, '[i]f [practices related to the negotiation of human mortality] do not fall within the scope of protected religion under the most recent American statutes designed to protect religion from government burdens, how can such laws be rationally defended?'[11]

The context

Sullivan's work is informed by a school of Religious Studies that questions the boundary between religious and non-religious ways of being. According to this narrative, 'religion' is not a universal feature of human life that manifests differently in different times and places, but an academic category of fairly recent origin. In this reading, religion has no core or essence; any practice, belief or subjectivity can be 'religious' – or, indeed, non-religious – so long as it is apprehended as such by those who study it. In the oft-cited words of Jonathan Z Smith, this understanding of religion posits it as 'solely the creation of the scholar's study'.[12] To call something 'religion' or 'religious' is to perform an act of classificatory boundary-marking, one which ultimately reflects cultural assumptions about what 'religion' is and how it ought to look. These acts of classification can be fairly arbitrary, the only characteristic marking a behaviour out as religious, being the agreement of a group of scholars' that it is so. The category of religion, then, 'is created for the scholar's analytic purposes by his imaginative acts of comparison and generalisation. Religion has no existence apart from the academy'.[13]

There are many scholars of religion who share (some version of) this position, insofar as they would accept that the kinds of acts and beliefs that get read as religious reflect socio-cultural subjectivities rather than objective essences. In what follows, however, I will focus on the contributions made by the anthropologist Talal Asad[14] and the religious historian Tomoko Masuzawa,[15] both of whom have

11 Ibid, 9.

12 JZ Smith, *Imagining Religion: From Babylon to Jonestown* (University of Chicago Press, 1982) 11.

13 Ibid.

14 T Asad, *Genealogies of Religion: Disciplines and Reasons of Power in Christianity and Islam* (Johns Hopkins University Press, 1993); T Asad, *Formations of the Secular: Christianity, Islam, Modernity* (Stanford University Press, 2003).

15 T Masuzawa, *The Invention of World Religions: Or, How European Universalism was Preserved in the Language of Pluralism* (University of Chicago Press, 2005).

challenged the common sense understanding of 'religion' as it is used in popular discourse. These outlines are, of necessity, all too brief to convey the nuance of either Asad's or Masuzawa's work. I include these overviews here, however, to highlight the academic context in which Sullivan's work was published, and to flag up two points that are of particular relevance to the argument put forward in *The Impossibility of Religious Freedom*. The first, which I hope to illustrate by reference to the work of Asad, is the recognition that there is no neutral, apolitical means of approaching 'religion' or its others. According to an Asadian position, religion must be understood as a category with a history. This history feeds into our willingness to declare a practice or object – such as a graveyard ornament – 'religious' or otherwise.

The second point, and building on what has come before, relates to questions of cultural, racial and religious hierarchy. In Masuzawa's analysis, the nineteenth-century domestication of non-European 'world religions' as equivalent species of the same religious genus as Christianity works to shore up a Protestantised European hegemony. This hierarchy of religious practice continues to shape the experience of non-Protestants before the law, particularly when religious claimants engage in ritual behaviours that might trouble archetypically Protestant assumptions about agency, materiality and embodiment. As Sullivan shows, it is of little surprise that the *Warner* plaintiffs were primarily Catholic and Jewish, for these groups have traditionally provided the Other against which American white Anglo-Saxon Protestant (WASP) society defines itself. (The one Protestant involved in the case, a born-again evangelical, had converted from his natal Greek Orthodoxy after migrating from Lebanon in the late 1930s.)

Asad's seminal *Genealogies of Religion: Disciplines and Reasons of Power in Christianity and Islam*[16] is a mainstay of undergraduate and graduate courses in the Anthropology of Religion. His genealogical approach to concepts such as 'ritual' and 'religion' suggests that it is fruitless to search for an a historical understanding of these categories, at least insofar as this definition would apply in all times and all places: 'there cannot be a universal definition of religion, not only because its constituent elements and relationships are historically specific, but because that definition itself is the historical product of discursive processes'.[17] For Asad, the construction of the category of religion is part of the broader narrative of modernity, 'a particular history of knowledge and power', in which the designation of the title 'religion' to a set of beliefs and/or practices can be a political act.[18] In this telling, the Western academy's tendency to treat religion as though it had an 'autonomous essence' – that is, 'a distinctive space of human practice and belief which cannot be reduced to any other', and which should be kept separate from the categories of, say, politics and law – is 'the product of a

16 Asad, *Genealogies of Religion: Disciplines and Reasons of Power in Christianity and Islam*.
17 Ibid, 29.
18 Ibid, 54.

unique post-Reformation history', one in which religion is conceptually removed from the domain of power.[19]

A means of distinguishing religion from non-religion, however, is just what is needed in cases such as *Warner v City of Boca Raton*.[20] Whether they take place in local tribunals or international courts, even the most cursory look at the news demonstrates the variety of ways in which freedom of religion cases make headlines throughout the world:

> Schoolgirls in France seek permission to wear the hijab to school. Sikhs in Britain seek exemption from motorcycle helmet laws. Muslim women seek civil divorces in India on the same ground as their Hindu and Christian neighbours.[21]

Regardless of the content of the individual claim or the geographic location of the person or persons making it, each such case requires a representative of the State – such as 'a court or a legislature or an administrative official' – to confirm that the act in question is 'legally religious'.[22] If religious commitments and ways of being are to be protected in ways that non-religious commitments and ways of being are not, then the State must have a set of criteria by which to distinguish truly religious acts from others. Failure to do so would risk a form of legal anarchy, a cafeteria approach to State law, with citizens abusing the system by picking and choosing which regulations to follow according to their shifting (and selectively embraced) religious whims.[23] But if, as Asad suggests, there is no core or essence to religion, how should courts and legislatures separate out religion from its pretenders? If there is no neutral, objective way to determine what counts as religion in the twenty-first century, are these legal judgments inevitably value judgments? If religion does not exist as a separate sphere of life, how can it be legally protected?

Similarly, Masuzawa's *The Invention of World Religions: Or, How European Universalism was Preserved in the Language of Pluralism* begins by lamenting that '[i]n the social sciences and humanities alike, "religion" as a category has been left largely unhistoricized, essentialized, and tacitly presumed immune or inherently resistant to critical analysis'.[24] Although somewhat vaguely defined, it is typically assumed to be 'a universal, or at least ubiquitous, phenomenon to be found anywhere in the world at any time in history, albeit in a wide variety of forms and with different degrees of prevalence and importance'.[25] In this reading,

19 Ibid, 28.
20 *Warner v City of Boca Raton*, 64 F. Supp. 2d 1272 (S.D. Fla. 1999).
21 Sullivan, *The Impossibility of Religious Freedom*, 11.
22 Ibid.
23 Ibid, 151.
24 Masuzawa, *The Invention of World Religions: Or, How European Universalism was Preserved in the Language of Pluralism*, 1–2.
25 Ibid, 1.

the different 'world religions' familiar to religious education students throughout the Euro-American world – which typically include, *inter alia*, such diverse traditions as Buddhism, Christianity, Daoism, Hinduism, Islam, and Judaism – are but localised variations of a human constant called 'religion'. This egalitarian paradigm is often seen as a move away from the more overtly ethnocentric approaches to non-monotheisms popular in early sociological studies of religious life, which ranked societies along a sliding scale in which animism and magical thought would, over centuries of social development, evolve into enlightened, post-Protestant secularism.[26]

Masuzawa's argument, however, is that the apparently common-sense recognition that Hinduism is equal to Buddhism and Islam is equal to Daoism is the result of nineteenth-century European anxieties related to Christianity, and particularly to its increasingly unstable status as a source of exclusive, transcendent truth. While 'religion' had previously been approached through a four-fold schema (including Christianity, Judaism, Islam and 'the rest'), nineteenth-century theologians began to speak of a set of 'world religions', of which there were, perhaps, as many as twelve. Beliefs and practices that might previously have been seen as part of the cultural mass were now categorised as specifically religious. Rather than Christianity against its competitors, then, the ideological battle being fought became one of 'world religions' against the secular. And although we might associate this trajectory with 'a turn away from the Eurocentric and Eurohegemonic conception of the world, toward a more egalitarian and lateral delineation',[27] Masuzawa argues that this was not the case. By contrast, this move functioned to universalise the experience of European Christianity, thereby cementing it as the religious movement par excellence.

This is not to imply, of course, that the practices, beliefs and subjectivities we now associate with, say, Hinduism or Buddhism did not exist before scholars of religion began to categorise them as such. Nor is it to deny that a set of practices, once they have been declared constitutive of a named religion, cannot take on important institutional meanings. Hinduism provides a useful example here. Although the classification of beliefs and behaviours that are now seen to make up Hinduism are of fairly recent origin, the term has become a powerful idea in the politics of Indian identity. As Masuzawa puts it of the nineteenth-century Indian thinkers behind Hindu Modernism: 'According to their projective view, "Hinduism", though the term itself may be a neologism, refers to the ancient faith of India, a religion that was originally and essentially monotheistic, and whose ancient wisdom is encapsulated in certain select but voluminous canonical texts'.[28] Thus, to claim that world religions are 'invented' is not to claim that

26 EB Tylor, *Primitive Culture: Researches into the Development of Mythology, Philosophy, Religion, Language, Art and Custom*, Vol 1 (John Murray,1920); JG Frazer, *The Golden Bough: A Study in Magic and Religion* (Wordsworth Editions, 1993).

27 Masuzawa, *The Invention of World Religions: Or, How European Universalism was Preserved in the Language of Pluralism*, 13.

28 Ibid, 283.

religious terms are not now meaningful to the people about whom they are used. What Masuzawa's work suggests, however, is that the tendency to view 'Hinduism' as a local manifestation of a universal drive towards religion is of recent origin. Further, this process of rendering various Others equivalent functions, in subtle ways, to maintain European hegemony. By domesticating difference, she suggests, the invention of comparable 'world religions' made them familiar and unthreatening to a European audience.

Sullivan's work is, of course, vastly different from Masuzawa's in scope. While the latter takes centuries worth of theological and sociological discourse as her objects of analysis, the former focuses her attention on a single dispute in a single city at the close of the twentieth century. The two are connected, however, by their interest in the ranking of religious forms. While neither the world religions model nor the freedom of religion case law explicitly privileges one kind of religion over another, both *The Invention of World Religions* and *The Impossibility of Religious Freedom* suggest that this is, in practice, the outcome they produce. For Masuzawa, those beliefs and practices that become (re)classified as religion tend to reflect Christian, and particularly Protestant, images of what constitutes this now universal category. For example, world religions are often taken to require a sacred text – a body of scripture that functions as equivalent to the Protestant Bible. For Sullivan, too, it is 'small "p"' protestantism that is privileged in the American legal system through its preference for a form of religiosity that is 'private, voluntary, individual, textual, and believed'.[29] Such an understanding of religion is difficult to square with the religious lives of those, like the *Warner* plaintiffs, for whom religion is public, material, difficult to map onto a coherent theology, and deeply rooted in ties of kinship and friendship.

Religion, then, is not a neutral concept. It lacks a historical essence that can be found throughout time and space. While the quest to transcend mortality appears to be something approaching a human universal, this quest is neither limited to the 'religious' sphere nor a necessary part of what gets called 'religion' by scholars or practitioners. The question of naming is of central significance to Sullivan, who provides a concrete example of the difficulty of defining religion in a particular context, that of a late twentieth-century American court. As we shall see, her account of the *Warner* case is evidence of the ways in which this category can be rejected, reaffirmed and reworked through the invocation of the law – and, indeed, of the way in which 'secular law only appears secular' in practice.[30]

The significance

'This book is about the impossibility of religious freedom.'[31] Given the title of the work, this opening sentence might strike the reader as somewhat redundant.

29 Sullivan, *The Impossibility of Religious Freedom*, 7–8.
30 Ibid, 153.
31 Ibid, 1.

But Sullivan's starting point is far from eponymous tautology. After all, the existence – or, at least, the possibility – of religious liberty is enshrined in constitutions, bills of rights, and international treaties the world over. Article 18 of the Universal Declaration of Human Rights, Article 8 of the African Charter on Human and Peoples' Rights, Article 22 of the ASEAN Human Rights Declaration, and Article 9 of the European Convention on Human Rights all provide similar affirmations. That signatories to these treaties are often found unwilling or unable to put them into practice is typically read as a failure on the part of national governments, not as an existential impossibility on the part of abstract rights.

Indeed, the pursuit or protection of religious freedom is often seen to be a defining characteristic of the liberal democratic State. This is particularly true in the case of America. The realisation of religious liberty is a central element of the founding myth of the United States, while its exportation forms a core part of its foreign policy. Take, for example, the International Religious Freedom Act (1998), Section 2(1) of which states:

> The right to freedom of religion undergirds the very origin and existence of the United States. Many of our Nation's founders fled religious persecution abroad, cherishing in their hearts and minds the ideal of religious freedom. They established in law, as a fundamental right and as a pillar of our Nation, the right to freedom of religion. From its birth to this day, the United States has prized this legacy of religious freedom and honored this heritage by standing for religious freedom and offering refuge to those suffering religious persecution.[32]

In the United States, then, religion is assumed to be equal parts 'strong' and 'free'. Both Democratic and Republican politicians consistently link this freedom with stability, democracy, and the peaceful coexistence of different communities.[33] Given the cross-party support accorded rights-based assertions of religious liberty, Sullivan is surely right when she acknowledges that '[t]he impossibility of religious freedom is not obvious, nor is the advocacy of such a position popular'.[34]

Politically unpopular this idea may be, but *The Impossibility of Religious Freedom*'s thesis has been enormously influential for scholars of Law and Religion. Sullivan's expert use of the case method, when combined with her obvious sympathy for the grieving *Warner* plaintiffs, provides a particularly compelling example of the difficulties involved in translating lived religion into legally legible terms. Indeed, this was an issue faced not only by the claimants, but by lawyers on both sides. Take the following exchange, in which an ACLU lawyer, Lynn

32 The International Religious Freedom Act (1998), s2(1).

33 Barack Obama, 'The National Prayer Breakfast' (2014) available at https://www.youtube.com/watch?v=4KVbBxYA_Ps, accessed 26 August 2018.

34 Sullivan, *The Impossibility of Religious Freedom*.

Waxman, encourages one of the plaintiffs, Caridad Monier, to explain the significance of the boundary she had erected around her deceased brother's grave:

> Ms Waxman: Is there anything in the history of the Catholic religion that allows protecting a grave with ropes or teaches you that that is important for you to do?
>
> Ms Monier: I don't know if there is anything that's written anywhere. And I don't know in particular about the rope. But I know that Jesus' grave was protected, was guarded, and it was not allowed to be walked on. And we were created in his image.[35]

This brief extract encapsulates many of the factors working against the *Warner* plaintiffs in their efforts to convince the court that their grave decor ought to be viewed as an exercise of religion. Although Ms Waxman supported the grave owners, her question focuses on the role of religious authority in her clients' lives: was there something in Catholicism that '[a]llowed' Ms Monier to protect her brother's grave in her chosen manner? Had she been '[t]aught' to do so by 'the Catholic religion'? The very question suggests that religious sentiment must be induced by an authority outside the practitioner. It also sets up an implicit hierarchy between this authority – the subject that allows and teaches – and the Catholic herself, the object of toleration and instruction.

That the plaintiffs were required to answer in these terms led to exchanges such as the one above, in which Ms Monier had to admit that she was unsure if this particular practice was 'written anywhere'. Her statement acknowledges what she had already learnt through her cross-examination: that a religious practice was more likely to be accepted as legitimate if it could be shown to be contained in a sacred text. Similarly, her reference to the rope that marked the boundary of her brother's plot speaks to questions she had already been asked about the point in time at which the decorative objects used were thought to have acquired their religious purchase. The witnesses were repeatedly pushed to explain whether or not their decorations had, in the defence's terms, 'independent religious significance'.[36] This was particularly so with graves featuring boundary markers, such as ropes and stones, that did not depict recognisably 'religious' symbols such as crosses and Stars of David (which, despite the myriad meanings they might signify, seemed to be accepted as self-evidently religious). Objects that had acquired significance *in situ* seemed to trouble the court's understanding of a properly religious object, which would, presumably, have religious significance independently of its placement, channelling the divine in all places and at all times. Of course, the plaintiffs knew that their rocks and ropes and statues were, in a sense,

35 Ibid, 39.
36 Ibid, 43–44.

just that: rocks and ropes and statues. But that didn't exclude them from also representing 'all that was holy'.[37]

Ms Monier's answer also raises the issue of what I will refer to, for want of a better term, as religious 'truth'. Her testimony suggests that although there may be nothing 'written anywhere'[38] that compels or encourages the care of gravesites in this way, she knew that Jesus' grave 'was protected, was guarded, and it was not allowed to be walked on'. How it is that she knows this, she does not say; and, as Sullivan points out, the belief that Jesus' grave was protected in this way is not a part of official Catholic doctrine. From the position of her local catechist or parish priest, it may be that Ms Monier is mistaken. But, from her perspective, it relates to a fundamental theological truth: the belief that men and women are created in the image of God, and that their bodies – whether above or under ground – ought to be treated with respect. When one considers that the body in question was that of her brother, it is not difficult to imagine the centrality of this point to her religious life. That it did not reflect the official tradition of the Catholic Church says nothing about its significance to Ms Monier: 'No one made [the plaintiffs perform these actions] and yet they were compelled by the logic of their own religious, cultural, and psychological location.'[39]

There is, as Sullivan points out, a slight irony here. The Florida court's refusal to recognise the Warner plaintiffs' actions as legally religious is somewhat at odds with what she calls the 'dominant American Christian theology', a Protestant-inflected theology that celebrates individualism and rejects a more Catholic deference to 'centralised institutionalised authority'.[40] Indeed, this incongruity is particularly striking in light of the religious placement of the Honourable Kenneth L Ryskamp, the judge who heard the case. Judge Ryskamp is an active churchgoer, and at the time of trial was a member of the Coral Ridge Presbyterian Church in Fort Lauderdale, Florida.[41] The Presbyterian Church emphasises the authority of God over earthly leaders. Yet it was the inability of Ms Monier and her fellow plaintiffs to explain who had 'allowed' or 'taught' them to perform their actions, combined with the fact that they were not 'written anywhere' and that (some of) the objects in question did not (appear to) have 'independent religious significance', that ultimately led to their rejection by the Florida court.

What are the implications of this rejection? In the end, if the *Warner* plaintiffs were not engaged in 'real religion, legally', then there may be very little 'real religion' in the United States[42] – or, as those who have built on Sullivan's

37 Ibid, 143.
38 *Warner v City of Boca Raton*, 64 F. Supp. 2d 1272 (S.D. Fla. 1999).
39 Sullivan, *The Impossibility of Religious*, 142.
40 Ibid, 138.
41 Ibid, 32.
42 Ibid, 147.

work have argued, anywhere in the contemporary world.[43] As such, Sullivan puts forward a bold thesis: 'freedom and equality are better realised, and liberty better defended, if religion, qua religion, is not made an object of specific legal protection'.[44] While supporting the legal protection of 'life beyond the state', *The Impossibility of Religious Freedom* suggests that this might be better achieved through alternative means, such as the rights to freedom of speech, assembly, and the press, that would not require a court to rule on the (il)legitimacy of a religious practice. Not only would this counter the discriminatory effects of a legal instrument that protects some forms of religious life at the expense of others, but it would also prevent discrimination against those who do not choose to describe their ultimate commitments in these terms. Protecting religious practice under the guise of freedom of expression would require those making claims for exemptions from State law to have very strong reasons for doing so, thereby putting them on an equal footing with their fellow citizens.[45]

Although writing of a single dispute in the United States, *The Impossibility of Religious Freedom*'s detailed explication of the difficulty of proving one's religious credentials in court has been highly useful for those analysing freedom of religion in other contexts. For example, my own work on Article 9 of the European Convention on Human Rights (ECHR) as it is interpreted by the European Court of Human Rights (ECtHR) suggests that the Protestant assumptions Sullivan uncovers in American religious freedom judgments are equally prevalent in Europe, the birthplace of the Reformation.[46] Building on Sullivan's recognition of the implicitly textual, privatised, belief-centric, internalised vision of proper religiosity that is presumed by Anglo-American law, I have argued that the ECtHR's Article 9 judgments reflect these norms in a number of ways. This can be seen most easily in the law's treatment of material religion, or the use of objects in religious practice and identity formation.

As the anthropologist Webb Keane puts it, '[r]eligions may not always demand beliefs, but they will always involve material forms'.[47] Despite the Reformers' rejection of religious art and objects as idolatrous, this is so even for those claimants who identify as Reformed Protestants, that is, for the theological descendants of men like Luther and Calvin.[48] Yet the Court has repeatedly failed to protect this aspect of religious life, privileging internalised belief – or the *forum internum* –

43 E Shakman Hurd, *Beyond Religious Freedom* (Princeton University Press, 2015); M McIvor, 'Carnal Exhibitions: Material Religion and the European Court of Human Rights' (2015) 17 *Ecclesiastical Law Journal* 3.

44 Sullivan, *The Impossibility of Religious Freedom*, 138.

45 Ibid, 149.

46 McIvor, 'Carnal Exhibitions' (2015) 17 *Ecclesiastical Law Journal* 3.

47 W Keane, 'The Evidence of the Senses and the Materiality of Religion' (2008) 14 *Journal of the Royal Anthropological Institute* 124.

48 McIvor, 'Carnal Exhibitions' (2015) 17 *Ecclesiastical Law Journal* 4.

over religious manifestations – the *forum externum*. Through an analysis of Article 9 cases involving such diverse objects as cassette players,[49] incense,[50] crucifixes,[51] headstones[52] and cross necklaces,[53] I have suggested that the Court's valorisation of religion as belief contests lived religion in at least three ways. First,

> the privileging of intellectual assent over sensory experience; second, the denial of agency to religious objects; and third, the requirement that religious practices be closely connected to an underlying belief. It concludes that interpretations of Article 9 which emphasise internal belief over external practice are somewhat ill-equipped to deal with the experience of lived religion, prioritising, as they do, the immaterial over the material, and downplaying the centrality of objects in the creation and expression of religious worlds.[54]

Similar points have been raised by Lourdes Peroni,[55] who argues that the Court has a tendency to treat religious belief and religious practice as a binary. This has led to unequal outcomes for those claimants who prefer (or are compelled) to manifest rather than to internalise their religious commitments. Peroni suggests that the Court must adopt a more holistic, integrated approach to these two elements of religious life as a means of creating a more inclusive Article 9.

In terms of international law, Sullivan's claim that religious freedom is a conceptual impossibility has significant policy implications. Elizabeth Shakman Hurd, writing of efforts to export and enforce religious freedom in international politics, has gone so far as to suggest that these efforts may do more harm than good.[56] In her words, the international community needs to distinguish between 'an abstract and aspirational state of peaceful religious coexistence, and the official practice of promoting religious freedom'.[57] While accepting that the former is a valid goal, 'it is not the case that the latter actually helps to realise it, and . . . it may actively impede it'.[58] For example, writing of the genuine threat facing religious

49 *Austrianu v Romania* [2013] ECHR 396.
50 *Kovalkovs v Latvia* [2012] ECHR 280.
51 *Lautsi and Others v Italy* [2011] ECHR 2412.
52 *Jones v UK* [2014] ECHR 176.
53 *Eweida and Others v UK* [2013] ECHR 285.
54 McIvor, 'Carnal Exhibitions' (2015) 17 *Ecclesiastical Law Journal* 5.
55 L Peroni, 'Deconstructing 'Legal' Religion in Strasbourg' (2014) 3 *Oxford Journal of Law and Religion* 235.
56 E Shakman Hurd, 'The International Politics of Religious Freedom' (2014) *IIC Quarterly* 225; Shakman Hurd, *Beyond Religious Freedom* (Princeton University Press, 2015).
57 Shakman Hurd, 'The International Politics of Religious Freedom' (2014) *IIC Quarterly* 227.
58 Ibid.

minorities in revolutionary Syria, Hurd notes that American efforts to protect these groups often follow a narrative structure in which the Muslim majority is homogenised and pitted against its neighbours. Not only does this framing of the conflict implicitly accept the regime's spurious claim to be 'the only bulwark against sectarian warfare', but it 'makes sectarian violence more likely' by stressing religion as a crucial site of difference: 'This framing of the conflict energises categories of religious difference – Christian, Alawite, Sunni – that might not otherwise necessarily define it.'[59] When religious difference is seen as *the* difference that matters, minority communities may find themselves required to put forward claims for justice in problematically narrow identitarian terms.[60] As such, she argues against the American desire to export religious liberty through statutes such as the International Religious Freedom Act (1998).

Of course, Sullivan's work is not without its critics, particularly in terms of these implications for policy. If religious freedom is impossible in theory and unequal in practice, does it follow that scholars ought to campaign against efforts to enforce it, as Hurd does? Writing against this position, and against critiques of human rights law more broadly, David Little has argued that the fact that states do not always live up to the rights-based standards they espouse is no reason to reject them wholesale. [61] Indeed, he suggests, the fact that we feel compelled to critique courts and legislatures for this failure suggests that there is, in fact, something worth rescuing in these lofty goals. He continues to contend that state recognition of religious liberty is a force for good: 'There is strong empirical support for the proposition that human rights compliance in general, and religious freedom compliance in particular, expand the prospects for peace'.[62] The freedom of religion case law may show evidence of occasional poor decision-making on the part of judges, but this does not render the language of rights defunct.

Similarly, one of Sullivan's more admiring critics, Silvio Ferrari, has argued that the *Warner* case 'is not the proof that religious freedom is impossible, it is evidence that freedom of religion has been inadequately understood by a judge'.[63] While he accepts that Sullivan is likely correct in pointing to the fact that we lack 'a convincing legal definition of religion',[64] he doubts either that this is limited to the question of 'religion' or that it renders futile attempts to protect this kind of freedom. As a means of overcoming the possible inconsistencies in the application

59 Ibid, 228.

60 JL Comaroff, 'Reflections on the Rise of Legal Theology: Law and Religion in the Twenty-first Century' (2009) 53 *Social Analysis* 193.

61 D Little, 'Human Rights, Religious Freedom, and Peace' (2017) 4 *BYU Law Review* 1215; D Little, *Essays on Religion and Human Rights: Ground to Stand On* (Cambridge University Press, 2015).

62 Little, 'Human Rights, Religious Freedom, and Peace' (2017) 4 *BYU Law Review* 1220.

63 Silvio Ferrari, 'Who Needs Freedom of Religion?' in Frank Cranmer et al (eds), *The Confluence of Law and Religion: Interdisciplinary Reflections on the Work of Norman Doe* (Cambridge University Press, 2016) 185.

64 Ibid, 180.

of laws designed to protect religious liberty, he suggests a system of 'embedded neutrality', in which parity is ensured through a policy of objectivity on the part of the state. In this vision, although different states may adopt entirely different means of managing religious plurality – some forbidding the display of religious symbols in schools, say, while others permit them – so long as the rules are applied to all religions equally, fairness can be achieved. Ferrari submits that this approach would result in equality of outcome whilst still respecting the cultural heritage of the country in question, allowing it to privilege its own culturally relevant vision of the good (which may include a public sphere that is ostensibly free of religious symbols) while preventing direct discrimination. Embedded neutrality, he argues, can be both even-handed and country-specific.

It is hard to see, however, how such an approach would overcome the very difficulties Sullivan notes: both the question of determining who or what counts as religious, and the fact that efforts to treat religions equally might still lead to indirect discrimination. After all, as the European Court's ruling in the *Lautsi*[65] case shows, the line between religion and local history remains inherently blurred, leading to cases where even the Catholic Church is willing to frame a crucifix as being just as much cultural as it is spiritual.[66] And while it may be true that those identifying as Christian, Muslim or Scientologist would all be prohibited from wearing religious insignia in some circumstances, embedded neutrality fails to appreciate that this sort of prohibition may be experienced much more viscerally and injuriously by some than by others, both within and between religious traditions.

The Impossibility of Religious Freedom, then, asks us to acknowledge that religious freedom is an impossibility not only when the law gets it 'wrong', but even in those cases where it seems to get it 'right'. In other words, there is no level of religious literacy, human sympathy, or conscientious judgment that can render religious life intelligible before the law. We are left to conclude, as Sullivan herself puts it, that '[w]ith all the good will in the world and unlimited expertise, the religious life of the Warner plaintiffs (and, indeed, perhaps of most people at most times, but certainly today) resists legal definition in a fundamental way'.[67]

The legacy

The Impossibility of Religious Freedom has had a significant and lasting influence in fields as diverse as Religious Studies, Law, International Relations and Anthropology. Over a decade after its initial publication, it continues to provide a striking challenge to the very existence of what some believe to be America's 'first freedom', revealing the potentially discriminatory impact of efforts to protect

65 *Lautsi and Others v Italy* [2011] ECHR 2412.
66 E Oliphant, 'The Crucifix as a Symbol of Secular Europe: The Surprising Semiotics of the European Court of Human Rights' (2012) 28 *Anthropology Today* 10.
67 Sullivan, *The Impossibility of Religious Freedom*, 138.

certain visions of the good at the expense of others. In the years since its publication, however, cases involving the right to religious freedom have not decreased. If anything, and whether by choice or by circumstance, religious communities appear ever more likely to frame their grievances in these terms.[68] In this conclusion, I hope to briefly flag up one element of America's contemporary legal landscape to which Sullivan's work can be usefully applied: the burgeoning of local Religious Freedom Restoration Acts (or RFRA), which have themselves been accused of fostering intolerance and discrimination.

Warner[69] has a special place in the history of America's Religious Freedom Restoration Acts. When the case was brought in 1998, it was the first to be adjudicated under Florida's RFRA, which prohibits the government from 'substantially burdening' a person's exercise of religion unless there are both compelling government interests requiring said burden, and the burden is 'the least restrictive means of furthering'[70] that compelling interest. The Florida RFRA is a local version of a federal statute, the Religious Freedom Restoration Act 1993, that had been signed into law by President Bill Clinton before being declared unconstitutional. (The original Act had been introduced with the explicit intention of undoing the effects of a Supreme Court decision, *Employment Division v Smith*,[71] that many religious lobbyists saw as relying on an unduly narrow reading of the First Amendment. The Supreme Court struck down the RFRA at its first opportunity to do so, declaring that Congress had no right to second-guess the Court's interpretation of the Constitution.) In the wake of this anti-RFRA ruling, Sullivan suggests, 'pro-religion lobbyists, architects of the now essentially defunct federal RFRA, took their case to state legislatures, arguing that the states could do what Congress could not'.[72] The result was local RFRAs springing up throughout America – including, of course, in Florida.

Since these early battles of the 1990s, however, RFRAs have gained a new significance in American law. Much of this is due to their invocation in cases in which the right to religious freedom is pitted against the right to non-discrimination on grounds of gender or sexuality. Perhaps the most controversial local incarnation has been in the Midwestern state of Indiana (which is, incidentally, the state in which Sullivan now teaches). Indiana's Religious Freedom Restoration Act allows both individuals and corporations to use their religious beliefs as a defence against claims of what would otherwise be illegal discrimination, and was widely condemned during its passage as a thinly veiled attempt to legalise discrimination against LGBT persons. Thousands took to the streets of Indianapolis to protest

68 Shakman Hurd, 'The International Politics of Religious Freedom' (2014) *IIC Quarterly*; JL Comaroff, 'Reflections on the Rise of Legal Theology: Law and Religion in the Twenty-first Century' (2009) 53 *Social Analysis*.

69 *Warner v City of Boca Raton*, 64 F. Supp. 2d 1272 (S.D. Fla. 1999).

70 Sullivan, *The Impossibility of Religious Freedom*, 23.

71 *Employment Division, Department of Human Resources of Oregon v Smith*, 494 U.S. 872 (1990).

72 Sullivan, *The Impossibility of Religious Freedom*, 29.

against the then bill, and Indiana gained notoriety among LGBT rights organisations throughout the world.

Still, these protests had little impact. The Indiana bill was signed into law by the state's then Governor, Mike Pence, in 2015. With Mr Pence now serving as Donald Trump's Vice President, it seems that the politics of religious freedom – and the resulting definitional scramble – are here to stay.

9 *Law and Revolution*

Rewriting the narrative of law

Ed Morgan

The work

To most people, the question: 'What is law?' enjoys the same practical worth as issues of space, kinetics and/or hydro-dynamics; whilst momentarily intriguing, initial interest soon wanes in the face of practical realities and demands. This is not surprising. Experience has shown that where a person engages with 'the law'[1] in a direct way, the encounter is prompted not by philosophical inquiry, but rather the prospect of vindicating or defending an interest which is personal to her. In contrast, the architects and legislators of a legal system must necessarily look beyond the subjective and seek to accommodate certain realities specific to the community the legal system is intended to serve. A cursory historical survey attests to the fact that, sooner or later, communal lived experience generates questions relative to the rights and freedoms of members, and perhaps of greater significance, the aspirations, values and purposes, to which the community is *itself* collectively committed.

In our present times, the interaction between law and culture has moved centre stage. At the level of the European Community the social and legal construct is 'the democratic society'. The concept is far from static; were it otherwise, there would be no need for the 'margin of appreciation'. When one considers these two constructs as facilitative of communal and individual autonomy, their collaborative purpose becomes apparent: to promote the reception of 'law' in the service of *a community*. By this means, the idea of 'law' represents the articulation of communal self-awareness; the corner-stones of societal identity. Given this reality, it is not possible for a community to formulate *any* institutions of normative behavioural standard without prior identification of the values to which *that community* itself subscribes. This is some distance away from an understanding of 'law' as the imposition of a penalty, curtailment of individual freedom, or expression of social retaliation. As Oliver Wendell Holmes observed:

> The Law is the witness and external deposit of our moral life. . . . The practice of it, in spite of popular jests, tends to make good citizens and good men.[2]

1 In colloquial use, the term 'law' is used indiscriminately to denote a principle of law, constituent laws, and the machinery of the given legal system.
2 OW Holmes, 'The Path to the Law' (1897) x (8) *Harvard Law Review* 61.

From this perspective, law testifies to the moral health of the community in question. But Wendell-Holmes is also adverting to fact that law is invariably – at one and the same time the same time – both *aspirational* and *normative*. The identification of the aspirational and normative features of the law, serve as important co-ordinates in the location of the *intellectus*[3] of a given legal system. Self-evidently, the *intellectus* of a legal system is seldom formed overnight. This is true even in those communities where written constitutions[4] have been promulgated or civil codes adopted. Such constitutional documents are to be seen as the product of a refinement process; one in which custom, practice and lived experience have influenced the formation of principle, or, its revision. For the most part, those factors said to inform the refinement process have been viewed from the vantage point of a sole discipline or sphere of study. In this respect, Hervada has remarked:

> These differences in the very notion of law are not to be surprising, since one's notion of law depends on one's notion of the human person and of society. Our society has become so pluralistic that we make people call into question even these most basic ideas.[5]

As will be seen in what follows, through his *Law and Revolution – The Formation of the Western Legal Tradition*[6] and his other work, most notably *Faith and Order – The Reconciliation of Law and Religion*[7] and *Law and Revolution II*,[8] Harold J Berman offered a narrative which points to the system of law as the product of the interaction between the core concepts of law, person, community and belief. It is too easy to classify the interrelationship of these concepts as the outworking of an irreconcilable tension or conflict between opposing social combatants, each vying for precedence. The cinematic depiction of the rapacious overlord competing for jurisdiction with the corpulent bishop, whilst entertaining, bears no resemblance to the forces and influences which have sought to accommodate both the socio-political understanding of community and the transcendent dimension which is the dignity of the human person.

3 In the present context, this term is used to denote the inner meaning and/or purpose of a legal system which may be discerned from a proper construction of its constituent laws. For a modern discussion of this process of interpretation, see J Coughlin, *Canon Law: A Comparative Study with Anglo-American Theory* (Oxford University Press, 2011) 184–186.

4 Written constitution being used here to denote the creation and promulgation of a single document defining the role and foundational obligations of the State toward the private citizen (e.g. the American Declaration of Independence of 1776).

5 J Hervada, *What is Law? – The Modern Response of Juridical Realism* (Wilson & La Fleur, Montreal, 2009) 170.

6 HJ Berman, *Law and Revolution – The Formation of the Western Legal Tradition* (Harvard University Press, 1983).

7 HJ Berman, *Faith and Order – The Reconciliation of Law and Religion* (Eerdmans, 1993).

8 Berman, *Law and Revolution Vol II – The Impact of the Protestant Reformations on the Western Legal Tradition* (Harvard University Press, 2003).

In contrast, Berman offered an understanding of law which is rooted in the shaping of communities. His historical narrative is not comprised solely of civil subjection, disturbance and retaliation. Instead, it is an account in which the tradition emerges as the product of change: thesis-antithesis and synthesis; each from the perspective of people, person, community and belief. He encapsulates his conclusions in the following observation:

> Law is not only a body of rules; . . . it is thus a living process of allocating rights and duties thereby resolving conflicts and creating channels of communication . . . All legal systems require not only that we recognise proclaimed legal virtues with our intellect, but also that we have come committed to them with our whole being.[9]

In this chapter, consideration is given to certain themes presented in Berman's works. It is important to sound a health warning. What follows is not a book review. Rather, the themes here presented are offered in support of two propositions, namely: first, that Berman presents a unique perspective of the provenance of the Western legal tradition and thus the values it has sought to espouse; and second, that within his exposition of the tradition, he locates and assesses the role played by religious belief in the formation of the tradition itself. To grasp the relevance and significance of Berman's work, a short survey of the understanding of 'law' as received in the emergence of the Western legal tradition is likely to be of some contextual assistance.

The context

Ancient Greece

Burckhardt[10] asserted that it was through the *polis* and promulgated laws (*nomos*) that the social ethos of Ancient Greece were defined, communicated and maintained;[11] with each individual expected to obtain a state of excellence (*arete*)[12] consistent with his condition in life. Whilst the precise content of the societal standard might vary,[13] it nonetheless included reference to 'moral

9 Berman, *Faith and Order – The Reconciliation of Law and Religion* (Eerdmans, 1993) 14.

10 Jacob Burckhardt (1818–1897) was one the founding fathers of cultural history as an academic discipline; a principal advocate of the idea that history had a meaning and was not merely 'a contingent set of random events'. See J Burckhardt, *Greeks and Greek Civilisation* (Harper Collins, 1998) 63.

11 As to the quality of this imposition, see D Kagan, 'Pericles of Athens and the Birth of Democracy' (Guild Publishing, 1990) 144.

12 This subject was of particular concern to Democritus. Scholars do not agree as to the precise meaning of the term. Whilst translated by some to denote a state of virtue, others have suggested the term is more consistent with the attainment of excellence.

13 Kenny has emphasised Plato's concession that law is in need of reform; citing *The Laws* VI at 774b for this purpose. See A Kenny, *A New History of Western Philosophy – Vol. 1. Ancient Philosophy* (Clarendon Press, 2006) 61.

worth' and 'nobility of character'. In doing so, Burckhardt depicted Ancient Greece as possessing the competence to shape the personal formation of each citizen and his societal contribution by means of law (i.e. a society in which laws were normative in character and purpose). For Sophocles, as for so many of the ancient Greeks, 'law' involved the imposition of rules, which translated to standards of social conduct. However, the rule was merely the form; the character of the law was what might be termed its *authority*.[14] Through the writings of Plato and Aristotle one encounters the notion of law as value-laden; directed to a specific end.

For his part, Plato started from the idea that laws were 'written copies of scientific truth',[15] crafted by the legislator whom he considered the architect of harmony,[16] the authority of such laws emanating from their quality of certainty. Thus, the Platonic vision comprises a cosmic order in which the protagonists are 'the gods' and men. Civic order was thus an essential component of the cosmic vision. If such order could not be achieved by encouragement and instruction, according to Plato, it ought to be imposed.[17] In the Platonic view, therefore, law was the dispenser of reason;[18] through which communal harmony might be achieved. This is an understanding of *law* serving (and thus prioritising) a communal necessity; any personal benefit to the individual citizen being entirely incidental.

For Aristotle, laws were consistent with the ambition of reason and Divine Will;[19] with judges serving as *ministers* of justice.[20] So understood, laws represented a means by which a person might be encouraged to act for his/her

14 In the present context, 'authority' is intended to refer to the inherent potential of the specific norm to secure compliance, not the status, jurisdiction or constitutional position of its author.

15 *Statesman*, 239d, 294a and 300c.

16 There being within a community, the universal requirement of morality: *The Republic*, 432a–c.

17 *The Republic* at 520a: Legislators should persuade or compel the members of a community to mesh together, should make every member share with his fellows the benefit which he is capable of contributing to the common welfare and should ensure that the community does contain people with this capacity; and the purpose of all this is not for the legislators to leave people to choose their own directions, but for them to use people to bind the community together. See also *The Republic* at 590d.

18 *The Laws*, 714a: 'The lesson is that we should make every effort to imitate the life men are said to have under Cronus; we should run out public and our private lives, our homes and our cities, in obedience to what little spark of immortality lies in us, and dignify the dispensation of reason with the name of law'. This should be read in conjunction with the requirement that it was for the legislator to *explain* his laws: 723a. This is not an explanation in the manner of justification, but rather by way of an appeal to the reason of the subject so as to more readily secure compliance.

19 'He who commands that law should rule may thus be regarded as commanding that God and reason alone should rule; he who commands that a man should rule adds the character of the beast'. E Barker, *The Politics of Aristotle* (Clarendon, 1946) Book III, 1287a.

20 *Politics* at 1287.

own personal virtue, whilst preserving personal freedom.[21] Aristotle considered law as discharging an educative function[22] in common with other communal instructions, save in one important respect: the quality of coercion which he considered the law was entitled to claim as its own. Further, Aristotle sought to identify those laws considered 'universal' and those termed 'particular'. The former arose from nature itself and were common to all mankind, being in no way dependent upon formulation by the legislator; capable of discernment by all men. In contrast, particular laws were the product of deliberation and reason. Aristotle was seeking to impress upon his audience the fundamental principle that consistency of law is itself a quality of *justice*. In addition, he was alluding to a more subtle issue: the need for a discernible cohesion in the values which laws seek to implement or encourage, such that each contributes to the architectural framework of *a system of law*. Aristotle contemplated two discrete matters, which modern lawyers might take for granted, namely: (i) the law – as distinct from individual laws – must exhibit an internal relational correspondence; and (ii) a system of law, properly so called, must possess not only a series of identifiable values with which the individual laws ought to correspond, but also a hierarchy, by reference to which any internal conflict or contradiction might be resolved.

In both Plato and Aristotle, there is the recognition of law as a necessary ingredient of the cosmic order. As indicated in *The Crito*, Plato viewed subscription and adherence to the laws as an act of assent, such assent being the outworking of social participation. Aristotle considered laws facilitative toward a particular end (i.e. the moral good which he had himself identified). The result, when properly analysed, is a *polis* in which the laws served first as an incentive to adherence and, in default, a means of potential compulsion. The compulsion was directed to social harmony, moral fulfilment and integrity (communal and personal) even if the general norm required adjustment to the particular circumstance.[23] Thus, it may be said that for the Ancient Greeks, the value of the person lay in his ability to contribute to the community. He had yet to be recognised as possessing or enjoying rights which might – superficially – require the relegation of the immediate community interest.[24]

21 Not some promiscuous heap of legislation: *Politics*, VII, 1324b. It is important to grasp that the cosmological vision adopted by Aristotle was predicated upon the pursuit of good (*eudaimonia* – virtue and happiness) without which the *polis* would be reduced to a mere aggregate of persons.

22 This is a key ingredient and supportive of Aristotle's view that was good for men was the acquisition of 'the good' through practice and habituation: *Nicomachean Ethics* II, 1103b.

23 Hence the reference to general rules: *Ethics*, Book III, 1103b, 30: 'Now, that we should act according to the right principle is common ground and may be assumed as a basis for discussion . . . But we must first agree that any account of conduct must be stated in outline and not in precise detail, just as we said at the beginning.'

24 Neither Plato nor Aristotle expressly consider the 'person' as a legal possessor of rights to which he may lay claim (i.e as the holder of rights antecedent to communal participation). The more fundamental question is whether the recognition of rights can enter into conflict with the common good is addressed below.

Rome

Roman law[25] has enjoyed an enormous influence on the development of modern-day legal systems. From the writings of Cicero[26] and Gaius,[27] one detects a significant intellectual shift; not only in understanding, but perspective and purpose. Whilst it may be said that the Greeks wrestled with foundational concepts, Roman law and its protagonists were concerned with the application of principles to aid the resolution of real, practical difficulties. Cicero's deliberations were centred upon the stuff of lived experience.[28] He understood 'reason' (and the natural law identified through its application) as the first common possession of gods and men.[29] But it was only through, and in, communities that Cicero considered man could realise his full potential.[30]

25 Precisely what we mean when we speak of Roman Law is not an entirely straightforward matter. It invariably relates to the codified principles to be found in the Institutes of Gaius, or works conducted under Justinian (ie. Code, Digest and Institutes). In each instance, there was a desire for consistency of principle for particular and practical application. As to the works of Gaius, one may look to the work of Professor Poste, *Institutes of Roman Law – Gaius* (Clarendon, 1904). In his introductory essay, Poste observed: 'The problems of the ultimate source and sanction of jus [sic] was not one that troubled the Roman to any appreciable degree at any period of history. He was content to regard it as the product of custom assisted by interpretation . . . Scarcely any people has had less of a gift or natural inclination for scientific legislation or the formation of a Code. The Roman's dependence on authority and skilled interpretation was, therefore, great'. As will be noted below, this work of interpretation – undertaken as it was by the *praetors* and the *jurisconsult* – bears strong similarity with patterns of judicial reasoning and adjudication in the common law tradition.

26 Three particular works lend assistance: *De Republica*, *De Legibus*, and *De Officiis*. It is reputed that Ambrose of Milan drew upon *De Officiis* when tendering advice to his priests: MT Griffin, *Cicero on Duties* (Cambridge, 1991). Some insight into the prioritisation of duty may also be gleaned from Cicero's *De Officiis* (Trans Miller, Loeb, Harvard, 1913) Book I, II: 'For no phase of life, whether public or private, whether in business or in the home, whether one is working on what concerns oneself alone or dealing with another, can be without its moral duty; on the discharge of such duties depends all that is morally right, and on their neglect, all that is morally wrong in life.'

27 The various commentaries speak with one voice as to the lack of information concerning the person of Gaius. It is nonetheless understood that he lived around the time of Hadrian (AD117–138); Dig. 34.5.7. However, Nicholas records the opening passages of the Institutes as including the following: 'Every people that is governed by statutes and customs applies partly its own peculiar law and partly law which is common to all mankind. For the law which each people establishes for itself is peculiar to it and is called *ius civile* as being the special law of that state (*civitas*) but the law which natural reason establishes among all mankind is observed equally by every people and is called *ius gentium* as being the law applied to all nations (*gentes*)': B Nicholas, *An Introduction to Roman Law* (Clarendon, 1975) 54.

28 This is evidenced in *De Republica* within its unqualified support of the Roman Constitution: R:1:70 and the fact *De Legibus* is set in Arpinum (south-east of Rome).

29 It being the rational soul which equipped man with his affinity to the gods: L:124.

30 In short, the Ciceronian view suggests man is actuated by an inner compulsion to form communities for purposes far beyond the reparation of individual weakness or the enhancement of personal security. This inherent motivation was likewise seen as a unifying facet of the human condition; a common denominator which points to a single universal natural law, which transcends positive law. See N Rudd, *Cicero – The Republic and The Laws* (Oxford University Press, 1998) xxviii.

Within the Roman treatment of the law, permanence and rigidity have yielded to the demands of practicality; the general concept has ceded to the particular application.

Far from seeking to define perfect laws, the Roman jurist was in search of principles of action. In short, a search for and reception of, principles from a wide range of sources:[31] legislation, determination and custom. Rules pervaded all levels of Roman life, such that in legal terms, it might be said this was an age of lists rather than explanations. It is clear, however, that whilst rules were intended to be normative in character, bringing order to a wide variety of social and commercial forms of interaction, there was no attempt on the part of a single body to impose a monochrome system of Roman law on all peoples in the Roman world; albeit the *ius gentium* changed in character from an early illustration in the resolution of 'conflict of laws' to a form of natural law of universal application. The Roman legal method was, however, one of accommodation, interpretation and application. The chief result was an amalgam of communities having the benefit of perhaps one of the earliest forms of legal pluralism;[32] parallel regimes operating as important contributors to legal and commercial efficiency.[33] This position was achieved by a variety of means, but its benefits could not have been maintained had the Romans not acknowledged *law* as having personal rather than territorial application. However, through the writings of Cicero and the works commissioned by Justinian, one is able to perceive a system in which both natural and positive law were recognised and accommodated. Both were seen as generating and supporting the imposition of rules of action; rules which were normative in character and served as direct means by which the *political vision*[34] of the community and/or its values might be adopted and preserved.

Judaism

Scripture[35] provides numerous examples of the understanding of law in the world occupied by Judaism.[36] One is presented with a community in receipt of law as

31 It has been suggested that this resulted *inter alia* in law which was subject to 'continuous, day-to-day adjustment': David Daube, 'Texts and Interpretations in Roman and Jewish Law' in *Collected Works of David Daube* (Volume 1, Berkeley, 1992) 174.

32 For a sociological perspective of this view, see: JA Crook, *Law and Life in Rome 90 BC–AD 212* (Cornell, 1976) 10.

33 In which, according to Buckland, the role and influence of morality was nothing more than an issue of public opinion: W Buckland, *A Manual of Roman Private Law* (Cambridge University Press, 1939) 27: 'Law may be called that part of morality which in a community it is thought desirable to make it compulsory.'

34 The term is used here in its etymological sense as a reference to a community (*polis*) rather than adherence to a partisan view as to be found in contemporary use.

35 The term 'Judaic Law' has been consciously avoided, by reason of the fact that, even in the times of Jesus, Judaism was far from uniform. In this respect, Neusner and Sonn have suggested the term '[S]tands for kindred religious systems': J Neusner and Sonn, *Comparing Religions through Law* (Routledge, 1999).

36 A detailed and informative analysis of this subject is provided in R Westbrook and B Wells, *Everyday Law in Biblical Israel* (Westminster John Knox Press, 2009).

a gift from God bestowed upon His Chosen People. Nonetheless it has application to a community in exile, seeking to articulate and maintain its own religious, cultural and moral identity in a world over which temporal powers exercise sovereignty and jurisdiction.[37] Added to which, according to Walzer, the Judaic legal system lacked any means of civil coercive power.[38] What then of the Hebraic understanding of law? The commandments of the covenant (*mitzvoth*) represented the currency of the relationship between God and man: *berit*.[39] The Old Testament scriptures may be seen as offering a narrative of both lived experience and legal practice;[40] with the legal system they relate presenting the expectation of Divine participation.[41] Moreover, the texts portray the application of law, the invocation of legal proceedings[42] and the promulgation of judicial or quasi-judicial deliberation. One is presented with a communal order in which rules are articulated for individual and collective compliance. Adherence to the law was considered inherent to the relationship between the people and their God and an expression of fidelity to the promise of the Divine covenant.

In this context, law served not only as a social measure of right conduct, but also – in the old Testament at least – as determinative of religious destiny. This was a community in which the actions of one could expose the whole to harm or adverse judgment. Equally, individual conduct might serve as an amelioration of some Divine sanction which might otherwise befall the community as a

37 There are numerous works, which seek to plot the evolution of Judaic legal tradition. Not infrequently they attempt to promote theories concerning Christ's attitude to Judaic law and the absence of single mode of observance. As to the former, and what Meier calls 'the riddle of Jesus and the Law', see JP Meier, *A Marginal Jew: Rethinking the Historical Jesus Vol IV – Law and Love* (Yale, 2009).

38 M Walzer, *Law, Politics and Morality in Judaism* (Princeton, 2006) 1.

39 D Novak, 'Law and Religion in Judaism' in J Witte and F Alexander (eds), *Christianity and Law – An Introduction* (Cambridge University Press, 2008) 35–36. Whilst the term *berit* is often translated in the form of covenant, the term is more consistent with the provision of a unilateral unsolicited promise. By this means, the *mitzvoth* represent the voluntarily bestowed gift of God to guide His people to life; a life which accords with man's dignity and his relationship with God, his creator.

40 Such as the irrevocability of the juridic act of blessing: Genesis 27:35: 'Your brother came with guile and he has taken away your blessing . . . Behold I have made him your lord . . . what can I do for you my son'. See also the proclamation of hierarchies: 1 Samuel 8.

41 According to Westbrook and Wells (R Westbrook and B Wells, *Everyday Law in Biblical Israel* (Westminster John Knox Press, 2009)) the Pentateuch contains no less than 613 'commandments' located within Exodus, Deuteronomy and Leviticus. The Ten Commandments [Exodus 20:1–17] are, of course, supplemented by a variety of instructions and ordnances which have all the hallmarks of responses to particular species of conduct considered injurious to the person, the community or the relationship with God. Westbrook and Wells emphasise that these extracts fall to be read with certain biblical narratives; thereby revealing the interpretation and application of those laws within the community (e.g. the parable of the negligent guard of 1 Kings 20:35 or the vineyard of Isaiah 5:1–7]. They readily concede: 'Nowhere are the tensions between different interpretations more acute than in the translation of biblical laws'.

42 See the arguments presented in 2 Sam 12:1–6 and Deuteronomy 22:13–19.

whole.[43] In short, a socio-political model in which laws articulated and retained a sacred duty and component. The Judaic community was disinterested in the formulation of social norms for the sake of communal order and stability alone. The Community was no mere aggregation of persons or coincidence of common interests. Rather, the social unit comprised the product of Divine election. Rules of conduct were, in consequence, normative only insofar as they were considered consistent with Divine Will. In the result: a world view in which the lived experience necessarily required reconciliation with the destiny to which the 'Chosen People' were directed.[44] In short: that the values of Divine Law found expression in the lived experience, individual and communal; consistent with the path or *halakhah*.[45] Accordingly, the law of Judaism was not rooted in any political ideology. It was directed to an eschatological purpose; the attainment of that purpose drawing upon individual obligation: *mitzvah* (*mitzvoth pl*). Community solidarity was *the product* rather than cause of this responsibility.

Christianity

Christ's attitude toward *the law* has dominated much of the works seeking to provide a fuller understanding of the 'historical Jesus'. In their various endeavours, certain scholars have cited texts said to confirm Christ's antipathy towards the law;[46] whilst others draw upon alternative texts for the contrary purpose.[47] However, for an understanding of the Christian influence upon the Western legal tradition, one must look to the writings of St Augustine of Hippo and St Thomas

43 As illustrated in the intercession of Abraham regarding the fate of the righteous of Sodom: Genesis 18:26 *et seq*.

44 The terminology of this legal culture was inextricably linked with this theological understanding; an understanding which defined, both person and community. As has been observed, the Judaic term for obligation (*mitzvah*) is 'bound up in a myth- the myth of Sinai. Just as the myth of the social contract is essentially a myth of autonomy, so the myth of Sinai is essentially a myth of heteronomy. Sinai is a collective – indeed a corporate – experience. The experience of Sinai is not chosen . . . All law was given at Sinai and therefore all law is related back to the ultimate heteronomous event in which we are chosen – passive voice.' And 'Indeed, to be the one who acts out of obligation is the closest thing to a Jewish definition of completeness as a person within the community'. See RM Cover, 'A Jewish Jurisprudence of the Social Order' in M Walzer (eds), *Law, Politics, and Morality in Judaism* (Princeton, 2006)

45 See Neusner and Sonn: 'Both Judaism and Islam believe that God governs in the here and now through revealed law. Each community of the faithful aspires to realize in this time and in this World God's will for humanity. Both make provision for human participation in, reception of, revelation, assign to sages and masters of the law a role in the process of reasoning and application of God's will': Neusner and Sonn, *Comparing Religions through Law* (Routledge, 1999)

46 Christ's declarations regarding the obligation of the Sabbath are frequently cited in support of such antipathy: Mark 2:23 et seq.

47 Most typically, Mark 12:17. For a broader analysis, see: J Witte and FS Alexander, *The Teachings of Modern Christianity on Law, Politics and Human Nature* (Cambridge University Press, 2006).

Aquinas. Neither requires an introduction. It is clear that, through the prism of Neo-Platonism, Augustine concluded the Celestial and Earthly cities were fundamentally irreconcilable. Social communities were, for Augustine, nothing more than an artificial construct (*societas*) where allegiance was formed for the purpose of enforcing man-made laws.[48] For Augustine, such 'laws' were primarily a counter to 'violence'. One is thus left with an Augustinian view of law as a necessary ingredient to social harmony, identified and imposed not because the norm is virtuous *per se* or consistent with the attainment of virtue, but rather a means of attaining an inferior form of peace,[49] through coercion. One will look in vain for any concession as to the educative qualities of human law.[50] The language used by Augustine is the vocabulary of deterrent and nothing more.[51] Whether his works paved the path taken by Luther is a different matter.[52] The Augustinian and Thomist perspectives could not have been more disparate. For Aquinas, law was the ordinance of reason directed to the common good.. Constituent laws were both normative and directive. Normative in that the law defined the conduct required (or prohibited), and directive by reason of the fact that they anticipated and required compliance. The coercion inherent to law was, however, not the deterrent of punishment, but the rational imperative seeking the restoration of reason and thus: order.[53]

In this way, law was consistent with Divine and natural order.[54] The Aquinian perspective looks beyond the executive power of a sovereign ruler or state constitution as the sole determinant of *law* and/or the quality of laws. In its place,

48 What Augustine viewed somewhat disparagingly: *City of God*, Book XV, 8.

49 'City of God', Book XIX, 17: 'The earthly city, which does not live by faith, seeks an earthly peace, and the end it proposes, in the well ordered concord of civil obedience or rule, is the combination of men's wills to attain the things which are helpful to this life. The heavenly city, or rather that of it which sojourns on earth and lives by faith, makes use of this peace only because it must . . .'

50 Righteousness was thus available only through the law of God: M Boulding, *The Confessions* (Hodder & Stoughton,1997) Book III, 7(13).

51 What has been termed elsewhere, the minatory nature of the law.

52 It is said Augustine was in fact Luther's favourite theologian: Harro Höpfl, *Luther and Calvin on Secular Authority* (Cambridge University Press, 1999) xiv. It has been noted that the identification of Luther's position on the relationship between Church and State is 'not a simple task'. One commentator has observed: 'However, the fact remains that, even if Luther did not teach radical separation of the two kingdoms, he, in fact, did distinguish between the kingdom of Christ and the kingdom of the world and this distinction led to a separation with sad consequences for church and government'. See P Coertzen, *Decently and in Order – A Theological Reflection on the Order for, and the Order in, the Church* (Peeters Leuven, 2004).

53 For a detailed conceptual analysis of Aquinas' treatise on law, and its modern-day relevance, see AJ Lisska, *Aquinas's Theory of Natural Law* (Clarendon, 1996), in which he attributes renewed interest to: 'Legal scholars . . . began searching for rational justifications of law beyond the theoretical accounts common to legal positivism' (at 8).

54 *The Summa Theologica*, 1a2ae, 90, 4: 'Natural law is promulgated by God so instilling it into men's minds that they can know it because of what they really are . . . '.

Aquinas offers a perception of law[55] that is more than a communal imperative or simply the vehicle of social convenience. In substantive terms, Aquinas makes clear that human laws should bear the hallmark of proportionality.[56] Proportionality is, of course, here used in a specific sense, which requires justification by reference to the end to which the law is directed. In consequence, in engaging with the power of human law (i.e. the *vinculo*) Aquinas reveals a fundamental truth, namely: it is not possible to classify an ordnance as 'law' without a prior determination of two matters: (i) whether the object to which the rule is directed is consistent with the common good; and (ii) assuming it to be so, whether the specific rule represents a proportionate means of attaining that objective. Any doubt on this matter is removed when regard is had to Aquinas' consideration of the properties of law and the moral response required where the legitimacy of a law is in doubt. As to the former, he addresses the character of law by reference to (i) the object of the rule under scrutiny; (ii) the provenance of the rule in question (i.e., the competent authority); and (iii) the form in which the rule is promulgated.[57] Aquinas was unequivocal: laws contrary to or inconsistent with the common good could not compel compliance.[58] There is no mistaking that these views, expressed as they are in an unparalleled systematic and comprehensive form, were the product not only of personal insight but the harvesting of the labours of others;[59] Christianising Aristotle as he did so.[60]

As with his predecessors, any reference to individual rights as we understand them today, is conspicuous by its absence. Nonetheless, through the writings of Aquinas, the concept of law made the transition from social and political norm to moral and ethical imperative; crafted toward personal and communal benefit as a whole and as such, deserving of adherence. On any analysis, Aquinas acknowledged law to be a central component in social order. But, moving from an Aristotelian perspective, Aquinas recognised law as fulfilling an essential role

55 For Aquinas, there are three species of law: divine, natural and positive. According to some commentators, Aquinas remains the bridge between natural law theories old and new: Knud Haakonsen, *Natural Law and Moral Philosophy* (Cambridge University Press, 1996) 15.

56 *The Summa Theologica*, 1a2ae 96, 1: 'Whatever is for an end should be proportioned to that end. For law the end should be the common good; Isidore remarks that it should be so composed for no private benefit but for the general welfare of the citizen. Therefore, human law should be proportioned to the common good.'

57 *The Summa Theologica*, 1a2ae 96, 4: 'Accordingly laws which apportion in due measure the burdens of responsibility are just, legitimate, and oblige at the bar of conscience.'

58 *The Summa Theologica*, 1a2ae 96, 6: 'As already stated, every law is ordained for the common well-being and to that extent gets the force and quality of law; in so far as it falls short it has no binding force.'

59 It has been said that Augustine was every medieval writer's first point of reference: G Rosemary Evans, *Fifty Medieval Thinkers* (Routledge, 2002). It is clear Aquinas would have had access to the writings of Ivo of Chartres (1040–1115) and Peter Lombard (1100–160); not to mention the impact of Gratian's Decretum (*c*1170).

60 That is to say, Aquinas drew upon Aristotle for the formulation of his own theories. See MM Keys, *Aquinas, Aristotle and the Promise of The Common Good* (Cambridge University Press, 2006) 15.

in the preservation of the common good, and by that means, the attainment of virtue. Law so viewed is, therefore, at the service of the community of persons, not their domination.

The English common law

It is sometimes suggested that legal systems invoke one of three foundational principles in support of autonomy and legal competence: religious belief (i.e. theocracy); monarchical sovereignty (i.e. the divine right of kings); or, political mandate (i.e. social contract theory). In historical terms, the common law tradition has experienced all three.[61] There is no mistaking the fact that prior to the enlightenment, the English common law was heavily influenced by natural law theory[62] of which royal prerogative was a necessary component.[63] For a time, this philosophical foundation gave way to utilitarianism;[64] much favoured by Benthamite perspectives and thereafter identifiable in the work of John Stuart Mill. In more recent times, common law jurists have been confronted with the same search for a non-religious conceptual foundational basis for law, as that which has vexed other traditions, particularly in the post-War period (i.e., to

61 For an excellent and highly readable account of the transformation of the absolute monarchy in England, see: RC Van Caenegem, *An Historical Introduction to Western Constitutional Law* (Cambridge University Press, 1995) 109 *et seq*: 'More and more people, in parliament and elsewhere, came to believe that the King eroded the ancient Constitution and the common law might fail to protect their persons against the incursions of the absolute prerogative' (at 111) and 'The Stuart era resulted in constitutional limits being imposed on the monarchy, and supreme power passing into the hands of parliament; thus the celebrated model of constitutional and parliamentary government . . . took shape'. It is important to record that theory of wider political mandate became a feature of British Constitutional theory as late as the nineteenth century with the emancipation of various classes of person previously denied any political mandate (e.g. the Catholic Relief Act 1829) said to have been prompted by the election of a Catholic (O'Connell) as Member of Parliament for Clare, who would otherwise have been unable to take up any seat in the House of Commons.

62 The influence of natural law theory may be deduced from a variety of sources and the recognition of certain species of rights enjoyed by the person; albeit the journey from recognition to meaningful protection has been somewhat meandering and spanned many centuries. The underlying philosophies can be detected in the writings of Fortescue, William of Ockham. It has been said that the first work specifically directed to the common law tradition was that of William Hooker, *Of the Laws of Ecclesiastical Polity*. Similar support for natural law theory may be found in the writings of Sir Edward Coke and Sir Matthew Hale's historical theory of law. The question of 'rights' is considered later in this chapter. It is necessary to sound a caveat against the scrutiny of Western constitutional thought in isolation from ecclesiology of the Church: B Tierney, *Religion Law and The Growth of Constitutional Thought 1150–1650* (Cambridge University Press, 1982).

63 It was reliance upon this prerogative that enabled Henry II to introduce legal institutions which were to have a vital role in the introduction of law and order. This mammoth task coincided with the compilation of Glanvill's *Treatise on the Laws and Customs of the Kingdom of England*.

64 The ascendancy of this view of law coinciding with the momentum of secular philosophies, which advanced the notion of the person as simply a component part of a wider political unit.

counter the excesses of positivism and legalism). Time and again, this endeavour has called for a re-evaluation of the human condition and the meaning of *personhood*.

Whilst not enjoying a written constitution, common law constitutional history is nonetheless peppered with documents which have shaped – if not determined – the communal understanding of law and secured legal accountability.[65] From these documents one is able to discern a reception of law as the safeguard of both the individual and communal interest, whilst also serving as a means of restraint against the arbitrary use of power or illegitimate conduct on the part of those exercising political authority. Thus, the common law offers a socio-juridical environment in which law as the articulation of value is afforded precedence; consonant with an anthropocentric perspective of law as *serving* the human condition. Within the experience of the common law and the conceptual constructs upon which it relies (e.g. promises, assurance or assumption of duty) there is evidence of a commitment to an underlying philosophical system in which integrity of personal and hierarchical interaction enjoy central position. But what has this to do with the study of Law and Religion today? The answer to this question is to be found within the works of Harold J Berman.

The significance

In *Law and Revolution*, Berman introduces a story which, from the outset, he acknowledges may not be universally welcome; even amongst those who recognise the narrative as true. In this respect, he has in mind those who might wish to depict the Western tradition as one harmonious and seamless line of progression. To the contrary, Berman's close historic analysis reveals a continuum of revolution–renewal–revival; a process in which 'each of the ancient of the ancient ingredients of Western culture was transformed by being mixed with others'.[66] That is to say, a living process of: '[A]llocating rights and duties and thereby resolving conflicts and creating channels of co-operation.'[67]

It is a detailed account which introduces the reader to the key historic events, movements and protagonists from the time of the Germanic tribes across the ensuing nine centuries. The terms of the introduction and the manner of its presentation challenge not only our understanding of the past, but our appreciation of the present. By way of example, Berman points to the influence of scholastic thought and the evolution of jurisprudence concerning matters as varied as the law of corporations, the law of contracts, inheritance and matters of procedure. In each, ecclesiastical polity is identified as having discharged a pivotal – not to say defining – role, with the church's own declarations and assertions of freedom

65 See for instance: Magna Carta (1215); The Petition of Right (1628); The Act of Habeas Corpus (1679); The Bill of Rights (1689).

66 HJ Berman, *Law and Revolution – The Formation of the Western Legal Tradition* (Harvard University Press, 1983) 3.

67 Ibid, 5.

from political domination ensuring legal pluralism and collaboration. It was this symbiotic existence between the law and belief which prompted the 'restorations of ancient liberties of Englishman as laid down in Magna Carta'.[68] But the fact that this was so was attributable not to some vague concession or toleration of religious belief, but to the simple reality that prior to the events of the seventeenth century the English common law was indistinguishable from the canon law practised elsewhere.[69]

However, Berman concluded that the vitality of this legal tradition (or *ius vigens*) was to be found in its built-in mechanism for organic change. In both the secular and canon law traditions, the barometer against which laws were measured remained a perception of the *common good*. These commonalities are not dependent upon mutual recognition or, indeed, upon any assertion of equality between the two regimes. Simply that the philosophical foundations underlying the two systems were not, in this respect, diametrically opposed. Indeed, both adopted an anthropocentric dimension and serve a teleological function. Such a conclusion is not quite as surprising as might first be thought; especially when regard is had to their shared heritage,[70] that is to say, their shared origins, influences and values. At first blush, such a statement may be considered anachronistic when viewed through a contemporary lens. However, this would be a mistake. As Berman has noted:

> Likewise, it is a serious oversimplification to categorise modern western legal systems as ideological reflections of capitalism. Much modern law is more feudal in character than capitalist. Much defies any characterization in socioeconomic terms. A more complex system of characterization is needed, which will draw not only on types of economic and political formations but also on philosophical, religious and other kinds of criteria.[71]

He continues:

> Law is not only fact; it is also an idea, or concept, and, in addition, it is a measure of value . . . The fact that law is, in its very nature, *both* material *and* ideological is connected with the fact that law *both* grows upward out of the structures and customs of the whole society *and* moves downward from the policies, values and rules of the society. Law helps to integrate the two.

It is this integration which has proven essential to the evolution of the Western legal tradition and is of central importance to its continued vitality. In our modern times, law and belief are all too often depicted as being in opposition.

68 See Berman, *Law and Revolution Vol II – The Impact of the Protestant Reformations on the Western Legal Tradition* (Harvard University Press, 2003) 206.
69 Ibid, 230.
70 M Bellomo, *The Common Legal Past of Europe 1000–1800* (CUA Press,1995).
71 Berman, *Law and Revolution – The Formation of the Western Legal Tradition*, 557.

Through the works of Berman, one is left in no doubt that this is not a modern phenomenon. Locating the coordinates which mark the intersection between religion and law can, however, all too readily obscure their mutual interdependence and interaction. It is in the region of their interaction that the legal tradition finds its most fertile terrain for future growth and continuity:

> The danger that faces us today, in contrast with earlier times, is, I believe, not the danger of excessive sanctification of law or excessive legalization of religion; it is not a crisis of their excessive integration but rather a crisis of their excessive fragmentation. We are threatened more by contempt for law than by worship of it, and more by skepticism regarding the ultimate meaning and purpose of life and of history than by some great all-embracing totalitarian eschatology.[72]

The legacy

Berman's work represents an invitation and opportunity to re-acquaint ourselves with the DNA of the Western legal tradition. It brings a new perspective to the narratives provided by the Greek, Roman, Jewish, Christian and common law approaches. It is a leading work, therefore, not only in terms of historicising the relationship between law and belief but also in terms of highlighting the importance of religion in legal studies: the relationship between law and belief over time has informed the question of 'what is law?' Berman's work stands as testament to the fact that the interrelationship between law and belief has played a central role in the development of the Western legal tradition. The capacity of the law to engage with the transcendent nature of the human person, requires that this should continue to be so. In his published works, Berman provides the student with the resources upon which he/she may draw to conserve this vital symbiosis upon which the Western legal tradition is so dependent. With Berman's analysis, he/she may do so in the certain knowledge that the issues which challenge this interrelationship today are not novel but have been experienced and tested by others. In the words of Cardinal Ratzinger:

> [T]he state receives its basic support from outside: not from a mere reason that is inadequate in the moral realm, but from a reason that has to come to maturity in the historical form of faith. This distinction must not be cancelled out.[73]

72 Berman, *Faith and Order – The Reconciliation of Law and Religion* (Eerdmans, 1993).
73 J Ratzinger, *Values in a Time of Upheaval* (Ignatius, 2006) 69.

10 *Religious Freedom, Religious Discrimination, and the Workplace*

Overlapping protections in changing contexts

Megan Pearson

The work

Religious Freedom, Religious Discrimination and the Workplace was first published in 2008 with a revised edition in 2016.[1] The author, Lucy Vickers, is a Professor at Oxford Brookes University and a qualified solicitor whose work focuses on employment and discrimination law. She has written extensively in this field, particularly on religious discrimination and, more recently, age discrimination, including contributing to reports on related topics for the European Commission and the Equality and Human Rights Commission (EHRC).

As the title would suggest, the work addresses the protection of religion and belief within the specific context of the workplace, an important context for reasons explained below. It takes the form of an academic monograph and the focus is on legal analysis rather than a sociological account of how religious freedom or discrimination is lived in the workplace, although there is course reference to relevant research carried out by others. While it is an academic work and not a practitioner guide to the law, the emphasis is practical rather than predominantly theoretical or jurisprudential. It has been referred to in decided cases[2] and in the EHRC's review and final report on the law relating to religion and belief.[3] However, it seeks not merely to explain the law but to consider its underlying principles and propose reform, partly through comparative analysis. It therefore differs both in content and structure and in its intended audience from practitioner works such as Knights' work on freedom of religion and minorities[4] and Dingemans *et al*'s more wide-ranging survey of the law relating to religious rights.[5]

Vickers begins by considering two foundational questions: the definition of religion and belief and the reasons for the protection of freedom of religion and

1 L Vickers, *Religious Freedom, Religious Discrimination and the Workplace* (2nd edn, Hart Publishing, 2016).
2 *Grainger plc v Nicholson* [2010] IRLR 4.
3 P Edge and L Vickers, 'Review of Equality and Human Rights Law relating to Religion or Relief' (Equality and Human Rights Commission Research Report 97, 2015)
4 S Knights, *Freedom of Religion Minorities, and the Law* (Oxford University Press, 2007).
5 J Dingemans, C Yeginsu, T Cross *et al*, *The Protections for Religious Rights: Law and Practice* (Oxford University Press, 2013).

belief. Both issues are extremely complex. For the first, given even the variety in beliefs which are uniformly considered to be religious, let alone identifying those beliefs which are not religious but which should be protected, it is difficult to move beyond, as with obscenity,[6] an 'I know it if I see it' kind of approach, if beliefs such as veganism are to be included but support for a football team is not. Secondly, justifications for protecting religion and belief tend to be either too over- or under-inclusive. If they focus, for example, on the protection of individual autonomy, this fails to identify why only particular kinds of beliefs and practices are protected, as opposed to protecting a general right to act in accordance with one's wishes. Other explanations, such as marginalisation and disadvantage of certain religious groups, only justify the protection of some, usually minority, beliefs. Nevertheless, Vickers argues, even if these issues cannot be answered wholly satisfactorily, sufficient answers to justify and enable legal protection can be given.

After addressing these preliminary issues, the main part of the book looks at how the law has and should operate in a range of workplaces: public sector, commercial, quasi-religious and religious. An important part of this discussion is the international context: the influence of the ECHR and, particularly in the second edition, the potential impact of the EU on domestic law, and comparisons with other jurisdictions, most notably Canada and the USA.

The context

This work is part of a (re?)surgence in interest in religion generally and from both an academic and practical legal perspective, that has occurred in the last 15 or so years. As Russell Sandberg puts it, 'at the dawn of the twenty-first century, something unexpected happened: religion became significant again'.[7] Partly this was due to changes in the law, most notably in the enactment of the Employment Equality (Religion or Belief) Regulations 2003,[8] which for the first time prohibited religious discrimination per se in employment. Some protection had previously been given by the law prohibiting race discrimination, most notably to Sikhs[9] and Jews,[10] but the partial and therefore discriminatory nature of this protection was unacceptable, particularly given the rise in prominence of Islamophobia and thus the need for specific legislation had become obvious. Nevertheless, it took a push from the EU in the form of Directive 2000/78/EC, establishing a general framework for equal treatment in employment and occupation, for domestic legislation to be enacted. Discrimination on the basis of religion or

6 *Jacobellis v Ohio (1964)* 378 U.S. 184 *per* Justice Stewart.
7 R Sandberg, *Religion, Law and Society* (Cambridge University Press, 2014) 7.
8 Employment Equality (Religion or Belief) Regulations 2003, SI 2003/1660.
9 *Mandla v Dowell-Lee* [1983] 2 AC 548.
10 *Seide v Gillette Industries Ltd* [1980] IRLR 427.

belief in the provision of goods and services was later prohibited by the Equality Act 2006.

In a form of dual overlapping but distinct protection, the tension of which lies at the heart of Vickers' book, this prohibition of religious *discrimination* ran alongside the protection of religious *freedom*. Whilst there had been numerous laws protecting religious freedom within specific contexts, religious freedom as a general right was given legal protection for the first time by the Human Rights Act 1998. This came into force in 2000 and incorporated the European Convention of Human Rights (ECHR) into domestic law, meaning that it was no longer necessary for claimants to go to Strasbourg to claim an infringement of their rights. Article 9 ECHR protects the right to freedom of thought, conscience and religion and a qualified right to manifest these beliefs. The meaning of this provision is far from determinate. The contested nature of what kind of religious freedom was protected by this provision was evident from the start, as can be seen even in the terms of the legislation. Owing to a fear that Article 9 might affect the freedom of religious organisations to choose their employees in line with their beliefs, section 13 of the Human Rights Act states that if a court's determination might affect the exercise by a religious organisation of its Convention right to thought, conscience and religion, the court must 'have particular regard to the importance of that right':[11] individual and collective religious freedom being potentially in conflict. In practice, however, this provision has been widely viewed as a dead letter.[12]

The Regulations and the Human Rights Act radically changed the legal scene. While law regulating or promoting religion is hardly new, these laws amounted to a radical 'shift from passive toleration to the active promotion of religious liberty as a right'.[13] This led to a process of 'juridification' of religion whereby 'conflicts are increasingly being solved by or with reference to law'.[14] This law not only increased the options for those with grievances but in doing so changed the ways these disputes were characterised by participants. Religious actors could for the first time perceive their actions or wishes not merely as morally and religiously right but also as *legally* justified. In this way, the law could, for example, be used as part of a broader strategy by conservative campaigning groups such as Christian Concern and the Christian Institute, in a way which had been an established part of political action in the USA for some time.[15] Religion therefore changed

11 Human Rights Act 1998, s.13.

12 *R (Amicus) v Secretary of State for Trade and Industry* [2004] EWHC 860.

13 R Sandberg, *Law and Religion* (Cambridge University Press 2011) 192.

14 Lars Chr Blicher and Anders Molander, 'Mapping Juridification' (2008) 14 (1) *European Law Journal* 36, 39 (as cited in Sandberg, *Law and Religion* (Cambridge University Press 2011)).

15 S Hunt, 'A Turn to the Rights: UK (Conservative Christian Lobby Groups and the Gay Debate' (2011) 6 *Religion and Human Rights* 291; and M Pearson, *Proportionality, Equality Laws and Religion* (Routledge, 2017).

to not merely a social phenomenon but also potentially a legal problem. These changes to the way religion and religious conflicts were perceived should be seen as part of a broader 'turn to rights' within UK law which had been nascent during the 1980s and 1990s and grew exponentially after these hopes were realised in the Human Rights Act 1998.[16] As Cranmer suggests, as the ECHR has become an integral part of English law, it would now be inconceivable to decide a case affecting religious rights without consideration of it, even though this would have been perfectly possible 30 years ago.[17]

As a result, there has been a rise in cases challenging believers' treatment within employment. The Regulations, of course, prohibited straightforward direct discrimination where there was no possible justification, such as a Muslim being denied a job with no religious connection due to Islamophobic stereotypes. But they waded into much murkier waters. Some cases raised clashes with the protection of other protected characteristics such as sexual orientation. Some involved a clash between a religious organisation's right to freedom of religion and the rights of an individual to non-discrimination and religious freedom. Some required consideration of the meaning of belief, particularly non-religious belief, and some a balancing of the interests of the employee with those of the employer, other employees or customers. Unsurprisingly, this new and fertile area became the source of much academic commentary, of which Vickers' work was an early part.

The vast increase in academic and popular interest in this area and the juridification of disputes does not though mean that claimants have been particularly successful. Rather, in a stream of cases which reached the higher courts, including but not limited to *Williamson*,[18] *Begum*,[19] *Playfoot*,[20] *Eweida*,[21] *Ladele*[22] and *Bull*,[23] the courts decided the case against the religious claimant. By their nature these cases raised controversial points of law and therefore would be less likely to be successful than more straightforward claims. At Employment Tribunal level, there has been some success for claimants, although there have been relatively few cases.[24] It is of course wrong to equate a successful discrimination law with

16 T Bingham, 'The ECHR: Time to Incorporate' (1993) 109 *Law Quarterly Review* 390; and D McGoldrick, 'The United Kingdom's Human Rights Act 1998 in Theory and Practice' (2001) 50 *International and Comparative Law Quarterly* 901.

17 F Cranmer, 'Religion, Human Rights and the Council of Europe: A Note' (2009) 162 *Law and Justice* 36.

18 *R. (on the application of Williamson) v Secretary of State for Education and Employment* [2005] UKHL 15; [2005] 2 AC 246.

19 *Begum (on the application of) v Denbigh High School* [2006] UKHL 15.

20 *R (Playfoot) v Millais School Governing Body* [2007] EWHC 1698 (Admin).

21 *Ewedia v British Airways Plc* [2010] EWCA Civ 80.

22 *Ladele v London Borough of Islington* [2009] EWCA Civ 1357.

23 *Bull and Another v Hall and Another* [2013] UKSC 73.

24 Annual Employment Tribunal and Employment Appeal Tribunal Statistics. Available at https://www.gov.uk/government/statistics/employment-tribunal-and-employment-appeal-tribunal-statistics-gb, accessed 27 August 2018.

high rates of formal legal proceedings rather than internal policy changes and informal ways of resolving disputes. However, a call for evidence by the Equality and Human Rights Commission (EHRC) found that many felt they had experienced discrimination, although the research methods used did not allow an analysis of how representative these experiences were.[25]

The other broader change, of which this new law on religion formed a part, was the, at least partial, longer-term change in the legal perception of the relationship between employee and employer beyond the traditional 'master' and 'servant' approach.[26] Thus, it can be seen in the same light as legislation granting the right to request flexible working or to emergency time off for dependents: as part of a move towards somewhat recognising the individuality of the employee as a person who has a life and obligations beyond the employment sphere. Partly this change was due to a normative move away from hierarchical societal structures, but there were also more instrumental considerations for such legislation, such as breaking down barriers to employment to encourage higher employment rates. This is not to say that this change applies consistently to all sections of the workforce as the rise of the '*precariat*' with zero-hour contracts or enforced self-employment suggests,[27] but it is still a relevant theme.

These changes in law combined with considerable political and social changes in religious belief. Whilst there has been a significant decline in church attendance with a fall from 11.7 per cent of the population in England attending church on a Sunday in 1979 to 6.3 per cent in 2005,[28] there has been a marked increase in membership of what were previously marginal religions as religious belief has become 'more varied and multifaceted'.[29] In fact, part of the reason for the increase in legal challenges may be that religious belief has declined and therefore to have a serious commitment to religion is perceived by many as unusual or even odd.[30] If it is accepted generally that apart from in emergency situations Sundays should be a day of rest, then there will normally be no conflict between a religious employee and an employer, but if this cultural understanding has broken down then conflict becomes more likely.

Religious belief has not only become less homogeneous but the type of religious belief has changed, with an increase in what Peter Berger has characterised as 'furious religion'.[31] Fears of radical Islam became a heated topic, particularly after the 7/7 London bombings which, it was argued, a lack of integration had

25 M Mitchell, K Beninger, A Donald *et al*, 'Religion or belief in the workplace and service delivery' (2015) Equality and Human Rights Commission.

26 *Johnson v Unisys* [2001] UKHL 13 and S Deakin, 'The Contract of Employment: A Study in Legal Evolution' (2011) ESRC Centre for Business Research, University of Cambridge.

27 G Standing, *The Precariat: The New Dangerous Class* (Bloomsbury, 2011).

28 L Woodhead and R Catto, *Religion and Change in Modern Britain* (Routledge, 2012) 5.

29 Ibid, 2.

30 A Bradney, *Law and Faith in a Sceptical Age* (Routledge, 2009).

31 P Berger, *The Desecularization of the World: Resurgent Religion and World Politics* (Eerdmans, 1999).

contributed to, leading to the growth of hard and soft law such as the Prevent strategy and a focus on 'British values'. [32] While the UK has not gone down the route adopted by some European countries of prohibiting by legislation the wearing of the Islamic veil either in public or in certain forms of employment,[33] clothing signifying religious difference has at times become a controversial topic in public discourse.

Vickers' work was the first book-length consideration of religious freedom which addressed this new law and social background within the context of employment, a particularly significant area. In doing so, this built on work by other commentators in this area, writing from a variety of perspectives, from explicitly evangelical Christian,[34] to those who take a more sceptical view of religion, particularly in its capacity to undermine other non-discrimination rights,[35] as well as numerous articles on particular points of law. Her book therefore contributed to the formation of Law and Religion as its own distinct sub-discipline, and not merely as part of Discrimination or Human Rights Law or the specialised field of Ecclesiastical Law. Whilst, of course, there had been research on issues relating to Law and Religion before this point, as Hall has argued in relation to medical law, simply studying a field related to law does not in itself make it its own sub-discipline.[36] Rather, this is formed by a process of academic work which is analytically coherent, permanent, and has a 'core substantive focus for the field and a core set of methods of inquiry'.[37] It is only fairly recently that Law and Religion as a field has gained its own specialist journals, research centres and undergraduate and postgraduate courses.[38] The creation of a sub-discipline is significant: while it means that research can be disseminated and used as the basis for further research, and the opportunity for collaboration is greater, it makes it harder to challenge assumptions relating to core principles of the field, appropriate research questions or methods of inquiry which have become taken for granted and may lead to the over-specialisation of knowledge.

It is significant that a second edition of Vickers' book was published, something of a fairly rare occurrence for an academic work as opposed to a textbook or a practitioner work. This is even more significant given that the law in one sense had not greatly changed between 2008 and 2016, given that the Equality Act 2010 largely consolidated rather than changed earlier legislation and there

32 L Woodhead and Rebecca Catto, *Religion and Change in Modern Britain* (Routledge, 2012).

33 C Joppke, *Veil: Mirror of Identity* (Polity, 2009).

34 R Ahdar and I Leigh, *Religious Freedom in the Liberal State* (Oxford University Press, 2005).

35 R Wintemute, 'Religion vs. Sexual Orientation: A Clash of Human Rights?' (2002) 1 *Journal of Law and Equality*. 126; P Johnson and R Vanderbeck, *Law, Religion and Homosexuality* (Routledge, 2014).

36 MA Hall, 'The History and Future of Health Care Law: An Essentialist View' (2006) 41 *Wake Forest Law Review* 347.

37 Ibid, 356.

38 Sandberg, *Law and Religion* (Cambridge University Press, 2011).

were no changes (although these were repeatedly threatened by many politicians) to human rights law. Yet, in another sense, the law could be said to have 'come of age' within this period.[39] This development is reflected in the fact that there are many more cases cited in the second edition than the first, from Employment Tribunal level up. If, as Sandberg argued, 'religious freedom died' with the *Begum* decision in 2006, which permitted a school to prohibit a Muslim pupil from wearing a jilbab on the basis that she could manifest her religion in other contexts, including by attending another school. Then it could be argued that it was resurrected by the ECtHR's decision in *Eweida v UK*[40] in 2013, holding that there was a violation of Article 9 taken with Article 14 in BA's refusal to allow her to wear a visible cross at work in contravention of its uniform rules.[41] Other landmark cases decided between the two editions included *Grainger v Nicholson*[42] defining the meaning of 'belief'[43] under the Regulations and now the Equality Act and the Supreme Court's analysis of the conflict between sexual orientation discrimination law and religious freedom in *Bull v Hall*.[44]

The significance

Religious Freedom, Religious Discrimination and the Workplace was therefore published at a significant time for Law and Religion. It is also significant in other ways. The first is in its particular subject matter. Employment situations are both important and distinct from other contexts where religious or other beliefs may be manifested. Employment is not only (usually) economically necessary but also provides social benefits and a sense of status. It is not a coincidence that an often-asked question when meeting someone is 'what do you do?', where the 'doing' automatically implies paid employment. Furthermore, as Vickers points out, in some contexts such as health or education, one employer, usually a state employer, is so dominant that it is not easy for an employee to find alternative employment. Whilst it is true that an employee may ultimately protect his/her rights by resigning, this does not by itself provide full justification for the interference with the right as had been initially held by the English courts under what was known as the specific situation rule.[45] This is an unsatisfactory approach to the protection of human rights and would clearly not be an answer to other forms of discrimination, such as race discrimination.

Nevertheless, Vickers argues that the employment context is a relevant factor in considering justification and greater restrictions on a person's manifestation

39 Sandberg, *Religion, Law and Society* (Cambridge University Press, 2014).

40 *Ewedia v British Airways Plc* [2013] ECHR 37.

41 Sandberg, *Religion, Law and Society* (Cambridge University Press, 2014).

42 *Grainger plc and others v Nicholson* [2010] EAT/0219/09.

43 Regulations and Equality Act 2010. Available at http://www.legislation.gov.uk/ukpga/2010/15/contents, accessed 27 August 2018.

44 *Bull v Hall* [2013] UKSC 73 On appeal from [2012] EWCA Civ 83.

45 *Copsey v WWB Devon Clays Ltd* [2005] EWCA Civ 932.

of their belief may be accepted in this area than in other contexts. This is firstly because these infringements exist only within a limited sphere. Whilst this should not provide a complete defence, it does mean the interference with a right is less than if the manifestation of the belief were to be prohibited entirely. More normatively, by accepting employment a person accepts some limitation on his/her personal autonomy, such as the hours they will work, the content of the work or the clothing they must wear. Restrictions on religious practices are therefore not unique.

Employment, then, is an important context, but it is also significant because of its complexity: indeed, the word 'complexity' is mentioned three times in the first couple of pages of the work. There is an intricate web of different interests to take into account, which, as Vickers points out, are 'seemingly infinite'.[46] Firstly, of course, there is that of the religious or non-religious employee. The nature of these interests will be multifarious. It may be the claim of an employee to be allowed to take up employment in a religious or quasi-religious organisation regardless of his/her religious or non-religious identity. Or it may involve religious beliefs in a more active way. Employees may wish to express their beliefs through proselytising to other employees or to customers, or in demonstrating their views in more subtle ways, through the wearing of religious symbols. Alternatively, an employee may claim to be unable to perform an aspect of their employment duties, such as handling alcohol, working at a precise time, or providing a service to gay people because this contradicts their beliefs.

Also relevant is the interest of the employer, with regard to ensuring the efficient and cost-effective performance of work tasks, or in maintaining a harmonious workforce, or for some religious employers, preserving a religiously observant workforce. In addition, other employees harbour concerns regarding the following: equal treatment in the distribution of work tasks and time off, non-discrimination, the protection of their own beliefs. Customers have interests in receiving an efficient non-discriminatory service that is in line with their beliefs. Further, the state's interests regarding full employment and non-discriminatory work practices cannot be forgotten. The decision-making process must therefore be capable of taking account of the multiplicity of interests.

Vickers' solution is based on the concept of proportionality, and in her discussion of this lies the work's second significance. The term 'proportionality' has become widely used in Discrimination Law, particularly that based on EU Law, as well as in Human Rights Law and Public Law generally. In her analysis, a proportionality enquiry requires a legitimate aim, and a consideration of 'whether there is a proportionate relationship between the means used and the aim . . . given the existence of competing interests'. She argues that this allows a structured approach to be taken to the necessary complex balancing of rights.

There is a large and expanding Public Law literature on this topic which considers the nature of proportionality and its advantages and disadvantages, which has

46 Vickers, *Religious Freedom, Religious Discrimination and the Workplace* (2nd edn, Hart, 2016).

developed alongside the great expansion in its use internationally. Vickers contributes to this field of research by giving a detailed account of how the process of proportionality can be worked out in the particular context of employment, especially in indirect discrimination claims where the discriminatory effect can be justified if it has a legitimate aim and is proportionate. By carefully outlining the various factors that need to be taken account of in this process, she not only provides guidance as to how cases in this area should be decided but also contributes to the wider debate on the appropriateness and value of proportionality. While proportionality has been strongly criticised on the basis that it does not provide sufficient guidance to judges and therefore leads to subjective and inconsistent decisions,[47] Vickers demonstrates that proportionality can be applied in a way which is fact sensitive but yet clear and consistent. As she points out, uncertainty is the price we pay for greater protection. Given the multiplicity of employment situations it would not be possible to say that there was, for example, a right to wear an Islamic headscarf for all work, without any kind of case-by-case analysis. The law would of course be clear if there were no right to wear a headscarf at work at all, but this would not be fair to some. As other commentators in the field of Public Law have pointed out, a rule may be fair in the vast majority of situations, but still create unnecessary hardship in a few cases.[48] A proportionality analysis allows relief to be given to these claimants.

Her analysis of proportionality also contributes to a different debate which is ongoing within discrimination law. An alternative to prohibiting indirect discrimination would be to use a reasonable accommodation approach, which is used albeit not in identical ways, as Vickers discusses, in the USA and Canada. A new right to reasonable accommodation, unless this would cause 'undue hardship', has received support from, among others, the EU-funded RELIGARE project,[49] the UN Special Rapporteur on Religion and Belief[50] and the Hepple Report,[51] which was extremely influential in paving the way for the Equality Act 2010. Some have argued that reasonable accommodation provides a more intuitive way of approaching these issues for employers and employees and avoids the difficulties in finding group disadvantage inherent in an indirect discrimination approach given the personal nature of many beliefs which may not be shared with others in the workplace.[52] Vickers also suggests that having a separate law which

47 GCN Webber, *The Negotiable Constitution* (Cambridge University Press, 2012).

48 K Möller, *The Global Model of Constitutional Rights* (Oxford University Press, 2012).

49 M Foblets and K Alidadi, 'Summary Report on the Religare Project' (2013). Available at http://www.religareproject.eu/system/files/RELIGARE%20Summary%20Report_0.pdf, accessed 27 August 2018.

50 H Bielefeldt, *Interim Report of the Special Rapporteur on Freedom of Religion or Belief* (A/HRC/28/66/Add.2 2014) United Nations General Assembly.

51 B Hepple, M Coussey, T Choudhury, *Equality: A New Framework Report of the Independent Review of the Enforcement of UK Anti-Discrimination Legislation* (Hart, 2000).

52 E Howard, 'Reasonable Accommodation of Religion and Other Discrimination Grounds in EU Law' (2013) *European Law Review* 360, and K Alidadi, 'Reasonable Accommodation for Religion and Belief: Adding Value to Art.9 ECHR and the EU's Anti Discrimination Approach in Employment' (2012) 37 *European Law Review* 693.

applies only to religious discrimination may be beneficial because to apply the same law to religion as to other protected characteristics, such as sex and race, may undermine their protection. This is because, it is argued, religion is different from these other grounds, and so a more generous approach to justification will be given, allowing for example economic arguments. Given the insistence that there is no hierarchy of rights, these cases will be 'read across' to other grounds, which will undermine the strict approach currently taken for other grounds of discrimination.

While the idea of reasonable accommodation may be easier to understand in the abstract than proportionality, it does not make easier the final decision as to whether to protect the employee or employer's interest. Rather, a reasonable accommodation test may instead lead to greater inconsistency in decision-making because there can be significant variation in considering what is 'reasonable', as can be seen from the very different emphasis in considering what amounts to undue hardship for employers between the USA and Canada. Ultimately Vickers rejects this approach because it would most likely replicate the current law on indirect distinction and proportionality is already capable of providing 'appropriate and balanced protection'.

At present, a proportionality test is used both to consider whether there has been a violation of the right to manifest beliefs and to consider whether there has been indirect discrimination. A further important way in which the work is significant is by analysing the distinction between religious freedom rights, protected by the ECHR, and the prohibition of religion and belief discrimination, contained in the Equality Act 2010 and which is ultimately protected in the UK by the CJEU until the withdrawal of the UK from the European Union (Brexit) is complete. These dual protections of course overlap. It is possible to view a refusal by an employer to give a day off work because an employee wishes to celebrate a religious festival as both interfering with the right of religious freedom, because the claimant cannot manifest their beliefs in the way they wish, and as indirect discrimination, because it will be harder for members of that religious group to comply with the requirement to work that day. Nevertheless, as Vickers makes clear, they have different aims and rationales. Prohibitions on religious discrimination focus on combating disadvantage and marginalisation, suggesting perhaps that it is particularly concerned with members of minority religions who may face structural barriers to employment. The rationales for protecting religious freedom are more concerned with personal autonomy and human dignity. For example, the claim of indirect religious discrimination was rejected in *Eweida v British Airways* on the basis that she could not show that Christians as a group were disadvantaged because of BA's uniform policy and individual disadvantage was held not to be sufficient. However, her claim that this policy violated her Article 9 rights taken with Article 14 was successful in the ECtHR.

Whether the theoretical differences underlying these two types of claim should affect a claim's success is less clear. Although some have suggested that there is an inevitable need to show group rather than individual disadvantage in indirect discrimination claims given this different focus and the text of the Directive on which the UK law is based,[53] this distinction may be less clear in practice.[54] This is partly because courts are under an obligation under the Human Rights Act to interpret legislation in accordance with Convention rights. Given that unique beliefs would be protected by the ECHR, Article 9 may require that discrimination law be widened to include them.

While religious freedom and religious discrimination claims may merge within the domestic sphere, there is of course a difference in where these cases may ultimately be heard. So far, the focus of claimants and of academic commentary has been on the ECtHR. While there is no right to individual petition in the CJEU, it is notable that English claimants have not asked domestic courts for a Preliminary Reference in indirect discrimination cases. However, we are on the cusp of a shift in attention. This can be seen by comparing the two editions of Vickers' work. In the first edition, Chapter 4 is entitled 'Freedom of Religion at Work and the European Convention on Human Rights'; in the second, it is broader: 'Freedom of Religion at Work: the European Dimension'.

The ECtHR has so far taken a deferential attitude to considering the justification put forward by member states in some contexts, particularly concerning prohibitions on religious dress. It has accepted, for example, that wearing an Islamic headscarf is, or at least can be, inherently proselytising and therefore prohibiting a teacher from wearing one was justifiable.[55] This deferential approach reached its height in *SAS v France*,[56] concerning the 'burqa ban' in public places which accepted an extremely vague justification that the ban was required to promote 'living together' (*le vivre ensemble*); a concept which had not previously been used by the court. As a supervisory international court, the ECtHR has made use of the 'margin of appreciation', allowing member states discretion in deciding social and cultural issues, but the CJEU does not use such a concept. Although it is, of course, aware of the political context in which it makes decisions and has at times sidestepped issues which are too controversial,[57] it has generally taken a proactive stance in combating discrimination and promoting equality.[58] Given this, it is perhaps surprising that more attention has not been paid to it up until now.

53 R McCrea, 'Singing from the Same Hymn Sheet? What the Differences between the Strasbourg and Luxembourg Courts Tell Us about Religious Freedom, Non-Discrimination, and the Secular State' (2016) 5 *Oxford Journal of Law and Religion* 183.

54 *Mba v Merton LBC* [2013] EWCA Civ 1562.

55 *Dahlab v Switzerland* [2001] ECHR 899.

56 *S.A.S v France* [2014] ECHR 695.

57 R McCrea, 'Singing from the Same Hymn Sheet? What the Differences between the Strasbourg and Luxembourg Courts Tell Us About Religious Freedom, Non-Discrimination, and the Secular State' (2016) 5 *Oxford Journal of Law and Religion* 183.

58 E Howard, 'Protecting Freedom to Manifest One's Religion or Belief: Strasbourg or Luxembourg?' (2014) 32 *Netherlands Quarterly of Human Rights* 159.

However, the cases of *Achbita*[59] and *Bougnaoui*,[60] suggest that this new frontier of discrimination law may not be that different from the ECHR. The issue in these cases was whether being forbidden from wearing the Islamic headscarf at work amounted to direct discrimination. The two Advocate Generals' Opinions reached very different conclusions.AG Kokott held in the first that this did not amount to direct discrimination because the prohibition of political, philosophical and religious symbols by the employer was a neutral rule and any indirect discrimination was justified by the employer's need to promote a religious or ideologically neutral image. AG Sharpston argued in *Bougnaoui*, however, that this amounted to direct discrimination and there was no applicable derogation from the principle of non-discrimination. The CJEU sided primarily with AG Kokott, holding that any indirect discrimination could be justified in order to enforce a policy of religious and ideological neutrality, although it did hold that if there were no such policy then it would not be legitimate to base a decision on the mere wishes of a customer not to have services provided by a worker wearing an Islamic headscarf. The final decision as to whether there had been discrimination was a matter for the Belgian and French courts and much depends on the way the judgment will be interpreted in future. Nevertheless, Vickers was right to sound a pessimistic note on the likelihood of the CJEU issuing a decisive stand allowing workers to wear the headscarf.[61]

Religious Freedom, Religious Discrimination and the Workplace is significant, therefore, not only because of its subject matter, thus contributing to the formation of Law and Religion as a field and providing the basis for further specialised scholarship, but because of the approach she suggests for resolving these issues and the contribution it makes in developing the literature on proportionality.

The legacy

As Vickers points out in the introduction to the revised edition, despite freedom of religion being well established internationally as a fundamental human right and legislation protecting against religious discrimination dating from 2003, the proper limits on religious freedom in the workplace and the interaction of these two sources of rights are still not fully clear. Certainly, there are references to far more decided cases in the second edition, reflecting the growth in this area, and these will provide greater guidance to employers and employees on matters such as working hours or the refusal to perform some duties, but there are still uncertainties. Some of these are inevitable given the huge variety of employment situations. For example, whilst it has been decided that it *can* be indirect discrimination

59 *Samira Achbita and Centrum voor gelijkheid van kansen en voor racismebestrijding v G4S Secure Solutions NV* [2016] CJEU C-157/15.

60 *Bougnaoui and ADDH* [2016] CJEU C-188/15.

61 T Loenen and Lucy Vickers, 'More is Less? Multiple Protection of Human Rights in Europe and the Risks of Erosion of Human Rights Standards' in S Morano-Foadi and L Vickers (eds), *Fundamental Rights in the EU: A Matter for Two Courts* (Bloomsbury, 2016).

not to change an employee's work patterns to accommodate her religious beliefs, whether it will be can only be decided based on the particular facts of the case. Given that Vickers' work provides a way of resolving these issues by laying out clearly the factors which should be considered, rather than attempting to provide prescriptive answers, this is not in itself a problem. There are, though, contexts where further exploration is necessary. Cases such as *Ladele*[62] and *McFarlane*[63] appear to have reached the conclusion that there is no 'right to discriminate'[64] in secular employment, but the answer is less clear when it comes to the right of religious organisations to discriminate, either in selecting employees or against service users. Especially, the anomalous position of teachers in faith schools, where discrimination is not subject to a proportionality test,[65] requires further consideration and empirical research to investigate how widely religious criteria are being used.

Vickers rejects, it is submitted correctly, a change to reasonable accommodation or a right to request accommodation along the same lines as the right to request flexible working. This was also rejected by the EHRC in its last report in this area. Given that the law has only recently had an opportunity to bed down, changing it would only add confusion, particularly given that the alternatives would themselves require much working out of their specific meaning. Furthermore, as Vickers demonstrates, whether reasonable accommodation or proportionality is used, the test only provides a basis for thinking about the complex balance of interests involved, rather than providing us with a readymade answer. Given that the concept of indirect discrimination has essentially incorporated a right to reasonable accommodation it seems unlikely that it would lead to radically different results. However, this is an ongoing debate.

As mentioned above, the book is particularly useful in outlining how a proportionality test could be used in this context and in describing its advantages, particularly its flexibility to respond to a range of circumstances. In doing so it has influenced my own work addressing proportionality's suitability in the specific context of the conflict between religious freedom and sexual orientation equality.[66] There is significant scope for further work on this principle. Whilst there is a considerable literature on proportionality within Public Law, and Discrimination Law is one of the main areas of law where proportionality is used, as I have demonstrated elsewhere,[67] there is only limited interaction between the two fields. The Public Law literature does not as a matter of course draw on the experience of Discrimination Law, even though this is a longstanding and detailed field of law, and could be used fruitfully to discuss issues such as whether the proportionality test is too uncertain and subjective, a problem which is recognised in both fields. Looking at it from the opposite perspective, the focus in discrimination

62 *Ladele v London Borough of Islington* [2009] EWCA Civ 1357; [2010] 1 WLR 955.
63 *McFarlane v Relate Avon Ltd* [2010] EWCA Civ 880; [2010] IRLR 872.
64 Sandberg, 'The Right to Discriminate' (2011) 15 *Ecclesiastical Law Journal* 157.
65 School Standards and Framework Act 1998.
66 Pearson, *Proportionality, Equality Laws and Religion* (Routledge, 2017).
67 Ibid.

law is more about the results of the proportionality enquiry or the benefits of proportionality compared to another test such as reasonable accommodation, rather than on the substantive nature of proportionality itself or its legitimacy as a method of adjudication, which have been the source of considerable academic analysis within public law theory.

This is partly due to the difference in context. There is a crucial difference in terms of the judge's role between a decision that the state has acted disproportionally and impermissibly and in a finding of disproportionality in a dispute between two private parties which is decided under the auspices of a legislative right and does not challenge the nature of the existing law. Discrimination disputes are more likely to be seen as a matter of law rather than, as may occur in Public Law, as a political dispute being illegitimately worked out through the courts. This thumbnail description of the distinctions between them may well be too stark, given that there may be a question of the institutional competence of the courts in both contexts, but this only serves to make the point that the issue is certainly worthy of further attention.

It is even unclear as to whether proportionality requires the same process of analysis in Human Rights Law as it does in Discrimination Law. In Discrimination Law there tends to be consideration of whether there is a legitimate aim and then the proportionality of the action is considered in a general way. In Human Rights Law, though, there is generally considered to be a four stage process: legitimate aim, rational connection between the aim and action taken, no less restrictive means of achieving the aim (sometimes referred to as a necessity test), and finally proportionality itself.[68] While the rational connection test is very rarely breached and where there is no rational connection then a policy will be obviously not proportionate, a consideration of alternative policies under the 'no less restrictive means' test before the final proportionality test changes at least the emphasis of the analysis and perhaps also the end result. Whilst there has been fairly significant work comparing the use of proportionality in different jurisdictions, far less has been written about how it applies between different areas of law.

Finally, Vickers is right to identify EU law as the new frontier of religious disputes, although its direct relevance to UK law may be short-lived. While the ECtHR has taken a generous approach in some employment contexts, as in *Eweida*, it has taken a very hands-off approach in cases which have a distinct cultural significance, such as in *Lautsi* and *SAS*. However, the CJEU's decision in *Achbita* and *Bougnaoui*, decided after the publication of the second edition of Vickers' book, demonstrates that hopes for a radically different approach may be unrealised. This decision is a fundamental step back for EU discrimination law which has up to this point been unafraid to challenge discrimination that was perceived as normal and culturally justified, such as pregnancy discrimination.[69]

68 *De Freitas v Permanent Secretary of Ministry of Agriculture, Fisheries, Lands and Housing* [1999] 1 AC 69; *Huang v Secretary of State for the Home Department* [2007] UKHL 11.

69 *Dekker v Stichting Vormingscentrum voor Jong Volwassenen (VJV-Centrum) Plus*, C-177/88 [1991] IRLR 27.

Vickers' most significant legacy in this work is in demonstrating the importance of considering religion and the workplace and in laying out a framework for deciding conflicts, which will remain relevant even given that new cases will always raise new issues and that the social and political context of religious and other beliefs are changing rapidly. It is interesting to think what a third edition in another eight years might look like. Perhaps there would be more similarities than between the first and second editions, even despite the loss of EU protection through Brexit, but only time will tell.

11 *A Note on the Theology of Burial*

A settled controversy

David Pocklington

The work

A Note on the Theology of Burial in relation to Some Contemporary Questions was written by the Rt Rev Christopher Hill when he was Bishop of Stafford. When considering the circumstances in which exhumation may be permitted in the case of *Re Blagdon Cemetery*,[1] the Dean of Arches requested Bishop Hill to prepare a *Note to the Court on the Theology of Burial* ('the Note'), and the work discussed here is the 'slightly expanded' version which was published in the *Ecclesiastical Law Journal* in 2004.[2] The article was written prior to Hill's translation to Guildford, but was two years into his chairmanship of the Ecclesiastical Law Society, a position he held until his retirement in 2013. In 2014, the Archbishop of Canterbury awarded Bishop Christopher with the Lambeth Doctor of Divinity in recognition of his 'long and distinguished ministry', which has focused on fostering ecumenical relations. The citation stated *inter alia*:

> Christopher's academic contribution to the field – always undertaken in the midst of heavy ministerial responsibility – has been remarkable. Together with Edward Yarnold he edited *Anglicans and Roman Catholics: the Search for Unity* (1994) and *Anglican Orders: the Documents in the Case* (1997). He has also written a large number of scholarly articles and essays on the subject of ecumenism as well as in the area of canon law.

Nevertheless, the Note does not address the issues of canon law *per se* but seeks 'to indicate some theological connection between the normal reticence of the ecclesiastical courts to agree to exhumations'.[3] Following the *Blagdon* judgment, most subsequent judicial considerations of exhumation have included an explicit or implicit reference to the Note.

1 *Re Blagdon Cemetery* [2002] Fam 299; [2002] 4 All ER 482.
2 C Hill, 'A Note on the Theology of Burial in relation to Some Contemporary Questions' (2004) 7 *Ecc LJ* 447.
3 Ibid.

The importance of the Note lies in its examination of the permanence of Christian burial and its reliance upon (non-legal) sources, primarily with reference to the Church of England; it was on this issue that Bishop Hill's Note was first sought, and based upon this the ecclesiastical courts have assessed the acceptability of exhumation under a wide range of circumstances, including the now-important issue of the re-use of graves. Whilst the courts' interpretation of *Re Blagdon Cemetery* has been expanded and finessed over the years, Bishop Hill's basic arguments regarding the permanence of Christian burial remain unchanged.

The context

An important pre-*Blagdon* analysis of the development of the law in this area is provided by Rupert Bursell's 'Digging up Exhumation',[4] in which he reviewed the development of judicial and other considerations from Gibson's Codex *Iuris Ecclesiastici Anglicani* in 1713[5] to his judgment *Re Christ Church, Alsager* in the Durham consistory court.[6] In this, he noted that:

> whilst Chancellor McClean's summary in *Re Stocks, deceased*[7] is a useful *aide memoire* . . . it seems unclear how strong the presumption against exhumation may in fact be, although it may also be thought that this might not matter so much in practice – especially as any such faculty is granted on its particular facts and should never be regarded as a precedent.

He concluded that:

> A definitive decision from the Court of Arches and [York] Provincial Court may, therefore, seem to be called for unless a consensus among chancellors can be found by other means. On the other hand, in some cases it would be quite possible to make the decision either way without infringing any legal principle.

The issue was given further consideration when in 1999 the Chancery Court of York (the Provincial Court of the Church's Northern Province), including Bursell himself with Sir John Owen (Auditor) and Chancellor TAC Coningsby QC, heard the appeal to *Re Christ Church, Alsager*.[8] In 'Exhumation Reconsidered' Chancellor Philip Petchey reviewed the Bursell article in the light of the *Alsager* appeal and two subsequent cases[9] in which the impact of Article 9 of the

4 R Bursell, 'Digging up Exhumation' (1998) *Ecc LJ* 18.
5 E Gibson, *Codex Iuris Ecclesiastici Anglicani* (London, 1713) 544.
6 *Re Christ Church, Alsager* (1997) 3 September, Durham Cons Ct, Bursell Ch (unreported).
7 *Re Stocks, deceased* (1995) 4 *Ecc LJ* 527; *The Times*, 5 September 1995. Cons Ct.
8 *Re Christ Church, Alsager* [1999] Fam 142.
9 *Re Durrington Cemetery* [2001] Fam 33 (Chichester Consistory Court); and *Re Crawley Green Road Cemetery, Luton* [2001] 2 WLR 1175.

European Convention on Human Rights (ECHR) had fallen to be considered.[10] Petchey noted that in its judgment, in addition to deciding the appeal before it, the Chancery Court formulated a test as to the circumstances in which exhumation might be appropriate, and commended a set of guidelines which it formulated, as well as providing general guidance.

The test asked: 'Is there a good and proper reason for exhumation that reason being likely to be regarded as acceptable by right thinking members of the Church at large?' This was 'severely criticized' by Petchey (according to Bursell)[11] on the ground that the court did not explain how the views of a right-thinking member of the Church might be ascertained, a criticism that was endorsed by the Court of Arches in *Blagdon*.[12] Petchey suggest that some of the guidance was questionable, and concluded:

> In the view of the writer, *Alsager* may come in time to be seen as the high water mark of the arguments against exhumation rather than setting a new and more restrictive norm.
>
> One may suspect that this is an issue which will not go away and that it is likely that in due course it will be addressed once again by the Chancery Court or Court of Arches.

As anticipated, the issue was soon addressed and on 6 October 2001 the Court of Arches (the Canterbury Provincial Court of the Church's Southern Province) considered an appeal under r6 Faculty Jurisdiction (Appeals) Rules 1998 against a decision of Chancellor Briden; in the first instance judgment on 16 February 2000, the Bath and Wells consistory court had refused to grant a faculty for the exhumation of the remains of Steven Whittle from Blagdon Cemetery, Somerset with a view to their re-interment in Stowmarket Cemetery, Suffolk.

The Arches Court comprised the Dean of Arches, the Right Worshipful Dr Sheila Cameron QC, sitting with Chancellor Christopher Clark QC and Chancellor Charles George QC. Mr Mark Hill appeared for the appellants, and Mr Philip Petchey appeared as *amicus curiae*, at the invitation of the Court. Judgment was handed down on 16 April 2002. The Arches Court noted that it was necessary '[to consider] a number of different matters, both as to the principles in relation to faculties for exhumation and reburial and the practical application of those principles'.[13] Importantly, the Arches Court stated:

> We agree with [the York Chancery] Court that exhumation cases do not 'involve a question of doctrine, ritual or ceremonial' . . . However, we

10 P Petchey, "Exhumation Reconsidered" (2001) *Ecc LJ* 122–134.

11 R Bursell, 'Aspects of Exhumation and Burial' (2017) 19 *Ecc LJ* 169.

12 However, in *Re Sam Tai Chan* [2016]ECC Dur 2, [22] Bursell observed that the civil courts have had no difficulties in applying such a notion.

13 *Re Blagdon Cemetery* [2002] Fam 299; [2002] 4 All ER 482, [9].

> consider that a summary of the theological principles can be usefully stated here so as to promote a better understanding of the theological reason for the approach taken by the Consistory Courts to applications for exhumation from consecrated land.[14]

The Court considered exhumation in relation to: the general principles concerning exhumation,[15] the theology of burial,[16] and the general approach of the courts to exhumation.[17] The themes developed by Bishop Hill (such as the Church's approach to the permanence of Christian burial) run throughout the judgment; more specifically, the Court noted:

> We have been greatly assisted by a paper on the Theology of Burial from the Right Reverend Christopher Hill, Bishop of Stafford. He drew attention to the fact that 'The funeral itself articulates very clearly that its purpose is to remember before God the departed; to give thanks for their life; to commend them to God the merciful redeemer and judge; to commit their body to burial/cremation and finally to comfort one another'.[18]

This went on to explain more generally that:

> The permanent burial of the physical body/the burial of cremated remains should be seen as a symbol of our entrusting the person to God for resurrection. We are commending the person to God, saying farewell to them (for their 'journey'), entrusting them in peace for their ultimate destination, with us, the heavenly Jerusalem. This commending, entrusting, resting in peace does not sit easily with 'portable remains', which suggests the opposite: reclaiming, possession, and restlessness; a holding on to the 'symbol' of a human life rather than a giving back to God.

In *Re Astwood Cemetery,* Dr Charles Mynors, Chancellor of Gloucester observed 'It is perhaps significant that the court quoted the first of those two paragraphs, but without the first two sentences [i.e. 'The biblical understanding of resurrection as expressed in 1 Corinthians 15 allows for real continuity and real discontinuity. There must be reverence and respect for human remains, but they are not ultimately what matters']'.[19]

14 Ibid, [22]
15 Ibid, [18]–[22].
16 Ibid, [23]–[27].
17 Ibid, [28]–[35].
18 Ibid, [23]
19 *Re Astwood Cemetery* [2014] Charles Mynors Ch (Worcester), [40].

The Court's application of the Note is summarised in the next paragraph of the judgment, which comments:

> In the light of his restatement of these theological principles the Bishop expressed the opinion that a reluctance by the Consistory Court to grant faculties for exhumation is well grounded in Christian theology.[20]

With regard to the issue of doctrine, the *Note* observes:

> In the original *Alsager* case the chancellor, on the basis of evidence from the archdeacon, had certified that the case did not involve a question of doctrine in accordance with section 10(3) of the Ecclesiastical Jurisdiction Measure 1963. The Chancery Court of York then commented that the archdeacon's evidence emphasised the pastoral aspect of the burial service and the importance of the committal of remains as underscoring the 'protective jurisdiction' of the ecclesiastical courts. This note is an attempt to indicate some theological connection between the normal reticence of the ecclesiastical courts to agree to exhumations, while allowing proper pastoral exceptions in individual cases.[21]

The sources employed by Bishop Hill are listed as: the worship of the Church; the Order for the Burial of the Dead in *The Book of Common Prayer*, and the more flexible provision found in *Common Worship: Pastoral Services.*[22] Bishop Hill considers that the most significant aspect of the 1662 *Book of Common Prayer* is the lesson from 1 Corinthians 15 at the interment, and in particular St Paul's analogy of the sowing of seed with the burial of the dead in verses 35 to 50. He observed:

> Two things are being said explicitly here. First, what is sown is not the body which is to be: 'it is sown a physical body, it is raised a spiritual body', i.e. 'if there is a physical body there is also a spiritual body' (v 44); the analogy is here the horticultural fact of the difference between seed and plant. Secondly, it is necessary to entrust to God the mortal remains of a human person on the analogy of trusting God to give growth and life to the 'dead' seed sown in the ground. Seeds need planting to grow.

20 Ibid, [24].

21 Hill, 'A Note on the Theology of Burial in relation to Some Contemporary Questions' (2004) 7 *Ecc LJ* 447.

22 He notes 'while the *Book of Common Prayer* remains a doctrinal standard alongside the *Articles of Religion* and the *Ordinal,* the material in *Pastoral Services* has hybrid authority, parts being authorised by the General Synod; other parts, not being alternatives to the *Book of Common Prayer* but additional, being commended by the House of Bishops for approval by the Ordinary pursuant to Canon B4'.

However, he regards *Common Worship* as:

> [giving] a considerably richer theology of death and dying than either the *Book of Common Prayer* or the superseded Alternative Service Book (1980), though the Pauline theology of the resurrection of the body remains central and an edited version of 1 Corinthians 15 is duly provided alongside other Scripture readings.

The theme of 'journey' is prominent in *Common Worship* in *Ministry at the Time of Death.* The Commendation of the dying, particularly, suggests the ancient (Christian and pagan) metaphor of journey, using traditional Western Christian prayers; this is followed by prayers of commendation suggesting the Pauline doctrine that 'nothing can separate us from the love of God in Christ and that the dying person is now in God's merciful arms, enfolded in mercy, rest and peace'; in the *Funeral Service* the use of the *Nunc Dimittis* is encouraged, which is suggestive of departing in peace; a translation of the Russian *Kontakion* is permitted, also suggestive of rest and that 'all of us go down to the dust'.

The *Note* then addresses the Church's services and prayers leading up to the burial (or cremation): reception of the coffin; the optional vigil service; the funeral service; the Commendation and Farewell; and the Committal. It states:

> The extensive *Common Worship* provision articulates very clearly that our purpose is to remember before God the departed; to give thanks for their life; to commend them to God the merciful redeemer and judge; to commit their body to burial/cremation and finally to comfort one another. The prayers of Commendation and Farewell speak of 'entrusting' the departed to God (and offer a wide variety of alternative prayers, including those already referred to at the time of death speaking of a journey). The Committal speaks of entrusting the departed to God's mercy and committing their body to the ground or for cremation in preparation for burial in the familiar words of the *Book of Common Prayer*. It speaks expectantly of resurrection and transformation. In summary, *Common Worship* restores to Anglican worship in relation to the burial of a body or cremated remains the ancient Christian metaphors of 'journey' and 'resting' to the expectation and hope of transformation and resurrection already found in the *Book of Common Prayer*.[23]

It then gives a brief review of burial practices, beginning with the early days of the Christian Church when Christian tombs were clustered round each other in otherwise pagan cemeteries; Christians wished to be buried proximately to both the saints (such as St Peter and other Christian martyrs in Rome) and a praying community; and when churches came to be built 'it was

23 Ibid, 449.

natural that Christians were buried close to them if possible'. Significantly, 'it was not thought wrong to remove Christian remains for safety' in times of unrest and social upheaval and migration; it was done for the 'relics' of the saints, although Hill adds: 'However, in such circumstances the relation between mortal remains and the living community continued: the whole community fled taking their "saints" with them.' The present-day relevance of these considerations to exhumation and the desire for 'portable' remains is expounded in the paragraph:

> The biblical understanding of resurrection as expressed in 1 Corinthians 15 allows for real continuity and real discontinuity. There must be reverence and respect for human remains, but they are not ultimately what matters. The permanent burial of the physical body/the burial of cremated remains should be seen as symbolic of our entrusting the person to God for resurrection. We are commending the person to God, saying farewell to them (for their 'journey'), entrusting them in peace for their ultimate destination, with us, in the heavenly Jerusalem. This commending, entrusting, resting in peace does not sit easily with 'portable remains', which suggests the opposite: reclaiming, possession, and restlessness; a holding on to the 'symbol' of a human life, rather than a giving back to God. The risen Lord in St John's Gospel says enigmatically to Mary Magdalene: 'Do not hold/cling to me' (John 20 vl7). In general, therefore, the reluctance to agree to faculties for exhumation is well grounded in Christian theology and eschatology. It is also right generally from the point of view of the mourner, who must learn to let go for their psychological and spiritual health.[24]

Bishop Hill notes that there are exceptions to the norm and gives a number of examples, including occasions in which there is a separation between the mortal remains of a person and their worshipping (or other) community. The examples given are: 'a burial ground somewhere on the East coast, where church and community have moved inland because of erosion by the sea';[25] and 'where the case of a deceased member of a religious community, when the residence of that community Moves', such as *Re Talbot*[26] which was noted by Bursell and more fully by Petchey. The principle here was 'the dead are buried close to the place of worship of the living community – part of our theology of the interrelation of the living and departed in Christian (especially Eucharistic) worship'.[27]

24 Ibid, 450.
25 Presumably this is an actual case, but there no indication of the location is given in the *Note.*
26 *Re Talbot* [1901] P 1, London Cons Ct.
27 A similar situation was reviewed by the Appeal Court in *Rudewicz, R (on the application of) v Secretary of State for Justice & Ors* [2012] EWCA Civ 499. Although the 'general presumption of permanence' of interment, as enunciated in *Re Blagdon Cemetery* was cited, the (secular) court held that 'the approach of [the Church of England's] consistory courts to

Considerations of the application of this principle in relation to *Blagdon* and in subsequent consistory court judgment are summarised, but not expanded, in the Note, which states:

> This principle established the *norm* of permanent burial but allows rare exceptions to the norm. These would include the legitimate desire for members of a family to be buried in proximity. The principle also has bearing in cases of mistake where a member of one faith community is accidentally buried in the burial ground of another.
>
> In cases of Christian burial according to Anglican rites, prescinding from cases where there has been a mistake as to the faith of the deceased or other exceptional circumstances, I would argue that the intention of the rite is to say 'farewell' to the deceased for their 'journey'; to commend them to the mercy and love of God in Christ to await the transformation of resurrection.
>
> Exhumation for sentiment, convenience, curiosity, or to 'hang on' to the remains of life, would deny this Christian intention.[28]

The Worshipful Mark Hill QC observed that the second of the above paragraphs was not reproduced in *Blagdon*.[29] The Note was written when the reuse of graves was under consideration by the Home Office and its consultation *Burial Law and Policy in the 21st Century* was in progress;[30] contemporary with this, the Legal Advisory Commission of the Church of England had completed a (legal) opinion on further burials in existing graves and in land already used for burials. With regard to this 'rather different question' of the disturbance for the deepening or reuse of graves, 'the Christian principle of the living and departed being in one communion and family would not seem to discourage the re-use of graves'.[31]

Examples (but not analysis) in support of this view include: the practice of continuous burial in churchyards 'until the eighteenth and nineteenth centuries, when monumental masons began to attempt the immortality of memorials'; family vaults (implicit); where burial space has been at a premium, such as the Isola di San Michele, Venice, where individual remains have been kept in individual tombs for only a limited time before reverent removal to a communal tomb; and

---

faculties for exhumation did not apply to the grant by the Secretary of State of licences under section 25 Burial Act 1857'.

28 Hill, 'A Note on the Theology of Burial in relation to Some Contemporary Questions' (2004) 7 *Ecc LJ* 447, 451. Emphasis in original.

29 *Re All Saints Beckley* [2006] Chichester Const Ct, Mark Hill Ch, [9].

30 Home Office, *Burial Law and Policy in the 21st Century: the Need for a Sensitive and Sustainable Approach*, January 2004. Available at:http://webarchive.nationalarchives.gov.uk/+/http:/www.dca.gov.uk/consult/buriallaw/buriallaw_cp.pdf, accessed 27 August 2018. This government response to the consultation was not available when the *Note* was published.

31 Hill, 'A Note on the Theology of Burial in relation to Some Contemporary Questions' (2004) 7 *Ecc LJ* 447, 451.

the 'many examples of the re-use of sarcophagi in Christian history'. From these, Bishop Hill concludes:

> While there are many questions of respect and reverence to consider in the necessary but limited disturbance involved in the deepening or re-use of graves, I can see no theological principle against the practice if done with proper care, respect and after due time.

The significance

The immediate importance of the Note is its restatement of the principle of Christian burial to the Court of Arches, and the Court's application in its consideration of the appeal of *Re Blagdon Cemetery.* Whilst the principle of the permanence of Christian burial was acknowledged in earlier considerations by the courts, it is clear from Bursell's comments in 'Digging up Exhumation' that a definitive decision on exhumation was required from the Court of Arches and Provincial Court.[32] Furthermore, the Court of Arches specifically requested Bishop Hill to provide a Note on this aspect of its considerations, rather than relying upon earlier case law. As indicated by its title, the content of the Note is primarily concerned with the theology of burial and the associated norm of permanence of Christian burial; the latter is clearly pertinent to exhumation, references to which feature strongly in the Note. Its analysis is based upon non-legal sources, and although these are primarily from within the Church of England, there is a strong commonality with other Christian churches.

Although some practical issues were addressed in the Note, the application of the principle of permanence was developed in *Re Blagdon*; the Arches Court reviewed the various factors considered by the Chancery Court of York in *Alsager* that can arise in connection with a petition for a faculty for exhumation; many of which had arisen in the instant case and the Arches Court 'had the benefit of argument upon them'. A total of six "Relevant Factors" were identified:

(i) Medical reasons which precluded the petitioner (and other relatives) from visiting the grave of the deceased.
(ii) Lapse of time between the interment and the petition for exhumation
(iii) Mistakes, a broad category encompassing those of the petitioner/relatives of the deceased, errors by funeral directors and other professionals.
(iv) Local Support.
(v) Precedent.
(vi) Creation of a family grave.[33]

The Arches Court judgment differed from that of the Provincial Court in relation to the nature of the test (specifically the wording), the emphasis placed

32 Bursell, 'Digging up Exhumation' (1998) *Ecc LJ* 18–33.
33 *Re Blagdon Cemetery* [2002] Fam 299 [36] (i)–(vi)

on local support, and subsequently, issues of precedent were raised. The Court concluded:

> there is much to be said for reverting to the straightforward principle that a faculty for exhumation will only be exceptionally granted. Exceptional means 'forming an exception',[34] and guidelines can assist in identifying various categories of exception. Whether the facts in a particular case warrant a finding that the case is to be treated as an exception is for the Chancellor to determine on the balance of probabilities.[35]

With regard to the case under consideration, the Arches Court concluded that there were a number of 'special factors' specific to the case which made it an exception to the norm of permanence.[36] In *Re Dunchurch St Peter*[37] Chancellor Stephen Eyre explained that the application of the approach in *Re Blagdon* to a particular case was essentially a two-stage process, and at each stage the consistory court must have regard to 'the straightforward principle that a faculty for exhumation will only be exceptionally granted':

> First, the consistory court must consider whether the matters raised are capable in law of amounting to special circumstances [and in] doing so the consistory court must take account of the guidance of the Court of Arches in identifying certain matters which can and others which cannot of themselves amount to such circumstances . . .
>
> However, the mere presence of a factor which is capable of being a special circumstance for these purposes does not necessarily mean that exhumations should be ordered in any particular case. The Court has a discretion and the second stage of the process requires the Court to consider whether exhumation is justified in the light of all the circumstances of the particular case and in the context of the presumption in favour of the permanence of interment.[38]

When the factors relied upon are included in the categories considered by the Court of Arches in *Re Blagdon Cemetery* 'that will often be a relatively straightforward exercise'. However, it has been observed that the exercise is not necessarily straightforward, and the courts have stated:

> When addressing a factor other than those considered there the Consistory Court has to assess it in the light of the approach laid down therein.

34 As defined in the Concise Oxford Dictionary.
35 Ibid, [33].
36 *Re Blagdon Cemetery* [2002] Fam 299 [37].
37 *Re Dunchurch, St Peter* (2014) 16 Ecc LJ 3 126, 12–13.
38 [13]–[14].

> It is . . . important to bear in mind, that the factors identified by the Court of Arches are not determinative, nor are they of necessity exclusive. They are guidelines rather than tramlines as to how the Court should exercise its discretion.[39]

Analysis of consistory court judgments reported by the Ecclesiastical Law Association for 2016 indicates that about a quarter are concerned with exhumation.[40] In the majority of these, the creation of family graves is the major issue; other cases involve problems of access, unlawful burial and errors in burial. A similar percentage of the cases reported for 2015 relate to exhumation, although these also include a number of different issues such as problems of access and errors in burial.[41] In all cases in the Southern Province and most of those in the Northern Province, the courts assessed whether the circumstances warranted an exception to the norm of permanence of burial, according to the criteria laid down in *Re Blagdon* with its reliance upon Hill's Note.

Cases involving exhumation and the disturbance of remains which do not fit readily into the *Blagdon* categories are nevertheless taken into consideration by reference to other aspects of the Note include: *Re St Leonard Beoley* (the 'Shakespeare's skull' case), *Re St James, Gorton* (investigation of grave for evidence on 'Moors Murderers'), *Re Astwood Cemetery* (time-limited provision for storage of ashes), and *Re Fairmile Cemetery Lower Assendon* (illegal practice of 'coffin sliding').[42]

In addition to Church of England churchyards, both the Note and *Re Blagdon* are applicable to any burial place subject to the jurisdiction of the church's consistory courts; this includes consecrated areas within municipal cemeteries, a common source of mistakes and misunderstandings on which the consistory courts are required to decide. In addition to the unwitting burial of remains within such areas (and petitions for their subsequent exhumation), the courts also consider the movement of ashes or remains: from consecrated ground to unconsecrated ground; to the churchyard of another denomination; scattering or strewing (of ashes); or into storage pending reburial. In such circumstances, the important criteria are the potential for a seemly exhumation and the conditions under which the remains will be reinterred subsequently. Although the consistory courts' jurisdiction does not extend to the specification of the conditions

39 *Re: Tunbridge Wells Cemetery* [2016] ECC Roc 11, [13], [15].

40 D Pocklington, Law and Religion UK, 'Ecclesiastical Court Judgments 2016' (30 December 2016) *Law and Religion UK* Available at http://www.lawandreligionuk.com/2016/12/30/ecclesiastical-court-judgments-2016/, accessed 27 August 2018.

41 David Pocklington, Law and Religion UK, 'Ecclesiastical Court Judgments 2015' (21 December 2015) *Law and Religion UK* Available at http://www.lawandreligionuk.com/2015/12/21/consistory-court-judgments-2015/, accessed 27 August 2018.

42 *Re St Leonard Beoley* [2015] Worcester Const Ct, Mynors Ch; *Re St James, Gorton* [2015] Manchester Const Ct, Tattersall Ch; *Re Astwood Cemetery* [2014] Worcester Const Ct, Mynors Ch; and *Re Fairmile Cemetery Lower Assendon* [2017] ECC Oxf 2.

for re-interment, its *vires* are such that it may decline a petition for exhumation where an equivalent level of care is afforded to the remains *post*-exhumation. In *Re St Swithun Cheswardine*,[43] Chancellor Stephen Eyre explained:

> The Court is concerned not just with the permanence of interment but also with the fact that remains which have been interred in consecrated land have been committed to the protection of the Church. Exhumation can only be permitted even in exceptional circumstances if the Court can be satisfied that appropriate arrangements are in place for the continuing protection of the remains.

In addressing what might be considered as 'appropriate arrangement', the Court in *Re Blagdon* noted that statutory control of unconsecrated ground had been introduced through the licensing system under section 25 of the Burial Act 1857. Local authorities are subject to the Local Authorities Cemeteries Order 1977[44] and:

> it can generally be assumed that local authorities carry out their legal responsibilities for care and maintenance of their cemeteries . . . it is reasonable for the Consistory Court to conclude (certainly in the absence of evidence to the contrary) that the new grave will be cared for in a seemly manner and will be protected in this sense.[45]

However:

> Re-interment in unconsecrated ground which is not in a local authority cemetery is a different matter. No general inference of the suitability for re-interment in such land can properly be drawn by the Consistory Court.[46]

Whilst exhumation from ground consecrated to the use of the Church of England engages the faculty jurisdiction whatever the faith of the person interred, in cases where Articles 8 and 9 ECHR are engaged, it is now necessary to take into

43 *Re St Swithun Cheswardine* [2015] Lichfield Const Ct, Stephen Eyre Ch, [7]–[8].
44 Local Authorities Cemeteries Order 1977, SI 1977/204.
45 *Re Blagdon Cemetery* [2002] Fam 299, [15].
46 Ibid, [16]. In the case of major infrastructure works, the enabling statutory measures often disapply the ecclesiastical and secular provisions concerning burial grounds, for example section 39(1) Channel Tunnel Rail Link Act 1996 and sections 27, 28 and Schedule 20 High Speed Rail (London – West Midlands) Act 2017. In cases such as these, the Church of England is limited to making its views known during the Bill's passage through Parliament. However, with regard to the re-use of graves under the London Local Authorities Act 2007, whilst s74(11) disapplies the requirement for a licence from the Secretary of State under s25 Burial Act 1857, the consistory courts retain their jurisdiction through s74(9 and 10); this applies both before and after exhumation/re-use of the grave.

account the manifestation of all religious beliefs.[47] The Human Rights Act 1998 requires all UK courts and tribunals to interpret legislation so far as possible in a way compatible with the rights laid down in the ECHR. Between the majority of the Act's provisions coming into force on 2 October 2000 that of 16 April 2002 (when the judgment in *Re Blagdon* was handed down on), the application of Convention Rights was considered by the consistory courts in relation to an humanists in *Re Crawley Green Road Cemetery, Luton*[48] and in relation to orthodox Jews in *Re Durrington Cemetery.*[49] Although these judgements were cited in *Re Blagdon,*[50] the Arches Court did not take the application of the ECHR into consideration into its deliberations. However, the relevance of the Convention has since gained prominence and in his 2014 judgement *Re Putney Vale Cemetery,*[51] Chancellor Petchey considered the potential engagement of Articles 8 and 9 ECHR. Citing the post-*Blagdon* judgments *Dodsbo v Sweden*[52] and *In re St Andrew's Church*, Alwalton,[53] he said that in his opinion, 'in cases of this kind, Article 8 rights are engaged, and that the Court of Arches, if it had to consider the matter again would hold that they were'. However, he noted:

> consideration of petitions for exhumation with reference to the European Convention is potentially circular: if the Chancellor is minded to refuse permission because he has not identified exceptional circumstances he will have the basis for saying that such a decision is justified on the basis of the limitations contained in Articles 8(2) and 9(2). Further, a Chancellor might say in any particular case that he would have given permission irrespective of whether the petitioner was able to rely on Articles 8 and 9.[54]

These and similar cases take into consideration the theology (or absence of belief) of non-Christian exhumation and reburial.[55] Nevertheless, this is still consistent with the *Note*, which stated:

> This principle established the norm of permanent burial but allows rare exceptions . . . The principle also has bearing in cases of mistake where a

47 D Pocklington, 'Permanence of Christian burial revisited – I' (22 March 2016) *Law and Religion UK* Available at http://www.lawandreligionuk.com/2016/03/22/permanence-of-christian-burial-revisited-i/, accessed 28 August 2018.

48 *Re Crawley Green Road Cemetery, Luton* [2001] 2 WLR 1175.

49 Ibid.

50 *Re Blagdon Cemetery* [2002] Fam 299.

51 *Re Putney Vale Cemetery* [2014] Southwark Cons Ct, Philip Petchey Ch.

52 *Dodsbo v Sweden* [2006] ECHR 38

53 *In re St Andrew's Church, Alwalton* [2012] PTSR 479.

54 [17].

55 *Re Putney Vale Cemetery* [2014] Southwark Cons Ct, Philip Petchey Ch [Buddhist]; *Re Putney Vale Cemetery* [2015] Southwark Cons Ct, Philip Petchey Ch [same family as 2014 case but different exhumation sought]; *Re Quoc Tru Tran Deceased* [2016] ECC Man 2 [Buddhist]; *Re Woolwich Cemetery* [2016] ECC Swk 2 [non-Christian, but faith not specified].

member of one faith community is accidentally buried in the burial ground of another.[56]

However, this does not imply that the courts are free to adopt a 'pick and mix' approach when considering the equivalent theology of other faiths; the petitioner must satisfy the court on both the justification for the exhumation and the conditions under which the remains would be re-interred. Consistory court petitions relating to equivalent (i.e. Roman Catholic) beliefs have been refused, as in *Re St Peter ad Vincula*,[57] whereas those involving dissimilar beliefs (i.e. Buddhist) have been permitted, for example *Re Quoc Tru Tran, deceased*.[58] Likewise, commenting on *R (Rudewicz) v Secretary of State for Justice*,[59] Mark Hill QC noted:

> the theology of burial is irrelevant to the exercise of a secular discretion, even if it could be extrapolated from the law of the Church of England to the praxis of a Roman Catholic order.[60]

The issue of precedent in relation to the relative binding nature of the *Alsager* and *Blagdon* rulings was given extensive consideration by Chancellor Bursell in his 2016 judgment *Re Sam Tai Chan*.[61] These comments were expanded further in a 2017 article in the *Ecclesiastical Law Journal*.[62] Chancellor Bursell suggested that his intervention might prove 'inconvenient',[63] but that the exhumation case raised 'the question . . . as to how rules of precedent apply within the two provinces'.[64] In his assessment of the potential for the disturbance of 'the tranquil operation of the post-*Blagdon* faculty jurisdiction', commentator Philip Jones argued that Bursell's assessment of the binding nature of *Alsager* was mistaken; he observed:

> [The judgment in *Alsager*] makes clear that guidance from the provincial court is: (1) not 'binding' in the way that precedent is; and (2) meant to assist all ecclesiastical courts, not just the courts in its own province.[65]

56 Hill, 'A Note on the theology of burial in relation to some contemporary questions' (2004) 7 *Ecc LJ* 447, 451. Exhumation and re-interment in the burial ground of a different Christian community has been permitted in in *Re Sam Tai Chan* [2016] ECC Dur 2 and in *Re Holy Cross Cemetery Wallsend* [2016] ECC New 2.
57 *Re St Peter ad Vincula* [2009] Chichester Const Ct, Mark Hill Ch.
58 *Re Quoc Tru Tran, deceased* [2016] ECC Man 2.
59 *R (Rudewicz) v Secretary of State for Justice* [2012] EWCA Civ 499.
60 M Hill, 'Grave Concerns', *Solicitors Journal*, 16 July 2013, 21.
61 *Re Sam Tai Chan* [2016] ECC Dur 2, 22, [8]–[22].
62 Bursell, 'Aspects of Exhumation and Burial' (2017) 19 *Ecc LJ* 169.
63 Ibid, 12.
64 Ibid, 8.
65 P Jones, 'Alsager v Blagdon: Binding and Guiding' (6 June 2017) *Ecclesiastical Law* Available at https://ecclesiasticallaw.wordpress.com/2017/06/06/alsager-v-blagdon-binding-and-guiding/, accessed 28 August 2018.

Jones also observed:

> *Blagdon* guidance did not engage the doctrine of judicial precedent. The guidance is just that – *guidance*. It does not 'bind' the consistory courts of either province. It merely seeks to *assist* them to avoid errors and appeals. Guidance is not binding precedent.[66]

However, these issues are likely to be resolved through the Church of England (Miscellaneous Provisions) Measure, section 7 of which will introduce a new section 14A into the Ecclesiastical Jurisdiction and Care of Churches Measure 2017; this section will provide that 'a decision of the Arches Court of Canterbury or the Chancery Court of York is to be treated by the other Court, and by the lower ecclesiastical courts in the province of the other Court, as if it were a decision which the other Court had itself taken'.[67]

In addition to these issues, Bursell's more recent article made a number of points specific to the theology of burial.[68] He suggested:

> the basic theology contained in, and reflected by, the Anglican burial services may be different from the theology surrounding a subsequent exhumation. In the *Alsager* case, no such possibility could be, or was, addressed, because to have done so would have lain outside the court's jurisdiction . . .
>
> the appeal court in *Blagdon* arguably went further than its jurisdiction allowed. Not only did the Dean of the Arches ask the then Bishop of Stafford, the Rt Revd Christopher Hill, to provide a paper on the 'Theology of burial' . . . but the court said: 'we consider that a summary of the theological principles can be usefully stated here as to promote a better understanding of the theological reason for the approach taken by the Consistory Courts to applications for exhumation from consecrated land'. Even if the appeal did not involve a question of doctrine, this seems to be a clear attempt by the Arches Court itself to decide on a matter of doctrine when the correct forum to make such pronouncements is the Court of Ecclesiastical Causes Reserved. This being so, its consideration by the Arches Court was *ultra vires*.

In addition to the issue of the *vires* of the Arches Court and the assertion of possible differences between the theology of burial and that of exhumation, Bursell's article made some pertinent comments on the nature of Bishop Hill's *Note* to the Court:

> By reason of the fact that the bishop was only asked by the Dean of the Arches to produce a paper on the theological aspects of burial, he was not

66 P Jones, 'Unprecedented Confusion: A Tribute to Chancellor Bursell' (12 September 2016) *Ecclesiastical Law* Available at https://ecclesiasticallaw.wordpress.com/2016/09/12/unprecedented-confusion-a-tribute-to-chancellor-bursell/, accessed 28 August 2018.

67 At the time of writing, a Report of the Revision Committee recommending the Measure had been circulated to General Synod for consideration in February 2018.

68 Bursell, 'Aspects of Exhumation and Burial' (2017) 19 *Ecc LJ* 169, 189.

> a witness before the court and he was therefore not cross-examined on its contents. No doubt, if either counsel had wished to challenge the bishop's conclusions, the bishop would have been made a witness of the court but the appellant clearly had no interest in challenging those conclusions and it was unlikely that the *amicus curiae* [i.e. Chancellor Philip Petchey] would do so in the circumstances.

In the event, both counsel would have had the opportunity to challenge Bishop Hill's conclusions, but neither did. Bursell also commented: 'in its judgment the Arches Court, having quoted only two passages from that paper, summarised the bishop's opinion (apparently with approval) "that a reluctance by the Consistory Court to grant faculties for exhumation is well grounded in Christian theology".' Yet, Bursell pointed out that the Note represents a 'relaxed attitude to exhumation' and is therefore likely to be compatible with Roman Catholic doctrine. This being so, the summary of the bishop's paper seems unlikely to reflect 'Christian theology' as a whole.

On the question of whether *Blagdon* was concerned with doctrine and reference should have been made to the Court of Ecclesiastical Causes Reserved, Charles Mynors makes a useful observation on the distinction between theology and doctrine.[69] He notes that in *Blagdon*, after holding that exhumation cases do not involve a question of doctrine, the court 'then went on to state that it had been greatly assisted by a paper on the theology of burial'. Likewise 'a considerable proportion of [the Arches Court's] decision in *Duffield, St Alkmund*[70] was taken up with careful consideration of differing views as to the theological significance of chancel screens', from which he observes:

> So doctrine would appear not to be the same as theology; although the dictionary definition of the former, so far as relevant is 'the belief or set of beliefs held and taught by a church', whereas the latter is 'the study of the nature of God and religious belief/religious beliefs and theory when systematically developed'.

The legacy

The legacy of Bishop Hill's Note is of relevance to two areas: its continued use in the ecclesiastical courts in cases where the permanence of Christian burial is at issue and in relation to the decreasing availability of burial space in England, and requirement for the courts to consider exhumation in this context. With regard to the former, the judgment in *Re Blagdon* was handed down on 16 April 2002 and since then, together with Bishop Hill's Note to the court, these have formed the primary reference in cases relating to exhumation and reburial. Despite recent

69 C Mynors, *Changing Churches* (Bloomsbury, 2016) 8.2.2.
70 *Re St Alkmund, Duffield*, [2013] Fam 158.

criticism of the *Blagdon* judgment and its use of the Note,[71] the guidelines in *Blagdon* have been used in both Provinces, with relatively few exceptions.

In addition to his own judgment in *Re Sam Tai Chan*, Bursell's article cites that of the Sheffield Chancellor, HH Sarah Singleton QC, in *In the matter of David Bell deceased*;[72] other Chancellors in the Northern Province apply the guidelines in *Re Blagdon*; not all refer to the criteria laid down in *Re Alsager*. On 16 January 2018, in *In the Matter of David Ernest Newton*,[73] HH Judge Sarah Singleton QC cited Chancellor Bursell's 2016 judgment, and stated:

> [2.2] . . . In the Consistory Courts, depending on the nature or location of a dispute there are three alternative appeal courts exercising a parallel but distinct reviewing jurisdiction . . . although *Blagdon* is an important and influential decision, the binding authority for the Province of York (including the Diocese of Sheffield) remains *Re Christ Church Alsager* [1998] 3 WLR 1394.

Nevertheless, in her conclusions she addressed *both* sets of criteria and concluded:

> [3]. I have decided that this Petition should succeed. I consider that the reasons for granting it satisfy the *Blagdon* test of being exceptional and the *Alsager* test of there being a good and proper reason such that most right thinking members of the church would agree.

The proposed changes to the Ecclesiastical Jurisdiction and Care of Churches Measure 2017 will make such references to *Re Alsager* unnecessary.

A recent consideration of the permanence of Christian burial and the application of *Re Blagdon* identified three issues in need of further consideration: areas highlighted in the judgments of consistory court chancellors which were not addressed by the Court of Arches (disputed petitions, scattering of ashes); those aspects which it did not cover in sufficient detail (Articles 8 & 9 ECHR); and issues on which greater consensus between the courts is required (family graves).[74] However, these are for the courts themselves to resolve and do not require a revision of the Note on the theology of burial. Whilst Charles Mynors' observation on theology compared with doctrine is clearly not intended to be conclusive, there is a general reluctance to refer issues of doctrine, ritual or ceremonial to the Court of Ecclesiastical Causes Reserved, the court having considered

71 Bursell, 'Aspects of Exhumation and Burial' (2017) 19 *Ecc LJ* 169.

72 *In the matter of David Bell deceased (2)* (n 41)

73 *In the Matter of David Ernest Newton* [2018] ECC She 1.

74 Pocklington, 'Permanence of Christian Burial Revisited – I' (22 March 2016) *Law and Religion UK* Available at http://www.lawandreligionuk.com/2016/03/22/permanence-of-christian-burial-revisited-i/; and 'Permanence of Christian burial revisited – II' (31 March 2016) *Law and Religion UK* Available at http://www.lawandreligionuk.com/2016/03/31/permanence-of-christian-burial-revisited-ii/, visited 28 August 2018.

only two cases[75] since it was established by the Ecclesiastical Jurisdiction Measure 1963. Although a future consideration of exhumation by the church's Provincial Courts would provide an opportunity to resolve some of the shortcomings and omissions in *Re Blagdon* identified by the consistory courts, it seems unlikely that a further assessment of the theology of burial would be sought. On the second point, the Note states:

> The expansion [of the note to the Court] largely concerns matters to do with the re-use of graves, an issue currently under consideration by the Home Office in relation to cemeteries in the current government consultation paper Burial Law and Policy in the 21st Century.[76]

A year earlier, the eighth report of the Select Committee on Environment, Transport and Regional Affairs, published in 2001, had argued for legislation to enable reuse on the grounds of the availability of burial space and the long-term financial viability of cemeteries.[77] Although successive administrations have done little to address these issues on a national scale, in recent years schemes have been introduced for the development of burial grounds, involving both the consecrated parts of municipal cemeteries, *Re Camberwell Old and New Cemeteries*,[78] and churchyards such as *Re St Peter Terwick*.[79]

In conclusion, in addition to the courts' on-going concerns with individuals' exhumation from relatively recent interments, Bishop Hill's Note is of relevance to the strategic development of burial grounds through the reuse of old graves. The Note's conclusion is still of relevance:

> Popular sentiment may often be antipathetic to such re-use [of old graves]. But theology and law offer no insuperable obstacles and a theology of the good stewardship of land may demand it in the future.[80]

75 *St Michael and All Angels, Great Torrington* (1985) Fam 81 and *St Stephen's Walbrook* (1987) 2 All ER 578.

76 Hill, 'A Note on the theology of burial in relation to some contemporary questions' (2004) 7 *Ecc LJ* 447.

77 House of Commons Environment, Transport and Regional Affairs Select Committee, Cemeteries, 2 April 2001, HC 91 2000–01, 127.

78 *Re Camberwell Old and New Cemeteries* [2017] ECC Swk 2.

79 *Re St Peter Terwick* [2017] ECC Chi 2.

80 Hill, 'A Note on the theology of burial in relation to some contemporary questions' (2004) 7 *Ecc LJ* 447, 451.

12 *Roman Canon Law in the Church of England*

Maitland's legacy on the study of religious law

Russell Sandberg

The work

Frederic William Maitland is usually viewed as the founder of the study of English legal history. As Milsom pointed out, Maitland's work remains 'a still living authority' providing 'the foundation of all we know about the history of common law'.[1] Historians of the common law still begin their study through the eyes of Maitland: 'Their questions still take the form: was Maitland right?' This chapter will argue that this is as true of the history of ecclesiastical law as it is of the common law. Moreover, it will contend that Maitland's work can be seen as the forerunner of Law and Religion scholarship. Maitland not only analysed the ecclesiastical law of the Church of England in the same way as he analysed the common law, but also explored the interplay between religiously-imposed and state-imposed laws. Maitland's work, therefore, deserves to be reclaimed and understood a leading work in Law and Religion studies. His work is authoritative and agenda-setting in terms of its subject matter and also inspirational, showing the importance of studying religious laws legally and demonstrating the importance of a historical approach.

Much has been written about the life and work of Frederic William Maitland.[2] His supposedly co-authored work on *The History of English Law* and his posthumously published lectures on constitutional history, the forms of action and equity are amongst the most important scholarly works ever published on the

1 SFC Milsom, 'Introduction' in F Pollock and FW Maitland, *The History of English Law* (2nd edn, Vol. 1, Cambridge University Press, 1968) xxiii, ixxi, xxiv.

2 See, e.g., HE Bell, *Maitland: A Critical Examination and Assessment* (Harvard University Press, 1965); GR Elton, *FW Maitland* (Weidenfeld and Nicolson, 1985); JGH Hudson, *FW Maitland and the Englishness of English Law* (Selden Society 2007); HAL Fisher, *Frederick William Maitland Downing Professor of the Laws of England: A Biographical Sketch* (Cambridge University Press, 1910) 2; CHS Fifoot, *Frederic William Maitland: A Life* (Harvard University Press 1971); M Reynell, 'Frederic William Maitland' [1951] 6 *Cambridge Law Journal* 67; RL Schuyler, 'The Historical Spirit Incarnate: Frederic William Maitland' (1952) 57 *American Historical Review* 303; M and JT Shotwell, 'Frederic William Maitland' (1907) 22 *Political Science Quarterly* 282; and AL Smith, *Frederick William Maitland Two Lectures and a Bibliography* (Clarendon Press, 1908).

history of English law.[3] However, less attention has been afforded to his collection of essays published as *Roman Canon Law in the Church of England*.[4] These essays can be regarded as a spin-off from *The History of English Law*. As Maitland explained in the preface:

> When, in co-operation with Sir Fredrick Pollock, I was at work upon certain chapters in a History of English Law, and, in particular a chapter on marriage, I found that, on pain of leaving the book shamefully incomplete, I was compelled to make an inclusion into a region that was unfamiliar to me, namely that of ecclesiastical jurisprudence.[5]

The essays published in *Roman Canon Law in the Church of England* show Maitland at the height of his powers. Unlike *The History of English Law*, Maitland is not confined here by the need to provide a comprehensive historical narrative. The wit and argumentation skills found in his posthumously published lectures are manifested here in a more polished form. *Roman Canon Law in the Church of England* was not the only place where Maitland paid attention to religious matters. In *The History of English Law* and his lectures on constitutional history, Maitland sketched the relationship between Church and State in medieval England and the penultimate section of his lectures was dedicated to 'The Church'.[6] However, it is in *Roman Canon Law in the Church of England* that Maitland made a stimulating and significant contribution to our understanding of the historical interrelations between secular and religious governance. The six essays all stand alone, but collectively they provide an argument that debunked conventional assumptions about the status of Papal law prior to the Reformation; an argument which has been simplistically labelled the 'Stubbs-Maitland debate'.

The Stubbs-Maitland debate concerns the status of catholic canon law prior to the Reformation. The argument attributed to William Stubbs, the Bishop of Oxford and historian, was that the papal law of Rome, though of great authority in the medieval period, was not binding upon the English Church, and that the Courts Christian applied the native law even where it was in conflict with the papal law. The argument attributed to Maitland was that the ecclesiastical courts accepted and applied Roman canon law as 'binding statute law', only refusing

3 Pollock and Maitland, *The History of English Law* (2nd edn, Cambridge University Press, 1968 [1898]); FW Maitland, *The Constitutional History of England* (Cambridge University Press, 1941 [1908]); FW Maitland, *The Forms of Action at Common Law* (Cambridge University Press, 1965 [1909]); FW Maitland, *Equity: A Course of Lectures* (Cambridge University Press, 1969 [1909]). See also, the often overlooked, FW Maitland and FC Montague, *A Sketch of English Legal History* (GP Putman's Sons, 1915).

4 FW Maitland, *Roman Canon Law in the Church of England* (Methuen & Co, 1898). This was not the only collection of his essays published. See also, for instance, FW Maitland, *Doomsday and Beyond* (Fontana, 1960 [1897]).

5 Maitland, *Roman Canon Law in the Church of England* (Methuen & Co, 1898) v.

6 Pollock and Maitland, *The History of English Law*; Maitland, *The Constitutional History of England*, 506–526.

to follow it in situations where royal law forced ecclesiastical practice to depart from canon law. As Smith has noted, the genius of Maitland was 'to treat this one controversial point . . . as the thread on which to build up a review of relations of Church and State and Papacy'.[7]

The context

The 'Stubbs-Maitland debate' label is somewhat misleading given that the name of Maitland's apparent adversary, Stubbs, appears only twice in the index of *Roman Canon Law in the Church of England*. Maitland spends much longer discussing the work of Lyndwood.[8] As Maitland noted in his preface, the first three essays 'state the reasons' that convinced him that the Catholic Canon law had 'an authority over the doings of the English Ecclesiastical Courts such as it is not commonly supposed to have wielded'.[9] They provide detailed accounts of particular issues.[10] And as Maitland noted in the preface, 'the other three [essays] deal with some minor but cognate matters'.[11] Yet, taken as a whole, the collection becomes greater than the sum of its parts. It provides a detailed rebuttal of the conventional view that downplayed the importance of the Papal law.

Despite being rarely named in the text, Stubbs is the elephant in the room. As Cameron has noted, Stubbs' was the orthodox view that Maitland's work questioned: 'When Maitland began to work on the subject of canon law in England, Bishop Stubbs, having both lectured on it at Oxford and compiled a memorandum for the Royal Commission on Ecclesiastical Courts, was the only authority in the field'.[12] In one of his two mentions of Stubbs, Maitland remarks that Stubbs was the author of the 'Historical Appendix' added to the 1883 Report of the Ecclesiastical Courts Commission, noting that he need not 'say that I regard

7 Smith, *Frederick William Maitland Two Lectures and a Bibliography*, 48–49.

8 Cam noted Maitland's study of Lyndwood's *Provinciale* during 'the summer of 1895, while working on a course of lectures on Canon Law for law students', was the catalyst for his interest in the issue: H Cam, *Law-Finders and Law Makers in Medieval England: Collected Studies in Legal and Constitutional History* (Barnes and Noble, 1963) 224.

9 Maitland, *Roman Canon Law in the Church of England*, v.

10 The first essay, 'William Lyndwood', set out Maitland's argument by detailed discussion of the *Provinciale* and other sources. The second, 'Church, State and Decretals', explored the space between the lay and spiritual jurisdictions. Of the third, 'William of Drogheda and the Universal Ordinary', Elton wrote that this 'hammered down the coffin lid on the false doctrine by demonstrating that William Drogheda, a leading English canonist of the early fourteenth century, totally accepted the "Hildebrandine" view of the Church according to which it was single empire ruled by the pope and not a federation of practically independent local Churches': GR Elton, *FW Maitland*, 72.

11 Some being more minor than others. Bell noted that 'Execrabilis in the Common Pleas' was 'little more than a note, and it has small importance except as an example of the kind of legal conundrum that from time to time exercised Maitland': HE Bell, *Maitland: A Critical Examination and Assessment* (Adams & Charles Black, 1965) 121.

12 JR Cameron, *Frederick Maitland and the History of English Law* (University of Oklahoma Press, 1961) 81.

that discourse with reverence and admiration'.[13] It is this Report which motivated Maitland's attack – although *Roman Canon Law in the Church of England* does not provide a close analysis or dialogue with the report. Rather, Maitland's concern is its underpinning assumptions[14] and one sentence in particular: 'But the canon law of Rome, although always regarded as of great authority in England, was not held to be binding on the courts.'[15]

As Maitland stated, the reference to 'the courts' here meant the ecclesiastical courts in the three centuries immediately prior to the Reformation.[16] He contended that, although 'the difference between "great authority" and binding force is somewhat fine', nevertheless, that sentence 'carefully worded though it be, is questionable and should be questioned'. It implied a relationship between domestic ecclesiastical courts and Rome as being based on 'respect, not of obedience', a relationship similar to the way in which English courts treat foreign law today. Roman canon law 'was not regarded as statute law by the English ecclesiastical courts; they did not conceive that it proceeded from a legislator whose commands they were bound to obey'. Maitland disagreed with this. For Maitland, this view was 'not yet beyond dispute' given that 'in all probability large proportions (to say the least) of the "canon law of Rome" were regarded by the courts Christian in this country as absolutely binding statute law'.

Maitland's important contribution was the way that he 'proceeded to positive arguments in support of his interpretation'.[17] He did not look for evidence of independence *per se*; rather he sought evidence of any 'situation where the ecclesiastical courts acted contrary to the formal canon law and where they were not constrained to do so by royal writs of prohibition or the threat of Praemunire'.[18] Maitland used Lyndwood's *Provinciale* (and other sources) not only to show the absence of native canonists following a 'national' line but to underline how doubting the Pope's legislative power or the binding force decretals was heretical. As Elton noted:

> He left no doubt at all that to those canonists the papal edicts constituted the source binding law; such provinces of the Universal Church as Canterbury and York could legislate as best by what Maitland called 'bye-laws' – local

13 Maitland, *Roman Canon Law in the Church of England*, 59.

14 Stubbs' argument had a political and religious motive. In claiming that the English ecclesiastical courts had been able to follow an independent line in the Middle Ages, Stubbs was able to argue that the Reformation was no true innovation: RH Helmholz, *Roman Canon Law in Reformation England* (Cambridge University Press, Cambridge, 1990) 4. This political/religious motive was still alive at the time of debates concerning disestablishment in Wales. A Ogle, *The Canon Law in Medieval England an Examination of William Lyndwood's 'Provinciale', in Reply to the late Professor F. W. Maitland* (John Murray, 1912) ix.

15 Report of the Ecclesiastical Courts Commission, Vol I (1883) xviii.

16 Maitland, *Roman Canon Law in the Church of England*, 2.

17 Cameron, *Frederick Maitland and the History of English Law*, 79.

18 Bell, *Maitland: A Critical Examination and Assessment*, 4–5.

> edicts which could only clarify or elaborate in detail where Rome had laid down general rule.[19]

Maitland's work also recast the issue by unpacking what was meant by the Commission's statement that catholic canon law 'was not held to be binding on the courts'.[20] Maitland wrote that there had been a tendency to confuse two propositions:

> The first is this: that in England the state did not suffer the church to appropriate considerable portions of that wide field of jurisdiction which the canonists claimed as heritage of ecclesiastical law. The second is this: the English courts Christian held themselves free to accept or reject, and did in some cases reject 'the canon law of Rome'.[21]

For Maitland, the truth of the first statement was beyond doubt: 'there are large portions of the canon law which, as a matter of fact, are not being enforced in England, because the temporal power will not suffer this enforcement'.[22] However, by contrast, Maitland found the second statement to be 'exceedingly dubious', asserting that he had looked 'in vain for any suggestion that an English judge or advocate ever called in question the statutory power of a text that was contained in any of the three papal law-books'.[23]

As Elton noted, Maitland's distinction was very helpful in that it 'cleared up an extraordinary confusion in part accepted and in part created by Stubbs', and showed that while there was 'much disputing between the king and Church', there was 'none between the Church and Rome'.[24] There seems to be some inconsistency, however, with the way in which Maitland describes the argument that he is debunking. His second proposition, that the English courts were 'free', seems much wider than the Commission's carefully worded statement that canon law was 'regarded as of great authority in England' but 'not held to be binding on the courts'. As Helmholz has warned, we need to be wary of the 'argument that the English Church considered itself "independent" of papal law during the Middle Ages', since, expressed that way, the argument is more extreme than that expressed by Stubbs and is 'anachronistic and even silly'.[25]

Helmholz's research has underscored the importance of Maitland's work by refining and questioning it. As Helmholz noted, Maitland only claimed a 'toe in the water' familiarity, since he was unable to examine sources revealing the kinds of

19 Elton, *FW Maitland*, 70–71.
20 Report of the Ecclesiastical Courts Commission, Vol I (1883) xviii.
21 Maitland, *Roman Canon Law in the Church of England*, 51.
22 Ibid, 9.
23 Ibid, 51.
24 Elton, *FW Maitland*, 71, 72.
25 Helmholz, *Roman Canon Law in Reformation England*, 5.

litigation that actually took place.[26] Looking at the primary sources in greater detail, Helmholz stressed how both Stubbs and Maitland thought in positivist terms that were not shared by medieval litigants and court personnel. For Helmholz, the relationship between the common law and Western canon law was much more fluid than either Stubbs or Maitland suggested. Canonical jurisprudence 'shaped the English practice at many points', not least in its allowance of flexibility.[27] The English Courts Christian 'tolerated a disparity between formal rule and local customary practice'.[28] Helmholz argued that the Stubbs–Maitland choice (either that Western canon law was binding statute law or that the English Church enjoyed an unfettered discretion) did not need to be made since in most cases there was no conflict between the canon and common law in relation to principle. The difference was to be found in the detail. An example of this could be found in testamentary law: Papal law required two witnesses to prove a will; the English practice permitted proof by one or two witnesses. The conflict was therefore technical; the substantive requirement that a will had to be witnessed was met under English church law. For Helmholz, there was little conflict in practice. The judges 'tacitly accepted a restriction of ecclesiastical jurisdiction based in subject matter'.[29] He found that:

> Whether the overall relationship between the common law and the spiritual courts can best be characterized in terms of conflict or of co-operation during the medieval period is not an altogether easy question. Certainly there was some of both. Maitland's generation tended towards emphasizing the conflicts; ours tends towards the co-operation.[30]

This is further underscored by the work of Donahue.[31] In his study of the records of the Consistory Court of York 1300–1399, Donahue identified three important variables, the institution, the time and the type of case. He found that the records revealed nothing about the king–Pope relationship but were informative about, first, the king–English Church relationship, and second, the English Church–Pope relationship. In respect of the king–English Church relationship, the records indicate that the Church courts were quite independent of the king. The Church courts turned to canon law, not the King's law, as authority. However, the Church courts depended on the king to support jurisdiction and sanctions. Litigants did not regard the choice of one forum as precluding the choice of the other. In respect of the English Church–Pope relationship,

26 Ibid, 5, 7; see also Elton, *FW Maitland*, 74.
27 Helmholz, *Roman Canon Law in Reformation England*, 11.
28 Ibid, 11–12
29 Ibid, 7.
30 Ibid, 20.
31 C Donahue Jr, 'Roman Canon Law in the Medieval English Church: Stubbs vs. Maitland Re-Examined After 75 Years in the Light of Some Records from the Church Courts' (1974) 72 *Michigan Law Review* 64.

Donahue found that the courts in Rome took most important cases themselves, meaning that the English Church courts exercised a filtering function. Donahue concluded that there were factors which needed to be taken into account but that overall the relationship between the English courts and Rome could be characterised as one of great deference but not of blind adherence. He endorsed what he called a 'Yes but' school, concluding that Maitland's view was to be preferred to Stubbs' but that a number of qualifications needed to be made.[32]

Generally, as Bell has noted, scholars following Maitland have found that he overstated the extent to which the royal and ecclesiastical courts were in conflict.[33] However, although subsequent work has modified some of Maitland's findings,[34] Maitland's view has been endorsed in the most part.[35] Indeed, these studies not only underline the continued importance of the subject matter identified by Maitland, but also explore the debate on his terms: Maitland has clearly set the agenda. As with Milsom's supposedly heretical comments on Maitland's account of the development of the common law,[36] recent scholarship has provided only slight modifications to Maitland's account. As Ibbetson has noted in that different context, 'Maitland was, as always, more or less right'.[37] Of *Roman Canon Law in the Church of England* in particular, Elton has commented that it is 'astonishing how well Maitland's book stood up through decades of quite intensive efforts to assail him on a front which he himself regarded as less well defended that it should have been'.[38] The immediate reaction to Maitland's revisionism was one of 'stunned amazement' and 'even Stubbs, no longer active as a historian, slightly amended some things he had said when a new edition of his lectures came out'.[39] It was suggested that 'the history of our medieval church

32 This was especially true in relation to Maitland's second essay, 'Church, State, and Decretals', where his assumption that the writs of prohibition constituted an example where the King's 'strong hand' tied the hands of the English judges has proved questionable given the absence of attempts to enforce this jurisdiction and the fact that courts had their own means by which to counter the writs.

33 Bell, *Maitland: A Critical Examination and Assessment*, 118.

34 This is particularly true of the second essay 'Church, State, and Decretals' where it now 'appears pretty conclusively that the courts Christian were much more active in this connection than Maitland realised' (Bell, *Maitland: A Critical Examination and Assessment*, 117. See also Helmholz, *Roman Canon Law in Reformation England*, 10–11.

35 Indeed, the fourth essay, 'Henry II and the Criminous Clerks' defied Maitland's expectations. Maitland wrote in a letter that 'I expect to be accursed by both parties' but actually 'its interpretation has met with overwhelming acceptance': Bell, *Maitland: A Critical Examination and Assessment*, 120–121.

36 SFC Milsom, *The Legal Framework of English Feudalism* (Cambridge University Press, 1976). On which see V Turner, 'Henry II's Aims in Reforming England's Land Law: Feudal or Royalist' in EB King and SJ Ridyard (eds), *Law in Medieval Life and Thought* (Sewanee Medieval Studies, 1990) 121.

37 D Ibbetson, 'The Challenges of Comparative Legal History' (2013) 1(1) *Comparative Legal History* 1, 2.

38 Elton, *F W Maitland*, 76

39 Ibid, 74.

would have to be rewritten in its light'.[40] As Cameron has noted, all writers on the subject since 'have either begun or assumed the general conclusions at which Maitland arrived'.[41] The fact that Maitland's account has now itself become the orthodox view is shown not only by Stubbs' revisions but also by the report of the Archbishops' Commission on Canon Law, which rejected the view of the Ecclesiastical Courts Commission, noting that: 'Maitland's point of view, for which support is abundant, whether in the text of legal treatises or in historical practice, has won general acceptance, and such opposition as it has met has been curiously ineffective'.[42]

The significance

In the preface to *Roman Canon Law in the Church of England*, Maitland modestly commented that the essays are based on 'some study, which must not be called prolonged or profound, but none the less was unprejudiced'.[43] However, it is clear that his work *was* profound. Maitland's identification of 'a not uninteresting tract of English history' has continued to attract scholarly attention and has become the starting-point on the subject.[44] As Cameron noted, Maitland's work was so foundational that 'it opened a whole new field of study'.[45] This in itself would be sufficient to designate the collection of essays as a leading work. However, the importance of Maitland's work is not reserved to its subject matter. The work is significant in demonstrating how religious laws could be subject to academic legal analysis and the importance of a historical approach to law.

Maitland's comment that his work was 'unprejudiced' was telling. As with most scholars who have written about religion, Maitland was aware that he was writing about a controversial topic. In the preface, he pointed out that he was providing a calm academic analysis:

> At a time when the perennial stream of Anglo-Roman controversy has burst its accustomed channels and invaded the daily papers, the assumption will be readily made that anyone who writes about these matters of which I have here written is an advocate of one of two churches, the English or the Roman. Therefore it may be expedient for me to say that I am a dissenter from both, and from other churches, Probably that fact will be, and I think

40 Bell, *Maitland: A Critical Examination and Assessment*, 123.

41 Cameron, *Frederick Maitland and the History of English Law*, 81.

42 *The Canon Law of the Church of England being the Report of the Archbishop's Commission on Canon Law* (The Society for Promoting Christian Knowledge, 1947) 36. That reference to opposition presumably refers to the one attempt to support the contrary view by Ogle: *The Canon Law in Medieval England an Examination of William Lyndwood's 'Provinciale' in Reply to the late Professor F. W. Maitland.*

43 Maitland, *Roman Canon Law in the Church of England*, v.

44 Ibid, vi.

45 Cameron, *Frederick Maitland and the History of English Law*, 63.

> it ought to be, of no interest to the readers of this book but I have reason to fear the repetition of a mistake.[46]

This has proved to be a much-quoted passage and has informed the simplistic depiction of Maitland as being the cold agnostic/atheist academic who debated with the Bishop and man of faith William Stubbs.[47] However, this passage says more than just that the author was not an apologist for either Church. It also underscores that the topic Maitland was looking at was not only an issue for people within the faith communities. As Donahue has noted, modern scholarship has seen an importance in the question 'beyond the polemical purposes to which its answer might be put'.[48] These questions are at the root of the literature on legal pluralism and the extent to which states should permit and protect religious difference. *Roman Canon Law in the Church of England* shows that issues concerning religious law are of legal importance. Maitland was one of the first scholars to be interested in religious law as law from an academic perspective. His great achievement was to show how matters of ecclesiastic legal history could be explored dispassionately. Maitland not only realised that the history of English law would be 'shamefully incomplete' without discussion of 'ecclesiastical jurisprudence'.[49] He also, crucially, subjected ecclesiastical law to the same level of analysis as any other form of law.

Helmholz has written that Maitland's work identified and distinguished two 'basic subjects': 'the relationship of English canonical practice to the formal canon law' and 'its relationship with English common law'.[50] As Helmholz observed, 'Maitland dealt with both in his work on the subject, and indeed they must provide principal themes for any serious study of the place of the canon law in English legal history'. These two themes also demanded different evidence to be surveyed: 'The first requires comparing practice with the texts found in what Maitland called "the papal law books". The second requires examination of specific examples of competition, conflict, and co-ordination between the two jurisdictions.' Both of these enterprises set the precedent for future Law and Religion scholarship. In the first, Maitland was subjecting Church law to the same scholarly scientific analysis as State law. This set a precedent for future scholarship on what I have referred to as 'religious law' (the internal rules, norms and rules made by religious groups).[51] In the second, Maitland was exploring the way in which

46 Ibid.

47 For a revisionist interpretation see R Sandberg, 'F. W. Maitland: Faithful Dissenter' in R H Helmholz and M Hill (eds), *Christian Jurists in English History* (Cambridge University Press, 2017) 301.

48 C Donahue, 'Roman Canon Law in the Medieval English Church: Stubbs vs. Maitland Re-Examined after 75 Years in the Light of Some Records from the Church Courts' [1974] 72 *Michigan Law Review* 647, 655.

49 Maitland, *Roman Canon Law in the Church of England*, v.

50 Helmholz, *Roman Canon Law in Reformation England*, 3.

51 Sandberg, *Law and Religion* (Cambridge University Press, 2011) chs 1 and 9.

religious jurisdictions interact with non-religious jurisdictions. Maitland's work, therefore, also sets a precedent for the study of what I have called 'religion law' (the external laws made by the State and how they interact with religious groups and individuals). As Donahue pointed out, Maitland was exploring the question whether it is 'possible for two different legal systems – canon law and common law – to operate simultaneously in the same geographic area, particularly when those two legal systems make overlapping jurisdictional claims'.[52] These questions continue to be of great interest, especially in recent years, given the focus on religious legal pluralism – or the fear of Sharia – that was reflected in and perpetuated by the 2008 lecture by the then Archbishop of Canterbury Dr Rowan Williams, leading to an abundance of literature on the topic.[53]

A claim could therefore be made that *Roman Canon Law in the Church of England* is the first work of Law and Religion scholarship. The influence of Maitland's approach can still be found today: the forensic legal analysis of Norman Doe and Mark Hill QC follows Maitland's example of subjecting the law of the Church to the same if not higher academic scrutiny as that afforded to the secular law while a whole literature on legal pluralism explores the interaction between different legal systems. Maitland's work also ensured that historical scholarship is a key aspect of Law and Religion studies. The works of Richard Helmholz and John Witte Jr, amongst others, carry on the Maitland legacy providing lucid historical accounts of ecclesiastical matters. As Cameron pointed out, Maitland 'was one of the first scholars to become interested in the history of the law for its own sake rather than as a mere adjunct to some other dominant concern'.[54]

The legacy

It is unfortunate, therefore, that the influence of Maitland's *Roman Canon Law in the Church of England* upon Law and Religion scholarship has been less than it could have been. Despite the growth of Law and Religion studies in recent years, it remains the case that little attention has been given to the study of religious laws in their own right as systems of law.[55] There are, of course, some exceptions. The study of the law of the Church of England has undergone something of a renaissance through the formation of the Ecclesiastical Law Society and the works of Doe, Hill and others, while important works on Islamic law, Jewish law and Hindu law have been published together with some work focusing upon

52 C Donahue, 'Roman Canon Law in the Medieval English Church: Stubbs vs. Maitland Re-Examined after 75 Years in the Light of Some Records from the Church Courts' [1974] 72 *Michigan Law Review* 647, 655.

53 R Williams, 'Civil and Religious Law in England – A Religious Perspective' (2008) 10 *Ecclesiastical Law Journal* 262. For an analysis see, e.g. the essays in R Sandberg (ed), *Religion and Legal Pluralism* (Ashgate, 2015).

54 Cameron, *Frederick Maitland and the History of English Law*, 62–63.

55 See further R Sandberg, 'The Reformation of Religious Law' (2017) speciale *Quaderni di Diritto e Politica Ecclesiastica* 97.

traditions within each faith. And there is a very small number of seminal works that seek to compare religious laws.[56] Yet, generally, religious law is rarely subjected to scholarly analysis as law. And as a result the importance of religious law is downplayed. As Rivers has argued: 'The idea that religions command respect on the part of secular government institutions because they consist of, or contain, autonomous systems of law is being lost in the inexorable rise of a dominant state–individual paradigm and the embrace of state regulation.'[57]

The general picture of neglect is especially unfortunate given that the establishment of the Church of England means that its law, the rules governing the established church including its doctrine and worship, are part of the law of the land enforced in Church courts which are part of the State court system.[58] Perhaps the development of Law and Religion as a distinct sub-discipline is partly to blame for this. Maitland's example shows that the study of these matters should not be regarded as a specialist matter, as shown by his preface mention that the study of marriage law is 'shamefully incomplete' without discussion of ecclesiastical jurisprudence.[59] Yet, for the most part Law and Religion scholarship has developed separately from other legal sub-disciplines such as Family Law.[60] Moreover, while there is a specialist literature within Law and Religion studies looking at the academic study of the law of the Church of England, little attention has been given to the academic study of religious law generally. *Pace* Maitland, the study of religious law needs to be understood as an indispensable part of legal analysis, being subject to the same level of scholarly scrutiny as the law of the State.

The distinct feature of religious law is its dual legal and religious nature.[61] This requires that religious law be subject to both rigorous legal and religious scrutiny. Religious law necessarily has a legal character. This is not to say that it must resemble state law or any other particular form of law. Rather, it is to insist that religious law includes legal as opposed to social or religious norms that are capable of enforcement in a way that is legal rather than social or religious (though, of course, the norms may well be social and religious too, and enforced in social and religious ways). Religious legal systems exist wherever there is a legal order; where there is not only a norm but also any mechanism, however informal, for resolving disputes about validity, interpretation and enforcement.[62] Law can be

56 Such as J Neusner and T Sonn, *Comparing Religions through Law. Judaism and Islam* (Routledge, 1999); A Huxley (ed) *Religion, Law and Tradition: Comparative Studies in Religious Law* (Routledge, 2002); and N Doe, *Christian Law* (Cambridge University Press, 2013).

57 J Rivers, 'The Secularisation of the British Constitution' (2012) 14 *Ecclesiastical Law Journal* 371, 394.

58 See Sandberg, *Law and Religion*, ch. 4.

59 Maitland, *Roman Canon Law in the Church of England*, v.

60 R Sandberg and S Thompson, 'The Sharia Debate: The Missing Family Law Context' (2016) 177 *Law & Justice* 188.

61 Sandberg, *Law and Religion*, ch. 9; R Sandberg, 'The Failure of Legal Pluralism' (2016) 18 *Ecclesiastical Law Journal* 137; Sandberg, 'The Reformation of Religious Law' (2017) speciale *Quaderni di Diritto e Politica Ecclesiastica* 97.

62 R Sandberg, 'The Impossible Compromise', in R Sandberg (ed) *Religion and Legal Pluralism*, 1. Cf. M Malik, *Minority Legal Orders in the UK* (The British Academy, 2012).

distinguished from other forms of social control by viewing law as a system of communications.[63] This shifts the focus from debates on the 'true nature of law' towards asking how law defines its own boundaries and where they are drawn.[64]

However, religious law does not only have a legal character. It also has a religious character. This insight is often lost. *Roman Canon Law in the Church of England* has much in common with most of the work on religious law in that it is addressed mainly to lawyers rather than to theologians. Yet, the religious nature of religious law is a key definitional attribute. Religious law has distinctive sources, purposes or functions and subject matters.[65] This is not to deny that religious laws do not share sources, purposes or content with other forms of law. However, there are elements that are distinctive and these flow from the religious character of religious law. In terms of sources, it is true that there are similarities between religious law and other forms of law. Religious law is not limited to the rules that adherents receive through sacred texts. It also includes 'internal' laws or other regulatory instruments that govern the activity of a religious group. These are the more practical rules, norms and laws – formal and informal, written and unwritten – that are constantly developed by group members to regulate their everyday life. In the Anglican context, the *Principles of Canon Law* distinguishes between 'fundamental authoritative sources of law', namely 'Scripture, tradition and reason', and 'formal sources' such as 'constitutions, canons, rules, regulations and other instruments'.[66] It might be thought that only the 'fundamental authoritative sources' of religious law are distinctive since the 'formal sources' of religious law have much in common with other forms of law. However, this would ignore the way in which some 'formal sources' of religious law are seen to be divinely inspired and that all of them are orientated towards a supernatural goal. The distinctive feature in terms of source is

63 Niklas Luhmann's social systems theory may be helpful here. Luhmann's social systems theory states that modern society is functionally differentiated into autonomous social systems such as law, religion, politics, science and the media. Luhmann sees these social systems as reproducing themselves by communication. Law, like every other social system (religion, politics, science and so on) becomes distinct and autonomous by developing its own function and its own binary code. Law's function is the 'stabilization of normative expectations' in the face of disappointment and its binary code is legal / illegal. Any communication that exercises this function using this binary code becomes part of the social system of law. Applying social systems theory, religious legal systems produce both legal and other communications but whenever they produce communications that uses the legal / illegal code and functions to achieve 'stabilization of normative expectations' then that is law. A systems theory approach, therefore, allows social norms to be distinguished from legal norms. It also allows the legal character of religious law to be understood. See further R Sandberg, 'Religious Law as a Social System' in Sandberg (ed) *Religion and Legal Pluralism*, 249; R Sandberg, 'A Sociological Theory of Law and Religion' in F Cranmer, M Hill, C Kenny and R Sandberg (eds), *The Confluence of Law and Religion* (Cambridge University Press, 2016) 66; and Sandberg, 'The Failure of Legal Pluralism' (2016) 18 *Ecclesiastical Law Journal* 137.

64 M King and C Thornhill, *Niklas Luhmann's Theory of Politics and Law* (Palgrave Macmillan, 2003) 42.

65 Sandberg, *Law and Religion* (Cambridge University Press, 2011) ch. 9.

66 *The Principles of Canon Law Common to the Churches of the Anglican Communion* (Anglican Communion Office, 2008).

rather that the ultimate foundation of the sources comes from a supernatural cause; a reality external to the individual. In terms of purpose or function, there is again an obvious overlap between religious laws and other forms of law. The purpose of religious law, like other forms of law, is to facilitate and order everyday life.[67] Yet, again, for religious law there is a deeper purpose. As Örsy writes: 'The purpose of canon law is to assist the Church in fulfilling its task which is to so reveal and communicate God's saving power to the world.'[68]

Although religious laws will often have much in common with other forms of law, reference to their sources and purposes shows that religious laws are distinctive because of their religious nature and context. Yet, the religious character by itself does not capture the phenomena of religious law. The unique thing about religious law is that it has both a religious character and a legal character. The definitional attribute of religious legal systems is not only the existence of both religious and legal phenomenon but also their fusion. It is impossible to neatly distinguish law and religion within religious legal systems. They are necessarily characterised by being both religious and legal and this is what makes them distinctive and what makes talk of a category of religious law useful and meaningful.

Roman Canon Law in the Church of England therefore provides an inspiration in that it shows how to take religious law seriously. As with the rest of Maitland's work, it also, of course, shows the value of a historically informed approach to the study of law. In English and Welsh law schools the subject of Legal History has been described as 'slowly and inevitably dying – or that it has been in a coma for the last 30 years, at least'.[69] As I have argued elsewhere, this decline has been reflected (and perpetuated) in the divided state of historical scholarship within law.[70] Legal History as a sub-discipline has tended to be self-contained, focusing on what is known as the 'old' or 'internal' Legal History: the study of the origins and early development of the common law using doctrinal legal methodology. It has failed to embrace the 'new' or 'external' historical work on law that has focused on the modern era and has explored legal developments 'as embedded in its context, typically its social or economic context; the history of the law in action'.[71]

At first blush, it would appear that Maitland and his work falls squarely within the camp of 'old' or 'internal' Legal History, giving a legal account of the development of the common law. Yet, this first impression would be misleading. As

67 For discussion of the facility and order theories see N Doe, *The Legal Framework of the Church of England* (Clarendon Press, 1996) 33 *et seq.*

68 L Örsy, 'Theology and Canon Law' in JP Beal, JA Coriden and TJ Green (eds) *New Commentary on the Code of Canon Law* (Paulist Press, 200) 2.

69 D Siemens, 'Towards a New Cultural History of Law' (2012) 2 *InterDisciplines* 18, 19.

70 R Sandberg and N Doe, 'Textual and Contextual Legal History' in N Doe and R Sandberg (eds), *Law and History – Critical Concepts* (Routledge, 2017) 1; R Sandberg, 'The Time For Legal History: Some Reflections on Maitland and Milsom Fifty Years On' (2018) *Law & Justice* 21.

71 D Ibbetson, 'What is Legal History a History of?' in A Lewis and M Lobban (ed), *Law and History* (Oxford University Press, 2004) 33.

Rose has pointed out, Maitland's work 'involves political, social, and economic contexts, as internal legal sources cannot be fully understood in a vacuum that ignores the external context'.[72] Therefore, 'Maitland is both the discipline's most important pioneer and one whose work connects with legal history's more recent manifestations'.[73] Maitland's work therefore bridges the gap between what has been variously styled the 'old' and the 'new', the' internal' and 'external', approaches to Legal History. Moreover, perhaps more so than the work for which he is widely known, *Roman Canon Law in the Church of England* provides inspiration in terms of its approach and tone. A further reason why Legal History is out of fashion in twenty-first century law schools is that it is inherently subversive. It challenges the assumptions that underpin the legal curriculum by showing that every line drawn in the law and every legal institution and practice is a historical construct. As Maitland expressed it, Legal History teaches 'the lesson that each generation has an enormous power of shaping its own law' and for students this means that the study of Legal History 'would free them from superstitions and teach them that they have free hands'.[74] Maitland's subversive nature is perhaps most evident in *Roman Canon Law in the Church of England*. Elton asserted that Maitland 'enjoyed the rumpus he had caused' and noted:

> The delight and bubbling irony which spring from the pages of the book did not come from nowhere: at the task Maitland ever went with a degree of mild malice that is not to be found elsewhere in his writings.'[75]

This 'mild malice' seems closely related to the late-twentieth-century development of what has been referred to as 'Critical Legal History'. This has been described as 'any approach to the past that produces disturbances in the field – that inverts or scrambles familiar narratives of stasis, recovery or progress; anything that advances rival perspectives (such of those as of the losers rather than the winners) for surveying developments, or that posits alternative trajectories that might have produced a very different present'.[76] *Roman Canon Law in the Church of England* can be reclaimed as a forerunner for such an approach. As Bell has noted, Maitland's work 'was never channelled in a single groove or pointed too single end; he has a lively, flexible mind that was always ready to follow a hint from the data that it happened to be processing'.[77] This included the questioning of received wisdoms and the 'spirit which causes one to go around

72 J Rose, 'Studying the Past: the Nature and Development of Legal History as an Academic Discipline' (2010) 31(2) *The Journal of Legal History* 101, 118–119.

73 Ibid, 114, 115 .

74 FW Maitland, 'Maitland to AV Dicey, c. July 1896' quoted in Fifoot, *Frederic William Maitland*, 143.

75 Elton, *FW Maitland*, 73.

76 R Gordon, 'The Arrival of Critical Historicism' (1997) 49 *Stanford Law Review* 1023, 1024.

77 Bell, *Maitland: A Critical Examination and Assessment*,108.

looking for skeletons in closets which might be exposed'.[78] As Bell put it, when Maitland 'became suspicious of the validity of any piece of received and traditionally accepted matter', he was always able to state his own conclusions 'with an admirable mixture of modesty and courage'.[79] His work, and *Roman Canon Law in the Church of England* in particular, provides an exemplar for historical legal scholarship, demonstrating its worth and the approach such work should take. Given that the inertia of Legal History has been caused in part by the splintering of different groups, Critical Legal History should not be regarded as a specialist form of Legal History. Rather, it should be seen as a necessary characteristic of Legal History, as an interdisciplinary endeavour. As the reference to 'disturbances' suggest, perhaps the word to describe this spirit is not 'critical' but 'subversive'.

Maitland's work in general, and *Roman Canon Law in the Church of England* in particular, has had a significant influence. It has placed the question of the authority of papal canon law in pre-Reformation England on the scholarly agenda and has debunked and overridden the previous pervasive assumptions. For these reasons alone, *Roman Canon Law in the Church of England* deserves the reputation afforded to Maitland's other works and deserves to be seen as a leading work in Law and Religion. However, it has achieved more than this. It has not been appreciated that Maitland provided the template for the legal analysis of religious law that blossomed a century after its publication. It rehearsed arguments concerning overlapping religious and secular jurisdictions that continue to exercise us today, albeit mostly in relation to a different context concerning Islam where today's moral panics are often an echo of the moral panics of yesteryear concerning Catholicism.

Moreover, *Roman Canon Law in the Church of England* has the potential to have an even larger effect upon legal scholarship, in two respects. First, by being regarded as an exemplar of how religious laws could be subject to the same level of academic scrutiny as other forms of law, the work has the potential to provide an inspiration for the further study of religious law as a category of law that has a distinct dual and fused religious and legal character. Second, the way in which Maitland's essays fuse precise doctrinal legal analysis with historical, theological and social insights shows not only the value of a historical approach but the need for a particular approach to the history of law; one which has the potential to reawaken Legal History from its self-induced coma.[80] A subversive Legal History disturbs the field in unsettling ways, showing that political, cultural, social and legal change is possible. *Roman Canon Law in the Church of England* underscores that Maitland should not be venerated only by legal historians; a claim can

78 He added that, 'Perhaps it is putting it too strongly to imply that Maitland had a polemic spirit, but there is no doubt that when he thought he saw a historical truth, he hewed to the line and let the chips fall where they might': Cameron, *Frederick Maitland and the History of English Law*, 65.

79 Bell, *Maitland: A Critical Examination and Assessment*, 108.

80 Cf. D Siemens, 'Towards a New Cultural History of Law' (2012) 2 *InterDisciplines* 18, 19.

be made that it is the first work of Law and Religion scholarship by subjecting religious law to academic legal scrutiny and by foreshadowing the debate upon religion and legal pluralism.

This points to a much larger issue: the effect of the development to date of Law and Religion. Its development as a sub-discipline within law schools with the usual ways of distinguishing itself from other sub-disciplines (the specialist journals, book series, conferences, courses and so on) has limited its reach. Not only has Law and Religion been constrained by its place within law schools; it has also been restricted by its limited interaction with other areas of law. Regarding and developing Law and Religion as a specialism has quickened its development in a host of ways but has come at a cost. The cost of this ghettoisation of Law and Religion is not only felt by experts in the field. Individual scholars can, of course, break out of the ghetto and already do, given that they need to be able to teach other topics. The larger cost, perhaps, is that the mainstream legal discourse still pays insufficient attention to religion. It is seen as a specialism rather than something that interacts with a whole host of areas of law and which all who analyse, practice or study law need to be aware of in a multicultural and multi-creedal society.

Maitland grasped the importance of religion and Religious Law historically but made the error of assuming that the same was not true of the society in which he lived. In his lectures subsequently published as *The Constitutional History of England*, he uttered the line that 'religious liberty and religious equality [was] complete'.[81] Generations of lawyers have assumed likewise, accepting the narrative of secularisation. The moral panics about the place of religion in the public sphere and concerns about terror attacks said to be in the name of religion have not sat well with this narrative. They do not, of course, mean that the narrative is irrelevant but they do question it; they nuance it in a way that was previously underappreciated. This has opened the door for an increase in attention to religion (or at least some manifestations of religion) by legal scholars. However, those who have gone through that door have closed it behind them by making it a specialist field. The general interest and potential have not been fulfilled. It is noticeable that work on inequalities and considerations based on gender have taken a different path to the work on religion. Scholarship on gender has not presented itself as a closed field. An edited collection by Auchmuty shows that the opposite is true.[82] The book is structured around legal sub-disciplines, each chapter 'identifying gender issues in traditional legal subject areas' with the aim that 'all law students [would] emerge from university recognising the importance of gender in everything they study, seeing it not as an optional add-on for a few people interested "in that kind of thing" but integral to law-making and the legal

81 *Maitland, Constitutional History of England*, 520.
82 R Auchmuty (ed), *Great Debates in Law and Gender* (Palgrave, 2018).

process, as well as to their own lives'.[83] There is much more to be done in relation to emphasising gender in the Law curriculum, but gender is increasingly (and belatedly) being seen as being important because it is not being marginalised as a specialism. It is rather seen as a factor that interacts with all areas of law and which provides a critique, an alternative way of looking at Law which changes the outlook, not just on the specific matter being looked at, but generally.

Maitland's work as a whole relished in moving from one topic to another not only within Law but also more widely. He would not have thought of himself as an interdisciplinary scholar but he was, not only in terms of History but also Political Science. This should provide an inspiration, highlighting a need for Law and Religion to develop as an interdisciplinary field. This is not just about bringing in insights from Theology and Religious Studies – seeing Law and Religion in Witte's words as a 'dialectical interaction' which includes reading law religiously as well as understanding religion legally[84] – it is also about bringing in insights from History following Maitland and from the social sciences.[85] However, talk about interacting disciplines has the risk of obscuring the issue. The important thing is not the choice of disciplinary bedfellow. Indeed, monogamy is probably to be frowned upon. It is the openness of approach that is crucial. It is all about bringing in the methods, insights and approaches from other disciplines and from schools of thought within Law itself and from other disciplines.[86] Bradney's description of Law as a 'parasitic discipline' might be taking things too far or at least might be unfortunate in terms of tone,[87] but Law and Religion academics need to look outwards to the work and ideas not only in law schools but in other parts of the University and beyond. The increased marketisation and obsession with metrics in Higher Education threatens to narrow the gaze of academics. The system rewards the asking of narrow questions that can be dealt with in fewer than 10,000 words and developing a niche specialism. But this needs to be resisted. We should look instead at the intellectual curiosity of Maitland and his willingness to dip a toe into unfamiliar waters. *Roman Canon Law in the Church of England*, seen within the context of his work as a whole, is a leading work not only in terms of substance but in terms of approach, motivation and ambition.

83 R Auchmuty, 'Introduction' in R Auchmuty (ed), *Great Debates in Law and Gender* (Palgrave, 2018) xi, xii.
84 J Witte, Jr., 'The Study of Law and Religion in the United States: An Interim Report' 14 (2012) *Ecclesiastical Law Journal* 327, 328.
85 See R Sandberg, *Religion, Law and Society* (Cambridge University Press, 2014).
86 Such as feminism, on which see Chapter 13.
87 A Bradney, 'Law as a Parasitic Discipline' (1998) 25(1) *Journal of Law and Society* 71.

13 *Multicultural Jurisdictions*

The need for a feminist approach to Law and Religion

Sharon Thompson and Russell Sandberg

The work

Arguments for women's rights and equal status in law can be traced back many centuries,[1] but it was not until the 1980s that the field of feminist legal studies was established as 'a significant body of scholarship' in many Western countries.[2] Yet, the influence of feminist approaches upon legal scholarship has been uneven. Public Law has been said to have been 'peculiarly resistant to feminist analysis', even though its core tenets of citizenship, rights, sovereignty and democracy have been central to much feminist legal critique.[3] This resistance can also be found in the Law and Religion literature (where the focus, at least initially, was upon the constitutional position of religious groups).[4] Where Law and Religion work has interacted with legal or political theory it has tended to gravitate towards accounts of natural law and liberalism respectively and has failed to acknowledge the relevance and value of feminist insights.[5] This has gone uncorrected by many feminist legal scholars, who Failinger, Schlitz and Stabile argue have mostly 'avoided the study of the difficult place in which religious women find themselves – pulled apart by family expectations for their lives, feminist critiques of their choices, and religious demands on their consciences and loyalties'.[6] Although there are,

1 E Jackson and N Lacey, 'Introducing Feminist Legal Theory' in J Penner, D Schiff and R Nobles (eds) *Introduction to Jurisprudence and Legal Theory* (Butterworths, 2002) 779, 780.
2 J Conaghan, 'Reassessing the Feminist Theoretical Project in Law' (2000) 27 (3) *Journal of Law and Society* 351, 352.
3 A Bottomley and S Sheldon, 'Preface' in S Millns and N Whitty (eds), *Feminist Perspectives on Public Law* (Cavendish, 1999) v.
4 With some notable exceptions such as the essays in MA Failinger, ER Schlitz and SJ Stabile (eds) *Feminism, Law, and Religion* (Ashgate, 2013).
5 See e.g., R Sandberg, 'Towards a Jurisprudence of Christian Law' in N Doe (ed) *Christianity and Natural Law: An Introduction* (Cambridge University Press, 2017) 220, and R Ahdar and I Leigh, *Religious Freedom in the Liberal State* (2nd edn, Oxford University Press, 2015).
6 MA Failinger, ER Schlitz and SJ Stabile, 'Foreword' in MA Failinger, ER Schlitz and SJ Stabile (eds) *Feminism, Law, and Religion*, xiii.

of course, exceptions,[7] this has meant there have been relatively few attempts to explore Law and Religion debates from a feminist perspective.

The lack of attention given to feminism in the Law and Religion canon is troubling given that Failinger *et al* view religious women as being 'not only part of religious communities [but] arguably, essentially DNA from which many rich religious cultures are built'.[8] A feminist perspective is particularly important in the context of the 'minorities within minorities' debate. This concerns the protection that ought to be afforded to members of religious groups who are vulnerable because of their minority status within that religious group, for instance, as women or as homosexuals. The 'minorities within minorities' debate explores whether the state should play a role in ensuring that members of religious groups should not be denied the rights that they would ordinarily enjoy by virtue of their citizenship of the state, where the polity of the group differs from that of the state as regards gender roles.

Although the 'minorities within minorities' debate is a legal issue, most of the academic writings on the subject come from a political science perspective.[9] This is surprising given the debate has come to the fore in Law and Religion scholarship in recent years. In a number of jurisdictions there have been high profile moral panics about the operation of religious courts and tribunals. In Canada in 2004 a report authored by the former Attorney General, Marion Boyd, stating that the 'Arbitration Act [1991] should continue to allow disputes to be arbitrated using religious law',[10] led to riots in major Canadian cities and a statement by the Premier of Ontario, Dalton McGuinty, that: 'There will be no shariah law in Ontario. There will be no religious arbitration in Ontario. There will be one law for all Ontarians'.[11] While in London in 2008, a lecture by the Archbishop of Canterbury, Dr Rowan Williams,[12] in which he suggested that 'we have to think a little harder about the role and rule of law in a plural society of overlapping identities', was illustrated on the news with footage of stoning and led the Prime Minister Gordon Brown to state that 'in Britain, British laws based on British values applied'.[13]

7 See for example, the essays in Failinger, Schlitz and Stabile (eds) *Feminism, Law, and Religion*.

8 Failinger, Schlitz and Stabile, 'Foreword' in Failinger, Schlitz and Stabile (eds) *Feminism, Law, and Religion*, xiii.

9 See, e.g, the essays collected in A Eisenberg and Spinner-Halev (eds), *Minorities within Minorities: Equality, Rights and Diversity* (Cambridge University Press, 2005).

10 M Boyd, *Dispute Resolution in Family Law: Protecting Choice, Promoting Inclusion* (Ministry of the Attorney General, 2004).

11 LE Weinrib, 'Ontario's Sharia Law Debate: Law and Politics under the Charter' in R Moon (ed) *Law and Religious Pluralism in Canada* (UCB Press 2008) 239 at 250.

12 R Williams, 'Civil and Religious Law in England – A Religious Perspective' (2008) 10 *Ecclesiastical Law Journal* 262.

13 For an analysis of the media reaction to the Archbishop's lecture, see ch. 7 of NA Kabir, *Young British Muslims* (Edinburgh University Press 2010) and R Grillo, *Muslim Families, Politics and the Law* (Ashgate, 2015).

These moral panics have resulted in a body of Law and Religion scholarship which has explored how certain religious tribunals have operated and how they currently and ought to be made compatible with the State legal system.[14] Although concerns about gender disadvantage have been ever-present in this literature, it has rarely been in the foreground. For this reason, the work of Canadian political scientist Ayelet Shachar has proved particularly influential because it takes an explicitly feminist approach.[15] The fact that Rowan Williams in his 2008 lecture discussed and praised her debut monograph *Multicultural Jurisdictions: Cultural Differences and Women's Rights*[16] as a 'highly original and significant' work and endorsed her call for 'transformative accommodation' has meant that her work has also become often cited (but less frequently discussed) within the Law and Religion literature.[17] This chapter will contend that Shachar's monograph should be regarded as a leading work because it serves as an exemplar of the need for a feminist approach to Law and Religion studies and that it should play a more influential role in the Law and Religion literature.

The context

Shachar's work is concerned with the 'minorities within minorities debate'. Her focus is on *nomoi* groups, that is, 'minority communities that generate sets of group-sanctioned norms of behavior that differ from those encoded in state law';[18] and what she refers to as 'the paradox of multicultural vulnerability':[19] the concern that those who are inside *nomoi* groups are denied the rights that they

14 This has included several empirical studies, most notably S Shah-Kazemi, *Untying the Knot: Muslim Women, Divorce and the Shariah* (Nuffield Foundation, 2001); S Bano, *Muslim Women and Shari'ah Councils* (Palgrave, 2012); and G Douglas *et al*, 'Social Cohesion and Civil Law: Marriage, Divorce and Religious Courts', available at http://www.law.cf.ac.uk/clr/research/cohesion.html, accessed 28 August 2018.

15 Educated at Tel Aviv and Yale Universities, she is currently Canada Research Chair in Citizenship and Multiculturalism and Professor of Law, Political Science and Global Affairs at the University of Toronto, Canada.

16 A Shachar, *Multicultural Jurisdictions: Cultural Differences and Women's Rights* (Cambridge University Press, 2001). The book had already been much lauded by political scientists. It won the 2002 First Book Award, American Political Science Association, Foundations Political Theory Section and was also cited by the Supreme Court of Canada in *Bruker v Macovitz* 2007 SCTT 54.

17 R Williams, 'Civil and Religious Law in England – A Religious Perspective' (2008) 10 *Ecclesiastical Law Journal* 262, 274. See, e.g., A Bradney, *Law and Faith in a Sceptical Age* (Routledge-Cavendish 2009) 51–52; B Jackson, '"Transformative Accommodation" and Religious Law' (2009) 11 *Ecclesiastical Law Journal* 131; M Malik, *Minority Legal Orders in the UK* (The British Academy, 2012) 36. For an exception see R Sandberg, *et al*, 'Britain's Religious Tribunals: "Joint Governance" in Practice' (2013) 33(2) *Oxford Journal of Legal Studies* 263.

18 Shachar, *Multicultural Jurisdictions*, 2.

19 Ibid, 3.

would ordinarily enjoy by virtue of their citizenship of the State.[20] Her argument is that the state should not endorse a strong version of multiculturalism whereby *nomoi* groups 'are to be granted extensive, formal, legal and constitutional standing so that they may govern themselves in accordance with their *nomos*' which would turn a blind eye to gender and other inequalities within the group. However, neither should the state adopt the other end of the spectrum where 'a uniform secular state law is imposed upon all citizens in family law matters, regardless of those citizens group affiliation(s)'.[21] For Shachar, this would relegate 'religious traditions to the margins, labelled as unofficial, exotic, or even dangerous (unrecognized) law'.[22] In her view, inactivity on the part of the state perpetuates the paradox of multicultural vulnerability. A stance of '"non-intervention" may effectively translate into immunizing wrongful behaviour by more powerful parties'.[23]

Shachar's work focuses on when and in what circumstances the state should intervene. She rejects what is often called the 'right to exit' argument which states that the role of the state should be limited to ensuring that at-risk group members are able to leave if they do not agree with their group's practices. Like many feminist scholars,[24] Shachar argues that this 'right to exit offers no comprehensive approach at all' because it imposes 'the burden of solving conflict upon the individual' whilst 'relieving the state of any responsibility for the situation'.[25] As she puts it: 'The right to exit rationale forces an insider into a cruel choice of penalties: either accept all group practices – including those that violate your fundamental citizenship rights – or (somehow) leave'.[26] Shachar is critical of how this approach is predicated upon a 'binary' notion of identity whereby an individual is either an adherent of the group or a citizen of the state. As Shachar points out, this is based on the premise that individuals cannot simultaneously be members of both the state and the group. It presumes that group members 'have relinquished the set of rights and protections granted to them by virtue of their

20 This refers to the way in which 'the same policy that seems attractive when evaluated from an inter-group perspective can systematically work to the disadvantage of certain group members from an intra-group perspective': Ibid. While *inter*-group equality is concerned with establishing equal treatment between cultural and religious *intra*-group inequalities is concerned with establishing equality within cultural and religious groups.

21 Ibid, 13, 63, 72–73.

22 A Shachar, 'Privatizing Diversity: A Cautionary Tale from Religious Arbitration in Family Law' (2008) 9 (2) *Theoretical Inquiries in Law* 573, 593.

23 Ibid; Shachar, *Multicultural Jurisdictions*, 37, 40.

24 Phillips, for example, denounces the 'right to exit' rationale as not attaching '*enough* significance to cultural belonging': A Phillips, *Multiculturalism without Culture* (Princeton University Press 2007) 133. She writes that it is based on a 'constructivist account of culture and universalist account of human nature' (ibid, 135).

25 Shachar, *Multicultural Jurisdictions*, 41. As Levy points out, 'to have a culture whose exit is entirely costless . . . is to have no culture at all': JT Levy, *The Multiculturalism of Fear* (Oxford University Press 2000) 112.

26 Shachar, *Multicultural Jurisdictions*, 41.

citizenship'. Shachar is opposed to any oversimplified 'either-or' understanding of legal authority which is not tailored to respect individuals' manifold identities.[27]

Shachar's significant achievement is to call for 'an alternative way of practicing multiculturalism' which 'seeks to enhance the autonomy of distinct *nomoi* communities, whilst at the same time providing at-risk individuals with viable legal-institutional tools to enhance their leverage within the group', challenging the power relations within their minority groups' traditions.[28] She writes that we should recognise those people within religious groups – whom she referred to as 'citizen-insiders' – as being both 'culture-bearers *and* rights-bearers'.[29] This is an important step forward in two respects. First, her work reminds us that there are 'three parties to the multicultural triad'.[30] Although Shachar follows Will Kymlicka,[31] Charles Taylor[32] and Iris Young[33] in arguing in favour of respecting group-based cultural differences, she makes an important step forward because the 'earliest proponents of multiculturalism too often forget the position of the citizen-insider, who simultaneously belongs to, and is affected by, both the group and the state authority'.[34] Second, her work highlights the agency of the citizen-insiders.[35] Shachar criticises the caricaturing of 'women who remain loyal to minority groups' cultures as victims without agency. She calls for attention to be paid to what she called the 'complex and multi-layered nature of multicultural identity'.[36] She asserts that we cannot 'remain blind to the web of complex and overlapping affiliations which exist between these competing entities'.[37] This means accepting that religious adherents are not 'cultural dopes': their religious affiliation does not mean that they do not want to enjoy and exercise citizenship rights. It is not simply the case of understanding how citizen-insiders are affected by their joint membership of the group and the state, we need also to understand the actions, desires and intentions of citizen-insiders themselves.

27 Ibid, 12.
28 Ibid, 7, 71.
29 Shachar, 'Privatizing Diversity' (2008) 9 (2) *Theoretical Inquiries in Law* 573, 593.
30 Shachar, *Multicultural Jurisdictions*, 5.
31 Shachar draws in particular on Kymlicka's concept of 'differentiated citizenship rights': W Kymlicka, *Multicultural Citizenship: A Liberal Theory of Minority Rights* (Oxford University Press 1995) 26. Note, however, that in this publication at least, Kymlicka does not seek to explore institutional models. See Susan Moller Okin's famous critique of Kymlicka's liberal theory on minority rights in SM Okin, 'Is Multiculturalism Bad for Women?' in SM Okin *et al.* (eds) *Is Multiculturalism Bad for Women?* (Princeton University Press 1999) 7.
32 See, in particular, his ground-breaking essay, C Taylor, 'The Politics of Recognition' in A Guttmann (ed) *Multiculturalism: Examining the Politics of Recognition* (Princeton University Press, 1994) 25.
33 See, e.g., I Young, *Justice and the Politics of Difference* (Princeton University Press, 1990).
34 Shachar, *Multicultural Jurisdictions*, 6.
35 As Phillips forcefully points out, reference to minority cultures is now 'widely employed in a discourse that denies human agency': Phillips, *Multiculturalism without Culture*, 9.
36 Shachar, *Multicultural Jurisdictions*, 15.
37 Ibid, 5.

Shachar therefore introduces her concept of 'joint governance'. This describes the idea that people can belong to, show allegiance to and follow norms from more than one source of authority at any given time.[38] Joint governance seeks to overcome the problem of 'artificially compartmentalizing the relationship between the group and the state into a fixed inside-outside division [which] conceals the extent to which both are in fact interdependent'.[39] It 'promises to foster ongoing interaction between different sources of authority, as a means of improving the situation of traditionally vulnerable insiders without forcing them to adhere to an either/or choice between their culture and their rights'.[40] Rather than creating clear winners and losers as a result of a conflict of rights, principled compromises will be reached that will be fact and context specific.

Multicultural Jurisdictions reflects many of the concerns that can be found within feminist legal studies literature. Although feminist approaches to law are varied,[41] Shachar's approach shares some core values of a feminist approach, for as Conaghan notes, it is possible and 'useful to identify some common, recurring features of feminist academic engagement with law and to do so without either essentializing feminism or denying the complexity and contestability of the features thus described'.[42]A feminist approach 'presupposes that gender has a much greater structural and/or discursive significance than is commonly assumed, a significance which is ideologically but not practically diminished by its relative invisibility'.[43] By choosing to explicitly recognise this, in other words, to not be

38 As Shachar puts it: 'Joint governance promises to foster ongoing interaction between different sources of authority, as a means of improving the situation of traditionally vulnerable insiders without forcing them to adhere to an either/or choice between their culture and their rights': ibid, 81.

39 Ibid, 40.

40 Ibid, 88.

41 This includes the identification of particular schools of feminist thought such as liberal, radical, cultural and postmodern. As Munro has argued talk of such classifications runs the risk that we 'lose sight of the basic and fundamental convictions that continue to animate and unite theorists across these divides': V Munro, *Law and Politics at the Perimeter: Re-evaluating Key Debates in Feminist* Theory (Hart, 2007) 11. This does not deny that feminist legal studies employ a range of methodologies which are not necessarily distinct. Conaghan's work on labour law shows how feminists use 'a multitude of methods to interrogate labour law – empirical, doctrinal, textual, and so on' and share methodology with other critical theoretical approaches: Conaghan, 'Labour Law and Feminist Method' (2017) 33(1) *International Journal of Comparative Labour Law* 93.

42 Conaghan, 'Reassessing the Feminist Theoretical Project in Law' (2000) 27 (3) *Journal of Law and Society* 351, 358–359. See also Wishtik's framework for inquiry for feminist jurisprudence: H Wishnik, 'To Question Everything: The Inquiries of Feminist Jurisprudence (1986) 1 *Berkeley Women's Law Journal* 64, 72–75.

43 Conaghan, 'Reassessing the Feminist Theoretical Project in Law' (2000) 27 (3) *Journal of Law and Society* 351, 359–360. It is possible to identify a shift in feminist legal literature moving from a focus on 'women and law' to 'law and gender'; moving on from identifying a particular 'women's perspective' to instead regarding 'the framework of gender divisions as a general category for critical legal analysis' which has 'opened up the possibility that law's contribution to the gendering of its subjects might interact with other social forces'.

silent on the gendered dimensions, issues of power are placed at the core of the discussions rather than on the margins. This questions and debunks conventional and traditional understandings about law and talk of law. For Conaghan, 'the application of a gender lens works to: (1) expose the operation of gender bias and neglect; (2) destabilise the normative and conceptual infrastructure; and (3) historicise and contextualise the field'.[44] The feminist approach, therefore, is one of critique. It is, in the words of Jackson and Lacey, 'an interpretative approach which seeks to get beyond the surface level of legal doctrine and legal discourse, and which sees traditional jurisprudence as ideological – and hence as an apologia for the status quo'.[45] Feminism is to be understood not as a discrete approach characterised by a fixed set of principles.[46] Rather, it is a dynamic '*process* of engagement or interaction – a dynamic *movement* of ideas',[47] which 'places distinctive substantive issues on the agenda of legal scholarship and legal theory'.[48]

As a result, Shachar's work can be characterised as adopting a feminist perspective because it stresses the need to take gender as 'a central organising principle of social life' and emphasises how power affects social relations.[49] In doing this, Shachar makes visible the gendered dimension of the 'minorities within minorities' debate. This distinguishes her work from that of other Law and Religion scholars, whose neutral treatment of the subject serves to obscure the lived experiences of those affected by gendered power. Instead, Shachar's feminist approach highlights the gendered aspects of law whilst probing what Conaghan refers to as 'characterizations positing themselves as neutral and, more specifically, ungendered'.[50] Shachar's is therefore a leading work in Law and Religion, for whether or not we choose to recognise it, gender is never absent from a discussion about where fundamental values in law come from, particularly when examining the wider context of social relations in which values are constituted and accepted. The conversation changes depending on whether we choose to emphasise or ignore gender. By refusing to accept gender as external to law, a feminist approach to Law and Religion, such as that adopted by Shachar, makes

---

Katherine O'Donovan's 1985 book *Sexual Divisions in Law* (Weidenfeld & Nicolson, 1985) is said to have 'represented a watershed in British feminist legal scholarship': Jackson and Lacey, 'Introducing Feminist Legal Theory' in Penner, Schiff and Nobles (eds) *Introduction to Jurisprudence and Legal Theory*, 779, 781.

44 Conaghan, 'Labour Law and Feminist Method' (2017) 33(1) *International Journal of Comparative Labour Law* 93, 100.

45 Jackson and Lacey, 'Introducing Feminist Legal Theory', 779, 789–790.

46 Ibid, 789; Conaghan, 'Reassessing the Feminist Theoretical Project in Law' (2000) 27 (3) *Journal of Law and Society* 351, 356.

47 Ibid, 356 fn 17.

48 Jackson and Lacey, 'Introducing Feminist Legal Theory' in Penner, Schiff and Nobles (eds) *Introduction to Jurisprudence and Legal Theory*, 779, 789.

49 S Millns and N Whitty, 'Public Law and Feminism' in Millns and Whitty (eds), *Feminist Perspectives on Public Law* (Cavendish, 1999) 1.

50 Conaghan, 'Reassessing the Feminist Theoretical Project in Law' (2000) 27 (3) *Journal of Law and Society* 351, 359.

gender 'analytically central' to and 'deeply constitutive' of law.[51] Furthermore, it acknowledges that ideas about gender are both affected by and effect legal ideas.

Shachar's focus on the 'paradox of multicultural vulnerability' provides an alternative lens to understand both the roles of the group and the state. Her work fits into a rich feminist tradition of exposing the binary constructions that are often pervasive in masculine-dominated public discourse, such as the artificial boundaries between public and private spheres. A feminist perspective is critical of such dichotomies and highlights the connectedness and integrated nature of human existence, and in doing so, demonstrates that 'lives that are not splintered between private or public, personal or professional'.[52] This rejection of artificial binaries in law can be found in Shachar's work. *Multicultural Jurisdictions* recognises the importance of the multiple, nuanced ways in which agency can be exercised by minorities within minorities in line with the feminist legal studies literature. Shachar does this by emphasising the 'complex and multi-layered nature of multicultural identity'.[53] Shachar's perspective also forms part of the literature on intersectionality whereby the focus has 'shifted away from the concept of gender as an isolated category of analysis towards a concern with the way in which gender intersects with other categories of identity for purposes of understanding and combating inequality.'[54] This focus represents 'a growing recognition of the need to broaden the representational base of feminism to take better account, substantively and strategically, of differences between women' buoyed by 'a keen suspicion of categories of categories in general and of the category 'woman' in particular'.[55] However, Conaghan is critical of the literature on intersectionality for being premised upon identity 'as a core unit of analysis, with gender, race and other inequality "grounds" being repositioned as "dimensions" of identity which law fails adequately to capture and reflect'.[56] She is concerned that this has 'had the unfortunate effect of directing feminist efforts away from concrete, empirically-based legal research with a socio-economic or distributive focus

51 This accepts and furthers Cotterrell's work in the sociology of law which argues that the legal and the social cannot be separated; rather legal and social ideas constantly penetrate one another: R Cotterrell, *Law, Culture and Society* (Ashgate, 2006).

52 Failinger, Schlitz and Stabile, 'Foreword' in Failinger, Schlitz and S J Stabile (eds) *Feminism, Law, and Religion*, xiii, xv.

53 This fits with the ground-breaking work of Judith Butler and in particular her theory of performativity, which highlighted how gendered understandings are perpetuated by women's subjective understandings of themselves and the construction and reconstruction of their social and legal identities: J Butler, *Gender Trouble: Feminism and the Subversion of Identity* (Routledge, 1990); J Butler, *Bodies that Matter: On the Discursive Limits of 'Sex'* (Routledge, 1993).

54 'This shift is in large part spawned by rejection within feminism of 'essentialist' invocations of sex and gender and the corresponding collapse of the category 'woman' as a core unit of feminist engagement and critique': J Conaghan, 'Intersectionality and the Feminist Project in Law' in E Grabham, D Cooper, J Krishnadas and D Herman (eds), *Intersectionality and Beyond: Law, Power and the Politics of Location* (Routledge, 2009) 21.

55 Ibid, 23.

56 Ibid, 30.

towards more abstract theoretical encounters with gendered cultural and legal representations.'[57] As we will discuss, this criticism can be levelled at Shachar's work too.

The significance

The flaw with Shachar's schema is that, although she correctly identifies the problem, her proposed solution perpetuates the problem rather than helping to resolve it. In emphasising how individual identity is negotiated through membership of overlapping (and sometimes competing) groups, her account fails to give adequate attention to the citizen-insider. The minority within the minority is treated as the object that the group and state fight over.[58] Shachar's focus upon competition has been criticised for taking a 'rational actor view of the world' which is 'written in the language of the marketplace'.[59] When this perspective of the 'individual rights-bearer' is employed it arguably rests upon and perpetuates a liberal legal idea of the autonomous rational person.[60] This fails to appreciate the nuances that the language of the marketplace obscures. Shachar's diagnosis – that gender and agency must be central to understandings of the minorities within minorities issue – is sound. However, by viewing the state and the group as two competing entities, her solution ignores individual agency and the gendered nature of decision-making. It ironically suffers from some of the very problems she is keen to avoid.

Although Shachar presents 'a repertoire of accommodation designs which can be combined and applied in creative ways according to different social needs and arenas',[61] the first four variants of joint governance she identifies are portrayed as 'straw' arguments.[62] Her preference is clearly for the fifth variant, transformative accommodation. Shachar describes transformative accommodation as being based on four key assumptions: first, 'group members living within a larger political community represent the intersection of multiple identity creating affiliations'; second, 'in many real-life circumstances both the group and the state have normatively and legally justifiable interests in shaping the rules that govern behavior'; third, 'the group and the state are both viable and mutable social entities which are constantly affecting each other through their ongoing

57 Conaghan, 'Reassessing the Feminist Theoretical Project in Law' (2000) 27 (3) *Journal of Law and Society* 351, 370.
58 Sandberg *et al*, 'Britain's Religious Tribunals: "Joint Governance" in Practice' (2013) 33(2) *Oxford Journal of Legal Studies* 263, 291.
59 Phillips, *Multiculturalism without Culture*, 153.
60 Conaghan, 'Reassessing the Feminist Theoretical Project in Law' (2000) 27 (3) *Journal of Law and Society* 351, 360–361.
61 Shachar, *Multicultural Jurisdictions*, 7.
62 Namely federal-style accommodation, temporal accommodation, consensual accommodation and contingent accommodation. For discussion see R Sandberg *et al*, 'Britain's Religious Tribunals: "Joint Governance" in Practice' (2013) 33(2) *Oxford Journal of Legal Studies* 263, 274–282.

interactions'; and fourth, 'it is in the self-professed interest of the group and the state to vie for the support of their constituents'.[63]

These assumptions show that Shachar sees transformative accommodation as a competitive model. She observes that 'each entity must "bid" for these individuals' continued adherence to its sphere of authority'.[64] This takes a very passive and rational-minded approach to the question of agency and ironically leads Shachar to adopt the sort of binary solution which she is herself critical of. She argues that there is a need to establish 'clearly delineated choice options through which constituents can express approval or disapproval of state or group decisions'.[65] However, she presents this as the possibility to 'opt in' or 'opt out' of specific group positions and describes this possibility of opting in or out in such a way that it makes it appear that such movement will be exceptional.[66] It is difficult to see how the right to 'opt-out' does not suffer from most of the defects of the right to exit. This is an 'either-or' type understanding of legal authority which will be of little help to the vulnerable minority who is a matter of fact unable to leave. This and other problems with transformative accommodation means that Shachar's work fails to achieve its ambitions.[67]

Transformative accommodation therefore fails to solve what Hadfield has referred to as a 'feminist puzzle' or 'dilemma of choice'[68]: whether it is possible 'to protect women from the oppressive consequences of harmful, constrained choices . . . without divesting women of agency?'[69] In other words, the dilemma Shachar confronts in her work, but does not overcome, is how the agency of minorities within minorities is facilitated, whilst simultaneously appreciating the effect of gendered power issues that may have coerced or constrained the decision-making process. Recognising joint governance *and* agency is ambitious but it is achievable. Feminist scholarship should prove influential here: a grounded approach is one of the characteristics of such work. As Conaghan puts it, feminist theory is built 'from the ground up, from the shared experience of women talking from personal testimonies, story-telling, consciousness-raising, and other revelatory techniques aimed at highlighting perspectives ignored by

63 Shachar, *Multicultural Jurisdictions,* 118.

64 Ibid, 117.

65 Ibid, 121.

66 'The purpose is not to fracture group solidarity so that members can opt out at the slightest opportunity. The initial division of authority between group and state must remain meaningful and presumptively binding on its individual': ibid, 123.

67 Sandberg *et al*, 'Britain's Religious Tribunals: "Joint Governance" in Practice' (2013) 33(2) *Oxford Journal of Legal Studies* 263, 286–289.

68 G Hadfield, 'The Dilemma of Choice: A Feminist Perspective on The Limits of Freedom of Contract' (1996) *Osgoode Hall Law J.* 337.

69 G Hadfield, 'Expressive Theory of Contract: From Feminist Dilemmas to a Reconceptualization of Rational Choice in Contract Law' (1998) 146 *University of Pennsylvania Law Rev.* 1235, 1237.

traditional narratives'.[70] A feminist approach is normative.[71] It questions traditional assumptions made by recognising the lived-in reality and particular ways in which power is exercised in relationships. By choosing to explicitly recognise this, one places the issues of power at the core of discussions rather than at the margins.

This does not assume that men necessarily have an oppressive role but it recognises that there is a power dimension between men and women in social life as a whole and especially when they are legal actors given the gendered nature of legal institutions, discourse and practices.[72] A theory that protects women *qua* women (and therefore as oppressed) fails to recognise the different contexts in which power imbalance occurs. Just because there are situations where women as minorities in minorities have less power and less autonomy, this does not mean these women are vulnerable or have less power because they are always weak in the face of inevitable male dominance. Indeed, it would be a mistake to presume a lack of agency when there is evidence of oppression or systematic subordination. As Meyers has argued, individuals experiencing multiple forms of oppression and structural inequality can still be partially autonomous and it should not be assumed they are unable to be autonomous because of structural constraints.[73] A more worthwhile use of feminism is instead to focus any concerns on the interests of people who are affected by power imbalance. The context of any situation must be assessed in a way that recognises gender without creating gendered stereotypes, and where both men and women have the power 'to truly make autonomous decisions because the context of agreements is recognised above formality'.[74]

70 Conaghan, 'Reassessing the Feminist Theoretical Project in Law' (2000) 27 (3) *Journal of Law and Society* 351, 364.

71 'It is concerned not just with describing or interpreting social arrangements but also with changing them, that is, with prescribing and effecting transformation, informed by a range of normative ideals including sexual equality, social justice, and individual self-development': Conaghan, 'Reassessing the Feminist Theoretical Project in Law' (2000) 27 (3) *Journal of Law and Society* 351, 375. However, there is a difference between feminism in the academy and feminism in the political realm. We agree with Conaghan that 'feminist academics and politics are situated within different validatory frameworks': 'as a scholarly engagement, feminism (seeks to) acquire(s) respectability and legitimacy through its explanatory and interpretative power; as a political movement, however, it gains its legitimacy through its ability visibly to bring about political change' (ibid, 355). As Conaghan puts it, 'feminism in the academy, then, is both expressive and interrogative of feminist politics' (ibid, 356).

72 S Thompson, *Prenuptial Agreements and the Presumption of Free Choice: Issues of Power in Theory and Practice* (Hart/Bloomsbury 2015) 9.

73 D Meyers, 'Intersectional Identity and the Authentic Self? Opposites Attract!' in C Mackenzie and N Stoljar (eds), *Relational Autonomy: Feminist Perspectives on Autonomy, Agency and the Social Self* (Oxford University Press, 2000) 151.

74 Ibid.

As we have argued elsewhere,[75] an approach previously created and applied by Thompson in relation to prenuptial agreements provides a way forward to overcome the weaknesses in Shachar's argument: Feminist Relational Contract Theory (FRCT). FRCT builds upon the strengths of both relational autonomy and relational contract theory. Relational autonomy as developed in the feminist literature and applied to Family Law in the work of Jonathan Herring[76] stresses the constraints on an individual's ability to exercise autonomy that exist as a result of various pressures in relationships. Indeed, ultimately the term 'relational autonomy' is a paradox: it recognises by definition that complete autonomy cannot be achieved since we are all shaped and limited by our social interactions with one another.[77] However, relational autonomy (especially as applied by Herring) would not have the desired practical impact of both facilitating agency and recognising relational inequalities and there is evidence to suggest that a relational autonomy approach does not lead to significantly different outcomes in practice.[78] Relational Contract Theory (RCT), as developed by Ian Macneil,[79] provides a step forward by shifting the focus away from autonomy to focus on the situations where social agreements are formed; where, in the words of Martha Fineman, 'individuals are given the means to voluntarily and willingly assume obligations and gain entitlements'.[80] Like Herring's explanation of relational autonomy, RCT brings the relationships of the parties to the fore. While orthodox and legalistic understandings of contract are imbued with flawed notions of autonomy, RCT instead repurposes contract in a way that recognises the relational context in which individuals make decisions. For Macneil, highlighting the parties' relationship necessitates a focus on important contextual factors in commercial transactions, such as duration and trade customs. This replaces neo-liberal assumptions that depict contracting parties as being purely self-interested and disconnected individuals with a relationship-orientated approach. However, this does not go far enough. It does not question the structures that exist and the power disparities and inequalities that exist as a result. Although some work has extended it beyond this setting,[81] the commercial

75 Thompson, *Prenuptial Agreements and the Presumption of Free Choice: Issues of Power in Theory and Practice*; Sandberg and Thompson, 'Relational Autonomy and Religious Tribunals' (2017) *Oxford Journal of Law and Religion* 137 and S Thompson, 'Feminist Relational Contract Theory: A New Model for Family Property Agreements' (2018) 45(4) *Journal of Law and Society* (forthcoming).

76 J Herring, *Relational Autonomy and Family Law* (Springer, 2014).

77 Sandberg and Thompson, 'Relational Autonomy and Religious Tribunals' (2017) *Oxford Journal of Law and Religion* 137, 148.

78 L Buckley, 'Relational Theory and Choice Rhetoric in the Supreme Court of Canada' (2014–2015) 29 *Canadian Journal of Family Law* 251, 256.

79 See, e.g., IR Macneil, 'Relational Contract: What we do and do not Know' (1985) *Wisconsin Law Review* 484; IR Macneil, 'The New Social Contract: An Inquiry into Modern Contractual Relations' (1996) 15(1) *Journal of Public Policy & Marketing* 157 and the essays in D Campbell (ed) *The Relational Theory of Contract: Selected Works of Ian Macneil* (Sweet & Maxwell, 2001).

80 M Fineman, 'Contract and Care' (2001) 76(3) *Chicago-Kent Law Review* 1403, 1408.

81 E.g., on marriage law: L Cohen, 'Marriage, Divorce and Quasi Rents; or, "I Gave Him the Best Years of My Life"' (1987) 16 *Journal of Legal Studies* 267; R Leckey, 'Relational Contract and other Models of Marriage' (2002) 40 *Osgoode Hall Law J.* 1, 5.

context in which RCT was forged means that it is unlikely to be sensitive enough to the numerous power imbalances experienced by minorities within minorities, particularly on gender lines.[82] And this is where FRCT steps in.

FRCT incorporates feminist perspectives that explicitly address power imbalances (especially those that are gendered) where RCT otherwise would not, directing critical fire at how social and legal structures reinforce power imbalances. For Campbell, a leading advocate of RCT, feminist contract theory is 'something of an oxymoron' because in his view it sacrifices the liberal values implicit in RCT (most notably the respect for individual autonomy) for the prioritisation of feminist equality.[83] However, FRCT is designed to overcome this incompatibility by building upon RCT but recognising as problematic and discarding the liberal values implicit in RCT. By applying an explicitly feminist approach, FRCT not only pays attention to the tacit understandings affecting intimate relationships, but also allows us to critique and subvert them. Focusing on gender creates 'disturbances in the field – that inverts or scrambles familiar narratives of stasis, recovery or progress' and 'advances rival perspectives'.[84] It emphasises the various overlapping relationships which people are in and the effect those relationships have. It involves examining social agreements within the wider context of multiple power relationships.[85] This involves exploring in detail not just the agreement and the conditions surrounding it, but a number of interlocking relationships over a much longer period.

In the context of religious tribunals this would include looking at the entire relationship between the individual member and the group, the relationship between the two parties the case is concerned with, as well as family and community pressures and the gendered aspects of the decision-making process and court personnel. Another important consideration would be the context spanning the whole period in which the parties were members of the religious community. Crucially, agency is not abandoned when feminist understandings of power are combined with relational contract's understanding of context. FRCT does not view choice as being a binary ultimatum between agreeing or disagreeing. It recognises instead that it is possible to follow a third route: staying within the group and negotiating a compromise.[86] FRCT can see that it may not be rational or

82 Sandberg and Thompson, 'Relational Autonomy and Religious Tribunals' (2017) *Oxford Journal of Law and Religion* 137, 156.

83 D Campbell, 'Afterword: Feminism, Liberalism and Utopianism in the Analysis of Contracting' in L Mulcahy and S Wheeler, eds, *Feminist Perspectives on Contract Law* (Routledge 2005), 161, 165.

84 Cf. R Gordon, 'The Arrival of Critical Historicism' (1997) 49 *Stanford Law Review* 1023, 1024.

85 Sandberg and Thompson, 'Relational Autonomy and Religious Tribunals' (2017) *Oxford Journal of Law and Religion* 137, 158.

86 Thompson, *Prenuptial Agreements and the Presumption of Free Choice: Issues of Power in Theory and Practice,* 129. For an application of a contextual approach see in *Thorne v Kennedy* [2017] HCA 49 as discussed by S Thompson, 'Thorne v Kennedy: Why Australia's Decision on Prenups is Important for English Law' (2018) 39(4)) Family Law 415. See also S Thompson, 'Feminist Relational Contract Theory: A New Model for Family Property Agreements' (2018) 45(4) *Journal of Law and Society* (forthcoming).

practical for minorities within minorities to walk away, and so this does not mean that we should presume that they lack agency.

There are a number of similarities between Shachar's concept of joint governance and FRCT. Both employ a feminist perspective to focus on issues of power (though FRCT places a feminist perspective to the fore). Both are based on the assumption that individualised notions of autonomy assume a level playing field that does not exist. However, unlike Shachar's variants of joint governance, and transformative accommodation in particular, FRCT advances matters in a way which unlocks the promise of recognising agency whilst simultaneously appreciating the effect of gendered power issues. Shachar stresses the importance of agency but her variants of joint governance do not achieve this: rather they focus on a rational economic understanding of the relationship between the state and the religious group relegating citizen-insiders to be the spoils whom they fight over. Ironically, the concept of joint governance is itself binary since it has been taken to imply two competing sources of authority: the group and the state. FRCT, by contrast, places agency to the fore. It fully recognises the web of relationships by regarding them as social contracts and accepts that power imbalances exist and that the role of the law is to decide when those power imbalances are significant enough to override freedom of (social) contract. Shachar's work stresses that 'the action and agency of individuals, groups and states is situational, that is, it varies in different institutions settings and to some extent is shaped by them'.[87] FRCT takes this further to regard action and agency as situational *and* relational; being shaped by complex interlocking social relationships and social statuses. FRCT therefore goes further than Shachar's work in that it provides a means by which courts and other decision-making bodies can recognise and take into account the various relationships involved and the resulting power imbalances. An approach based on FRCT overcomes this by recognising various forms of identity but providing a concrete legal way based upon contract that can provide practical solutions.

The legacy

A feminist perspective changes our view of Law and Religion scholarship drastically. It takes us away from an orthodox legal binary view of choice towards an understanding of the many and varied ways in which people really make decisions, and the social, economic and legal pressures they are under when making these decisions. Conventional understandings of legal actors as autonomous and rational decision-makers conjures up a monochrome painting of perfectly balanced scales. When we interpret this legal relationship from a feminist perspective, the picture suddenly becomes chaotic, disordered and is in bright technicolour because it depicts real people, real relationships and, importantly, the real issues with how power is exercised. *Multicultural Jurisdictions*, therefore, should be

87 Shachar, *Multicultural Jurisdictions*, 89.

seen as a leading work in Law and Religion studies because it uses a feminist perspective to highlight aspects of the minorities within minorities debate that would otherwise be rendered invisible. Shachar's paradox of multicultural vulnerability provides an alternative lens through which to view both the roles of the group and the state. Her work fits into a rich feminist tradition of exposing the pervasive binary constructions. Her argument for joint governance is compelling, as is her recognition of the ways in which multi-layered identities are constantly being constructed and reconstructed.

However, Shachar's aim of ensuring that agency is recognised is in the end unrealised. Her preferred variant of joint governance, transformative accommodation, ultimately adopts an institutional approach which focuses upon the interaction of state and group. The citizen-insider is simply the one over whom the group and state fight. The needs, motives and feelings of the citizen-insider are absent from the analysis. Her approach still does not place enough emphasis upon agency. This does not mean, of course, that *Multicultural Jurisdictions* should not be regarded as an inspiration. It remains a leading work. It shows the value of a feminist approach to Law and Religion studies but it also shows that a feminist approach allows us to go further still. A relational approach provides a step beyond this, recognising how 'identities are formed within the context of social relationships and shaped by a complex of intersecting social determinants, such as race, class, gender and ethnicity'.[88] FRCT grounds this analysis using notions of relational contract by focusing on gendered power relations. This provides real recognition of joint governance[89] in that, unlike Shachar's schema, FRCT takes into account not only the claimant's relationship with the religious group and the state but also considers the claimant's relationship with co-religionists. It focuses on questions of power and recognises the importance of facilitating the agency of minorities within minorities.

A characteristic of feminist legal studies, as a form of the critical legal studies movement, is that it highlights, challenges and disrupts understandings and narratives about law. The work of Lacey has shown that a feminist critique questions 'a number of assumptions common to positivistic and liberal legal scholarship': notions that legal reasoning is neutral, that law is a system of enacted norms or rules that have a unity and coherence and are rational, neutral, objective, autonomous and central to social relations.[90] A feminist approach exposes how 'the very fabric of law itself is gendered'.[91] This has two important consequences. The first is that it is crucial also to recognise that law is in part responsible for these imbalances because it is based on gendered norms and assumptions. The question

88 C Mackenzie and N Stoljar, 'Autonomy Refigured', in Mackenzie and Stoljar (eds), *Relational Autonomy: Feminist Perspectives*, 3, 4.

89 Or what might be more accurately called 'multi-governance' because there may be more than two sources of influence in play.

90 N Lacey, *Unspeakable Subjects: Feminist Essays in Legal and Social Theory* (Hart, 1998) 4.

91 E Jackson and N Lacey, 'Introducing Feminist Legal Theory' in Penner, Schiff and Nobles (eds) *Introduction to Jurisprudence and Legal Theory*, 779.

of how feminism can operate within law to produce solutions given that law is part of the problem is perhaps the greatest challenge for a feminist methodological approach in law.[92] The second, and related, consequence is that it is crucial to recognise that law is not disconnected from social norms and prejudices. Rather, law 'must be analysed in terms of the part it plays in conjunction with other regimes or "discourses" to regulate our familial and gendered lives'.[93] The co-existence of these two consequences means that the feminist critique of law cannot operate entirely separate from and outside conventional legal discourse. To transform law, a feminist approach needs to recognise that law and social ideas are inseparable and that the feminist project is shaped by and shapes both. This means that feminist legal methods are able to 'complement traditional legal method by incorporation of alternative views, experiences, perceptions and values which traditional method, in its insistence on logic and deductive thought, may exclude'.[94] A feminist perspective should not necessarily be placed in opposition to conventional accounts. Instead, it can improve those accounts by criticising the law whilst operating within its confines.[95] Feminist perspectives provide useful toolkits that we can use when building an analysis of law. However, as with any form of critique, feminism serves as an exercise in deconstruction and reconstruction. Feminist scholarship does not simply diagnose; its grounded nature means that it is especially well-placed also to be the needed medicine that rebuilds, re-strengthens and improves.

A feminist approach is critical not only of law as an institutional system but also law as a discourse, as a body of knowledge. Feminist legal scholarship disturbs both the narrative and the sources used by traditional accounts, being directly concerned with questions of power and focusing upon the agency of those that conventional accounts invariably overlook. This exposes the 'conceptual and normative architecture supporting the field of knowledge, thereby inviting its (critical) scrutiny'.[96] A feminist approach to legal sub-disciplines such as Law and Religion can be used to criticise processes of inclusion and exclusion, assumptions made, the authority given to certain voices and the importance afforded to particular topics and arguments. Indeed, the critique a feminist perspective proffers is likely to require the deconstruction and reconstruction of the field. This is likely to entail a deeper awareness of the ways in which the parties involved and implicated in religious relationships (adherents, group officials, State officials, those outside the group not to mention the family and cultural bonds that these

92 See C Smart, *Feminism and the Power of Law* (Routledge 1989).

93 A Diduck and K O'Donovan, 'Feminism and Families' in A Diduck and K O'Donovan (eds) *Feminist Perspectives on Family Law* (Routledge, 2006) 1, 3.

94 H Barnett, *Introduction to Feminist Jurisprudence* (Cavendish, 1998) 25.

95 V Munro, *Law and Politics at the Perimeter: Re-evaluating Key Debates in Feminist* Theory (Hart, 2007) ch. 2.

96 Conaghan, 'Labour Law and Feminist Method' (2017) 33(1) *International Journal of Comparative Labour Law* 93, 107.

people involved in negotiating and re-negotiating) interact, interpret and use (and are represented in) law. *Multicultural Jurisdictions* provides an important step forward in this regard and can properly be seen as a leading (and perhaps foundational) work. However, it does not go far enough in terms of its proposed solutions. Thompson's FRCT provides a means to capture, analyse and protect this. Such an approach would truly recognise the definition of religion law proposed by Sandberg as being 'concerned with the recognition and regulation of certain religious *relationships*'.[97]

Moreover, a feminist approach can question and dissolve disciplinary boundaries and sub-disciplinary demarcations within law.[98] As Bottomley notes, feminism 'gives rise to the recognition of the contingency of attempting to form of asserting or claiming subject status'.[99] As Conaghan points out, like any critical approach, a feminist approach 'troubles categories, blurs boundaries, subverts meanings and contests normative priorities'.[100] A feminist approach not only has the potential for dissolving demarcations within law, it also has the potential to debunk disciplinary demarcations. The infiltrated understanding of law and society as shaping and being shaped by one another means that a firm line between law and other disciplines cannot be made. As Conaghan puts it, 'law emerges simultaneously *gendered* and *gendering*'; both 'a repository of values replicating and reinforcing wider social and cultural arrangements – including gender-based attitudes, practices, and beliefs – and also actively implicated in the construction and maintenance of such arrangements'.[101]

A feminist approach to Law and Religion studies can therefore disrupt the narratives, values, structures, priorities and questions of the sub-discipline by centring upon gender and the questions of power this raises. Given the interactions between Law and Religion studies and other areas of law, a feminist approach can be used to question the historical development of frameworks, concepts and assumptions transplanted from those other areas of law and the erection and rigidity of sub-disciplinary dividing lines. As the prologue to this volume pointed out, this and the resulting 'ghettoisation' is a major concern and one that can be questioned, deconstructed and reconstructed using a feminist approach to the creation of knowledge and to the development of a Law and Religion discourse.

97 R Sandberg, *Law and Religion* (Cambridge University Press, 2011) 11 (emphasis added).

98 The growth of interdisciplinary literature and thought shows that the questioning and transcending of disciplinary distinctions is not exclusive to feminist approaches. As Conaghan notes, the 'blurring of legal disciplinary boundaries is not peculiarly feminist': Conaghan, 'Labour Law and Feminist Method' (2017) 33(1) *International Journal of Comparative Labour Law* 93, 111.

99 A Bottomley, 'Introduction' in A Bottomley (ed) *Feminist Perspectives on the Foundation Subjects of Law* (Cavendish, 1996) 1, 2.

100 Conaghan, 'Labour Law and Feminist Method' (2017) 33(1) *International Journal of Comparative Labour Law* 93, 114.

101 Ibid, 112.

A feminist approach to Law and Religion studies is therefore crucial. Developing Shachar's work and the literature of which it is part to provide a feminist approach to Law and Religion studies has the potential to cause a significant disturbance of unknown magnitude. A feminist critique in and of Law and Religion studies may well involve dismantling the status quo and creating something entirely new.

14 Afterword

John Witte, Jr.

This is a British Isles book. I mean that as a compliment. It's not just because the chapters herein sparkle with the elegant prose that still typifies much British and Irish academic work – much to the envy of us colonists. It's not just because the editor, Russell Sandberg, has rapidly emerged as Britain's brightest new academic star in the field of Law and Religion study – much to the delight of us veterans. It's also a compliment because many of the 'leading works in Law and Religion' featured in these pages are very much country-specific books. To be sure, Harold J Berman's *Law and Revolution*, translated into a dozen languages, is a top-tier title anywhere. Legal historians will know FW Maitland's name, if not his classic title, *Roman Canon Law in the Church of England* featured herein. A few left-wing scholars may have heard of Winnifred Sullivan's *The Impossibility of Religious Freedom*. A few legal pluralists will know Ayelet Shachar's pioneering work on *Multicultural Jurisdictions*, especially given Archbishop Rowan Williams's controversial comment in 2007 about the 'unavoidable' need for English courts to accommodate Shari'a and other faith-based family laws. Some comparative religious liberty experts will know Carolyn Evans' pioneering work on religious freedom in the European Convention on Human Rights, especially since the Strasbourg Court has become so active on these questions of late. But the rest of the scholarly names and titles featured on the foregoing pages – Kevin Boyle, Sir John Robilliard, Francis Lyall, David Maxwell Fyfe, Jean Baubérot, Lucy Vickers, The Right Reverend Christopher Hill, and others – are rather too little known outside the British Isles, although the chapter authors work hard to show how and why they should be part of the Law and Religion canon.

Calling this a very British and Irish book is also a compliment to the emerging global field of Law and Religion scholarship, which is now developed and diverse enough to have distinct national and regional accents, authors and literatures. The study of Law and Religion is relatively new in modern research universities in the West. A century ago, it was only a tiny boutique area of scholarship, focused mostly on religious laws, church–state relations, and religious freedom. Most universities had, if any, only a specialist or two scattered among the faculties of History, Divinity, Law, Politics or Anthropology. A half-century ago, even these early scholarly lights seemed to be dimming as university campuses came under the thrall of the 'secularist hypothesis' that the spread of reason and science would slowly eclipse the sense of the sacred and restore the sensibilities of the superstitious. Liberalism, Marxism, and various new critical philosophies were regnant on many university campuses. Even divinity schools and seminaries were arguing that 'God is dead' and organised religion is dying.

No longer. Over the past quarter-century, another great awakening of religion has broken upon us – now global in its sweep, startling in its diversity, and frightening in its power. Even if the Global North and Global West now feature more Nons, Neins, and Nyets on organised religion than ever before, the Global Middle and Global South have seen powerful new religious upsurges of old and new religions. Globalised media, migration, marketing and mission work have brought these religions to the Global North and West, too, sometimes with a vengeance. And they have brought with them a whole alphabet of new law and religion challenges –Apostasy, Blasphemy, Conversion, Defamation, Evangelism, Fundamentalism, Genocide, Hate Crimes, ISIS, Jihad, Kosovo, Migration, Neo-Paganism, Ostracism, Populism, Queer Rights, Refugees, Shari'a, Theocracy, Universal Rights, Value-Voters, Warfare, and Xenophobia. This alphabet of new challenges sits alongside an alphabet of more benign topics whose legal and religious dimensions are more familiar to Western readers but pressing again for more attention: Adoption, Baptism, Charity, Dignity, Education, Forgiveness, Grace, Hospitality, Intervention, Justice, Kindness, Love, Ministry, Negotiation, Obedience, Pastoral Care, Reconciliation, Sanctuary, Toleration, Uprightness, Virtues, Welfare, and more.

Scholars of Law, Religion, Politics, History, Ethics, Philosophy, and other social and humane sciences have taken note of these new movements and developments. More than 1500 serious scholars worldwide are now part of a rapidly growing scholarly guild of Law and Religion study. Some 50 centres and institutes of law and religion have popped up on campuses around the globe – more than half in the United States, but also with growing numbers in Europe, the Mediterranean basin, sub-Saharan Africa, Central and Latin America, Australia, New Zealand, Southeast Asia, and several lands on the Pacific Rim. These groups are being further integrated by international and regional consortia of Law and Religion studies and by dozens of periodicals and blogs on Law and Religion newly available. More than 1700 books on Law and Religion were published in English alone, worldwide, over the past 25 years and several new Law and Religion book series have been established by leading publishers.

While the global movement of Law and Religion study is collectively impressive in its sweep, the slower pace of the Law and Religion movement in the British Isles, noted by several authors herein, is quite typical of other lands. So is the preoccupation with some of the largely local concerns illustrated by these chapters, such as the ecclesiastical laws of burial, the clashes between Continental *laïcité* and Anglican establishment, or the tensions between the European Convention on Human Rights (ECHR) and common law jurisprudence. This has not been the case in the United States, with its stronger religious adherence and its longer tradition of interdisciplinary legal study in Law Schools. Today, more than 200 American law schools offer at least a basic course on religious liberty or religion–state relations. A growing number of law schools now also teach courses in Christian canon law, Jewish law, Islamic law, and natural law, and include serious consideration of religious materials in their treatment of Legal Ethics, Legal History, Jurisprudence, Law and Literature, Legal Anthropology, Comparative Law, Environmental Law, Family Law, Human Rights, and other basic courses. Religion is no longer just the hobbyhorse of isolated and peculiar professors principally in their twilight years and suddenly concerned about eternal life. It is no longer just the preoccupation of religiously-chartered Catholic, Protestant, Evangelical, Mormon or Jewish law schools. Religion now stands alongside Economics, Philosophy, Literature, Politics, History and other disciplines as a valid and valuable conversation partner with Law.

For the past few years, I have been periodically mapping the main themes in Law and Religion scholarship around the globe, at least as the work appears in Romance languages.[1] Herewith an updated map that will help situate the 'leading works in Law and Religion' featured in this volume:

First, by far the largest body of Law and Religion scholarship is devoted to issues of religious freedom and religion–state relations in national and international contexts. This topic courses through more than half the chapters in this volume, anchored by the religious freedom and non-discrimination provisions of the Human Rights Act 1998 and the ECHR, Article 9. In the United States, this is in part the law of the First Amendment guarantees of no establishment and free exercise of religion and related statutes. In other lands, these questions are topics of special constitutional provisions, concordats, treaties, statutes, regulation, and cases. Several international human rights instruments also include religious freedom norms, not least Article 18 in both the 1948 Universal Declaration of Human Rights and 1966 International Covenant on Civil and Political Rights, the 1981 UN Declaration on the Elimination of All Forms of Intolerance and of Discrimination Based on Religion and Belief, and the 1989 Vienna Concluding Document, Principles 16 and 17.

The legal, theological, cultural and personal issues arising under such provisions are perennial, profound and ever more pressing today. How to manage religious pluralism and protect religious and cultural minorities, particularly groups such as Jews, Muslims, Mormons, Jehovah's Witnesses, Scientologists and Indigenous Peoples, who often bring charges of private and state-based discrimination. How to define and set limits on religious and anti-religious exercises and expressions that cause offence or harm to others or elicit charges of blasphemy, defamation, or sacrilege. How to adjudicate challenges that a state's laws run directly counter to a party's core claims of conscience or cardinal commandments of the faith. How to balance private and public exercises of religion, including the liberty of

1 See, e.g., J Witte Jr, 'The Study of Law and Religion in the United States: An Interim Report' (2012) 14 *Ecclesiastical Law Journal* 327; J Witte Jr, 'The Interdisciplinary Growth of Law and Religion' in F Cranmer et al (eds), *The Confluence of Law and Religion: Interdisciplinary Reflections on the Work of Norman Doe* (Cambridge University Press, 2016) 247.

conscience of one party to be left alone and the free exercise right of another to proselytise. How to balance conflicts between the rights of parents to bring up their children in the faith and the duties of the state to protect the best interest of the child. How to discern the proper place of religion in public state schools, and the proper place of government in private religious schools. How to protect the distinct religious needs of prisoners, soldiers, refugees and others who do not enjoy ready access to traditional forms and forums of religious worship and expression.

Many religious freedom issues also involve religious groups, for whom the right to organise as a legal entity with juridical personality is itself often the most critical first issue. But here, too, myriad other questions have reached national high courts and international tribunals: how to negotiate the complex needs and norms of religious groups without according them too much sovereignty over their members or too little relief from secular courts in the event of fundamental rights violations by religious officials. How to balance the rights of religious groups to self-determination and self-governance with the guarantees of freedom from discrimination based on religion, gender, culture and sexual orientation. How to balance competing religious groups who each claim access to a common holy site, or a single religious or cultural group whose sacred site is threatened with desecration, development or disaster. How to protect the relations between local religious communities and their foreign co-religionists. How to adjudicate intra- or interreligious disputes over property, contracts, employment, or torts that come before secular tribunals for resolution. How to determine the proper levels of state cooperation with and support for religious officials and institutions in the delivery of child care, medical services, disaster relief, or humanitarian aid. How to define the lines of cooperation and jurisdiction between religious and political officials over fundamental institutions such as the family, school and charity that for many citizens have both spiritual and secular dimensions.

Secondly, and related to the above, various scholars now focus on the (contested) place of religion and religious freedom in the human rights pantheon. Several leading critical scholars today – jurists, historians, anthropologists, political theorists, and philosophers alike – argue that religion is too dangerous, divisive and diverse in its demands to be accorded special protection. Freedom of conscience claimants, they argue, unfairly demand the right to be a law unto themselves, to the detriment of general laws and to the endangerment of other people's fundamental rights and legitimate interests. Institutional religious autonomy is too often just a special cover for abuses of power and forms of prejudice that should not be countenanced in any organisation, religious or not. Religious liberty claims are too often proxies for political or social agendas that deserve no more protection than any other agenda. Religion, these critics thus conclude, should be viewed as just another category of liberty or association, with no more preference or privilege than its secular counterparts. Religion should be treated as just another form of expression, subject to the same rules of rational democratic deliberation that govern other ideas and values. To accord religion any special protection or exemption discriminates against the non-religious. To afford religion a special seat at the table of public deliberation or a special role in the implementation of government programmes invites religious self-dealing.

By sharp contrast, a number of leading scholars argue that religion is a cornerstone of human rights and that religious freedom is indispensable to constitutional order. Even in today's liberal societies, committed to policies of secularism, neutrality, or *laïcité*, religions still help to define the meanings and measures of shame and regret, restraint and respect, responsibility and restitution that a human rights regime presupposes. They help to lay out and tie down the fundamentals of human dignity and human community, and the essentials of human nature, human capacities, and human needs upon which human rights are built. Moreover, religious organisations stand alongside the state and other institutions in helping to implement and protect the rights of a person and community, especially at times when the state is weak, distracted, divided, cash-strapped, transitioning, or corrupt. Religious communities can create the conditions (sometimes the prototypes) for the realisation of civil and political rights of speech, press, assembly and more. They can provide a critical (sometimes the principal) means of vindicating rights to education, health care, childcare, labour organisations, employment and artistic opportunities, among other things. And they offer some of the deepest insights into duties of stewardship and servanthood that lie at the heart of environmental care and the rights of nature. Several detailed empirical studies have shown that the protection of 'religious freedom in a country is strongly associated with other freedoms, including civil and political liberty, press freedom, and economic freedom, as well as with multiple measures of well-being': such as less warfare and violence, better healthcare, higher levels of income, and better educational and social opportunities, especially for women, children, the disabled and the poor. By contrast, where religious freedom is low, communities tend to suffer and struggle, and human rights protection dramatically declines across the board.[2] This topic, too, comes through in some of these chapters.

Third, the internal religious legal systems of the great world religions have also captured growing attention in Law and Religion scholarship – and worries, too, in some quarters. Each of these world religions, especially Christianity, Judaism and Islam, has long had their its internal legal specialists who have been part of the broader Law and Religion discourse. But these topics are now becoming more mainstream in Law, Religion, Sociology, History and Anthropology departments of research universities and societies worldwide, with growing new attention to the place of law in various Asian and indigenous traditions, too. Books are beginning to emerge offering intra- and interreligious perspectives on discrete legal topics – Human Rights, Family Law, Constitutional Law, Private Law and more.

2 BJ Grim,' Restrictions on Religion in the World: Measures and Implications' in A Hertzke (ed), *The Future Of Religious Freedom: Global Challenges* (Oxford University Press, 2013) 86, 101.

A major new issue that many Western democracies are now facing squarely is the place of faith-based laws, tribunals and dispute resolution in secular legal regimes. How much deference do secular authorities owe to these religious authorities? How much involvement may secular authorities have in the adjudication of religious disputes and questions that come before them for resolution? These new questions join older questions about more overt state establishments of various forms of Christianity, Judaism, Islam, Shintoism, Confucianism and other faith traditions. How do modern nations square their state establishment or privileging of one faith with the universal human rights claims to religious freedom and equality for all?

Fourth, a small library of books has also emerged documenting the contributions of the world's religions and their religious legal systems to the secular legal systems around them, both historically and currently. Part of this inquiry concerns the exportation, transplantation or accommodation of discrete internal religious rules or procedures in secular legal systems. But more of this inquiry concerns the influence of religious ideas and practices on the complex doctrines of public, private, penal and procedural law of the state. In the Western tradition, numerous historians have documented the successive influences of Christianity on Roman law, Germanic law, medieval and early modern canon law, civil law, and the common law, and the eventual colonisation of these efforts throughout the world. Similar work is now being done on the cross-cultural legal influences of the laws of Judaism, Hinduism and Confucianism, and especially the tremendous influence of Islamic law on the secular laws of the 57 Muslim-majority states today and their political predecessors. The reality in many parts of the world, including in the secular West, is that religious ideas and institutions, norms and practices are part of the foundation and infrastructure of the positive laws of the state.

Fifth, as part of these last two points, a large body of literature has grown around the perennially contested issues of law, religion and family life. Three new questions are now attracting a great deal of new scholarly attention, a bit of which is reflected in this volume, too. The first question concerns the growing contests between religious liberty and sexual liberty. May a state require a minister to marry a gay or interreligious couple, a medical doctor to perform an elective abortion or assisted-reproductive procedure, or a pharmacist to fill a contraceptive prescription, when those required actions run counter to those parties' core claims of conscience or central commandments of their faith? May a religious organisation dismiss or discipline an official or member because of their sexual orientation or practice, or because they had a divorce or abortion? These are major points of contestation and litigation on both sides of the Atlantic and with likely implications for the global law and religion field.

A second question concerns religiously-based polygamy. For nearly two millennia, the West has rejected polygamy, from the ninth to the nineteenth century calling it a capital offence. These issues are back, with various Muslims, Fundamentalist Mormons, and traditional religions and cultures in Asia and Africa pressing their case for toleration, if not recognition, of polygamy on grounds of religious freedom, sexual autonomy, domestic privacy and equal protection. This, too, has triggered a small avalanche of writing.

A final question in this field of law, religion and family concerns the growing call by religious minorities to opt out of the state's Family Law system and into their own religious legal systems. This is raising a lot of hard legal and cultural questions. What forms of marriage should citizens be able to choose, and what forums of religious marriage law should state governments be required to respect? How should religious minorities with distinct family norms and cultural practices be accommodated in a society dedicated to religious liberty and self-determination, and to religious equality and non-discrimination? Is legal or normative pluralism necessary to protect religious believers who are conscientiously opposed to the values that inform modern state laws on sex, marriage and family? Doesn't state accommodation or implementation of a faith-based family law system run the risk of higher gender discrimination, child abuse, coerced marriage, unchecked patriarchy or worse, and how can these social tragedies be avoided? Won't the addition of a religious legal system encourage more forum-shopping and legal manipulation by crafty litigants involved in domestic disputes, often pitting religious and state norms of family against each other? Does the very state recognition, accommodation or implementation of a religious legal system erode the authority and compromise the integrity of those religious norms? Isn't strict separation of religious norms and state laws the best way to deal with the intimate questions of sex, marriage and family life? These hard questions are generating a great deal of important new scholarship. Comparable complex work can be found on the Law and Religion issues surrounding education, charity, poor relief, immigration, environmental care, sex trafficking, warfare, torture, terrorism and more.

Sixth, natural law theory is becoming a topic of growing interest again, having once dominated patristic, medieval and early modern Catholic, Protestant and Enlightenment thought before giving way to modern legal positivism. The renaissance of natural law theory began back in the mid-twentieth century. The horrible excesses of Nazi Germany and Stalinist Russia catalysed the modern international human rights revolution, which defined and defended the natural rights protections of human dignity and the natural law limits on state power. The rise of Catholic social teachings and the monumental reforms of the Second Vatican Council in 1962–1965 together gave further powerful impetus to Catholic natural law theories. A number of Jewish, Protestant, Eastern Orthodox and Muslim scholars are now also resurrecting the rich natural law teachings of their own traditions and developing new natural law theories to address fundamental legal questions today, in and on terms that others with different faith traditions can appreciate. And all these groups have found interesting overlaps with the burgeoning religion and science scholarship that is exposing some interesting natural foundations of human morality and sociability. Natural law theory, while still controversial, is becoming a promising new arena of interreligious and interdisciplinary dialogue.

Seventh, natural law arguments often inform a related area of continued importance in Law and Religion study: the topic of legal ethics, both by itself and in comparison with theological ethics, business ethics, medical ethics and more. Legal and theological ethicists have long recognised the overlaps in form and function of the legal and religious professions. Both professions require extensive doctrinal training and maintain stringent admissions policies. Both have developed codes of professional ethics and internal structures of authority to enforce them. Both seek to promote cooperation, collegiality, and *esprit de corps.* There are close affinities between the mediation of the lawyer and the intercession of the cleric, between the adjudication of the court and the arbitration of the consistory, between the beneficence of the bar and the benevolence of the diaconate. Ideally, both professions serve and minister to society. Both professions seek to exemplify the ideals of calling and community. Nonetheless, there can be strong tensions between one's legal professional duties and personal faith convictions. What does it mean to be a Christian, Jewish, Muslim, Hindu or Buddhist lawyer at work in a secular legal system? These topics now have attracted a small cluster of important new scholarship.

Eighth, this last question – about the place of the religious believer in the legal profession – has raised the broader question of the place of overt religious arguments in legal discourse altogether. This is in part an epistemological question: whether legal and political argumentation can and should forgo religious and other comprehensive doctrines in the name of rationality and neutrality. In America, this is also in part a constitutional question: whether the First Amendment prohibition on establishment of religion requires that all laws be based on secular and neutral rationales in order to pass constitutional muster. In the heyday of secular liberalism and strict separationism in the 1960s and 1970s, it was common to insist that all political debates sound in terms of rationality and neutrality. Today, a number of scholars have argued that religious and other comprehensive doctrines are essential parts of an enduring legal and political morality.

Finally, questions of law and religious language have also raised broader questions about the overlaps between legal and theological interpretation, translation and hermeneutics. Legal historians have long been intrigued by the overlaps between the scholarly methods used to interpret the Bible and the constitution, a code and a creed, a consistory judgment and a judicial opinion. The rise of modern literary theory and of form-critical methods of biblical interpretation has heightened this scholarly interest in how to discern the original meaning and understanding of authoritative texts. And with the rise of globalisation and the study of global law and world religions, a number of jurists have become keenly interested in the questions of translation, transplantation and transmutation of legal and religious ideas across cultural, disciplinary and denominational boundaries.

It will take a whole library to come to terms with these and related themes of Law and Religion scholarship. But the chapters herein provide a judicious and delicious sampling of the refined work that is now on offer in this growing field.

Index

For Product Safety Concerns and Information please contact our EU representative GPSR@taylorandfrancis.com
Taylor & Francis Verlag GmbH, Kaufingerstraße 24, 80331 München, Germany

www.ingramcontent.com/pod-product-compliance
Ingram Content Group UK Ltd.
Pitfield, Milton Keynes, MK11 3LW, UK
UKHW021302190926
475701UK00009B/607
* 9 7 8 0 3 6 7 6 6 4 2 5 1 *